RE-VISIONING MISSION

ISAAC HECKER STUDIES
IN RELIGION AND AMERICAN CULTURE

RE-VISIONING MISSION

The Catholic Church and Culture in Postmodern America

Richard G. Cote, O.M.I.

Paulist Press
New York / Mahwah, N.J.

The Publisher gratefully acknowledges use of an excerpt from "Little Gidding" in FOUR QUARTETS, copyright 1943 by T. S. Eliot and renewed 1971 by Esme Valerie Eliot, reprinted by permission of Harcourt Brace & Company and by permission of Faber and Faber Ltd. Richard G. Cote's chapter "A Spirituality for Crossing the Postmodern Divide" is adapted from the article "God Sings in the Night: Ambiguity as an Invitation to Believe" originally published in *Concilium* 4 (1992), pp. 95–105, and is used with permission of the publisher.

Cover design by Kathy McKeen.

Library of Congress Cataloging-in-Publication Data

Cote, Richard G., 1934–
    Re-visioning mission : the Catholic Church and culture in postmodern America / Richard G. Cote.
        p.   cm.–(Isaac Hecker studies in religion and American culture)
    Includes bibliographical references (p.   ) and index.
    ISBN-0-8091-3645-7 (alk. paper)
    1. Catholic Church–United States–History–20th century.   2. Catholic Church–United States–Missions–United States.   3. Christianity and culture–United States.   4. Missions–Theory.   5. United States–Civilization–20th century. I. Title II. Series.
BX1406.2.C68   1996
282′.73′09049–dc20   96-12355
                                                                              CIP

Published by Paulist Press
997 Macarthur Boulevard
Mahwah, NJ 07430

Printed and bound in the
United States of America

Contents

Part Three
Culture Revisited: A New Approach

Part Four
New Paths and Spirituality of Mission

PART ONE

Unresolved Issues

1 | Why a New Utterance About Mission?

With the numerous publications that have appeared on the subject of mission, particularly within the past decade, one may wonder why there is need for yet a new utterance about mission. In the first two chapters I wish to consider some of the major reasons why the question of mission, which in the past has always been very close to the heart and *raison d'être* of the church, must be re-visioned anew. In this first chapter, I will draw attention to several fundamental reasons why the notion of mission must be re-visioned again today and why Vatican II's dynamic statement that the church is missionary in its very nature has virtually fallen on deaf ears at the grass-roots level of the church, that crucial level where any renewed sense of mission must begin. In the next chapter, I will deal more specifically with the Catholic Church in the United States and why it is still unsure of itself and its mission, and why it lags behind some of the younger local churches in the third world in its missionary resolve and spirit. This will serve as an immediate introduction to the central focus of our study, namely, inculturating faith in the North American context.

The church's understanding of mission has often changed over the centuries and, foreshadowing these changes like a barometer, the Holy Spirit seems always to have elicited in the church some new utterance, some new word about mission, as though either to herald or to give added momentum to these changes. This should come as no surprise since the coming of the Christian gospel itself was initially a "speech-event," the "utterance" of a word that has since reverberated down the corridors of time. One must remember that even before the gospel was consigned to writing, the proclamation of the gospel took place by word of mouth. A certain Christian idiom and special speech-modes had already been developed in the oral preaching of the church, and the earliest Christian texts are clearly based on this idiom and these speech-modes.[1] St. Paul said that faith comes by "*hearing*," and on this score the church has never wavered; it has always considered *viva voce* communication and oral proclamation to be inextricably bound to the idea of mission however much its understanding of mission might otherwise change over the years.

It must also be acknowledged that the church has generally respected, though at times with considerable fear and caution, the initiating and creative power of words, how *new* words especially possess an uncanny ability to inaugurate a new "order" of things, often in ways that are unforeseen and even quite disturbing. The introduction of certain key words in the church's traditional discourse about mission has frequently been a prophetic "event" foreshadowing things to come. One remembers how the advent of such key words as "development," "social justice," and "liberation" in the church's discourse had a singular impact on mission theology and praxis. One can therefore understand the reluctance of a conservative magisterium to accept new words in its official lexicon or rhetoric (whether theological, liturgical or encyclical). It is keenly attentive to detect danger in the advent of any new linguistic expression in its inherited tradition. Yet for all its vigilance and guardedness, new words have been known to creep into and make their home in ecclesiastical discourse, words that subsequently went on to have a vivid spontaneous life of their own with far-reaching implications for the church and its mission in the world.

New words are subversively prophetic in any tradition or institution, and the reason for this is because certain words can and often do liberate the imagination of the faithful or what we will later refer to in this study as their "faithful imagination," that truly creative dimension which not only adheres to faith, but is a *constitutive* element of the very act of believing. It is precisely this re-visioning quality of faith that enables the believer to think the unthinkable, to conceive the inconceivable, and to imagine the imaginable, namely, "a new heaven and a new earth" (Rev 21:1). Words are very much a part of this process. What fascinates us about them is precisely their enormous suggestive power. Not only can they determine and pin down meaning, but as linguistic symbols they also suggest new ways of re-visioning conventional ideas and approaches, new ways of walking together into the future. James Hillman puts it beautifully:

> We need to recall the angel aspect of the word, recognizing words
> as independent carriers of soul between people. We need to recall
> that we do not just make words up or learn them at school, or ever
> have them fully under control. Words, like angels, are powers which
> have invisible power over us. They are personal presences....This

aspect of the word transcends their nominalistic definitions and contexts and evokes in our souls a universal resonance.[2]

Karl Rahner also makes the point succinctly:

> There are words which "fence off" and isolate. There are also, however, words which make an individual thing transparent so that we can see through to the Infinity of all reality. They are like sea shells in which, no matter how small they themselves are, the ocean of Infinity thunders. They illuminate us, not we them. They have power over us because they are gifts of God—not the makings of men—even if perhaps they do come to us through men.[3]

The initial surprise or resistance to any new vocabulary affecting the mission of the church is not unlike that which the paradoxical utterances of Jesus himself occasioned—the saying, for example, about losing one's life by finding it, about leaving the dead to bury their own dead, about receiving the kingdom of God like a child, or about how the first will be last and the last first. Considered rhetorically, such "hard" sayings all had the effect of breaking the continuity of existence of the hearer to the extent that he or she was suddenly left without a frame of reference. In other words, Jesus challenged his hearers "to say what cannot be said, to applaud what should not be applauded, to recognize in the reversal of human judgments and human situations the sign of the breaking in of God's Kingdom."[4] So it is with any new utterance about mission. At first, it generally tends to bewilder and dismay, provoking a certain disorientation in previously held positions about mission, positions inherited from the past that are only marginally open to risk and renewal of vision. Yet this creative disruption, however much it may throw us off balance, is where we must look in order to be able to "see through" and beyond the profound, even radical, changes that are taking place in our world as well as in our church.

If we truly accept the fact that we are presently experiencing—and will indeed continue to experience well into the third millennium—a great historical transition, an epochal paradigm shift from modernity to postmodernity, and assuming also that the risen Christ is still very much the "Lord of history," then certain consequences would seem to follow for the church, consequences that the present study will seek to explore. Among other things, I will be suggesting a new approach to the inculturation of faith, as well as a corresponding spirituality for today's church. I mean a "core" spirituality in tune with our changing times and one that is tailor-made for an exodus/pilgrim people about to enter a new historical landscape, the third millennium—a spirituality, in short, of real theological hope rather than one of ecclesiastical "containment." Damage control is one thing; walking in faith with God into the future is quite another.

As evidence of the transforming power of words, any serious discussion about mission today must take into account and contend with a host of new speech-modes, words and expressions like the following: *liberation, comunidades de base, inculturation, local theologies, new evangelization, world church, evangelization of cultures, creation spirituality, postmodern church, eco-feminism, New Age, cyberspace,* etc. In virtually each case, it is possible to fix a date and a specific name or occasion when these expressions first broke into present-day discussion about mission. And as linguistic symbols so often do, they presented themselves initially as discrete "signs of the times," as dynamic accelerators of change, never as full-blown "blueprints" of the future. They make their appearance first as intuitions that stir the imagination of the faithful; only later do they become mission programs. They seem to fall into the lap of the church, like "angels" from on high (and *angel* means originally "emissary," "message bearer"), and so prompt the church to ask, as Mary did when the angel Gabriel suddenly appeared to her, "what all this could possibly mean."

After considering some of the major reasons behind the need to re-vision mission yet again, the remainder of our study will attempt to suggest some new paths of mission for the church in the United States as we approach the third millennium.

Confusion About "Mission"

There is, first of all, considerable confusion surrounding the term "mission" itself. Amid the surprising escalation of literature on mission in recent years, as David Bosch rightly notes, "it remains extraordinarily difficult to determine what mission is." His own remarkable study, *Transforming Mission*, evolved, he says, "from the assumption that the definition of mission is a continual process of sifting, testing, reformulating and discarding."[5] One of the difficulties, of course, is the frequent disjuncture of mission theory and *praxis*. On the one hand there is considerable "high-level" academic discussion about mission, but this is often divorced from first-hand missionary involvement and practice. On the other hand missionaries in the field have little time or the "distancing" necessary to reflect critically on their own missionary past history and tradition. Hence the danger of remaining overly absorbed in the more immediate tasks at hand, a danger already deplored by Pius XI in 1924 and Pius XII in 1950.[6]

There is also the problem of the way we have generally come to understand the term "mission" in modern history. It can mean: (a) the sending of missionaries to distant lands, (b) the activity effected by that sending, (c) the result and fruit of such activity, such as evangelization and the establishing of local churches, and (d) the place or "mission field" where the activity occurs. In a more restricted sense, the term may be used to designate a local Christian community that is without a priest or minister (sometimes called "mission stations"), or a series of special services intended to deepen the faith of Christians (sometimes called "parish missions").[7]

The more crucial issue around which there is still much confusion today is what is meant exactly by saying that the church is *missionary in its very nature*.[8] Does it mean that everything the church is and does is essentially an act of mission? Or must the expression be more specifically reserved for certain particular activities of the church? This is not a purely academic question since, depending on the answer that one gives to it, the approach and *praxis* of mission either here at home or abroad will be conducted quite differently. Although David Bosch does well to raise the question in his study, he does not really answer it. Other authors do, maintaining, as one put it, that "mission is not everything in the church."[9] These authors seek support for their claim in Vatican II, *Ad Gentes* 6, where it is said: "Missionary work among the nations *differs* from the pastoral care of the faithful and likewise from efforts aimed at restoring Christian unity" [emphasis added]. However, this decree, promulgated back in 1965, contains many notions about mission that are obsolete and no longer valid today, including the above distinction between "missionary work," "pastoral work," and "ecumenical work." Moreover, as many commentators were quick to point out, this church document is replete with ambiguity and fails moreover to give us a coherent, unified vision and doctrine of mission.[10]

One should remember also that the word "mission" only appeared in the seventeenth century and did not initially designate the activity of those who were entrusted with the specific task of extending the faith beyond the geographical limits and boundaries of what was then considered "Christian Europe."[11] Nor was it at first seen as deriving from the "mission" of Christ,[12] or from what today is referred to as the *missio Dei*, God's lasting commitment to the world for its salvation. Before the seventeenth century, the church had a more integrated and "holistic" notion of evangelization and mission; its idea of *propagatio fidei* was inclusive and all-embracing rather than restrictive. In fact, it was virtually coextensive with the principal activities that constitute the very life of the church itself, namely: proclamation (*kerygma*), catechesis (*didache*), professing the faith (*homologia*), liturgical praise and thanksgiving (*doxologia*), witnessing (*martyria*), fellowship (*koinonia*), service (*diakonia*), and dialogue (*dialogos*). Thus what we now call evangelization and missionary work were not regarded as distinct activities alongside all the above, but rather were seen as constitutive of these. To evangelize, therefore, was simply "to be" church in the deepest, most defining, sense of this verb. All the above-mentioned ecclesial activities are but so many indivisible expressions of "being" church, namely, a community of believers that tries to articulate for itself first and then attempts to somehow disclose to the world the deep reasons for its profound and joyous hope. As someone lightheartedly yet so aptly put it: To evangelize is like one beggar telling another one where he or she has found food.

Clearly, one of the challenges of any postmodern theology of mission will be to show—and indeed show convincingly—how each of the vital activities of the church mentioned above is a *constitutive* act and celebration of mission. Only then will it be possible for the laity in particular to realize that every member of the church is a missionary in virtue of his or her baptism, and that, *as Christians*, their basic missionary character must be experienced as informing and coloring everything they do both in the church as well as in the world. Much of the confusion surrounding the term "mission" today stems from having lost sight of this all-pervasive, deeper, and essential unity of mission which constitutes the very being of the Christian community, making it truly missionary in its very nature. Having been for so long and so exclusively identified with "foreign missions," and still largely perceived as but one of several important yet distinct activities within the church, the term "mission" has become very problematic in today's changing world. Without overstating the case, one could say that it is a word which is once again looking for a new definition (or better still: a new vision). The question, in sum, is: should the term "mission" be retained or has it become too compromised by the many conflicting connotations it must now carry? Could it conceivably become a mobilizing symbol again in the postmodern church of the future, or is it destined to become, like many other archaic speech-modes in the church, a topic better left to research students in church history?

The confusion in mission terminology is explicitly acknowledged by John Paul II in *Redemptoris Missio*.[13] If one wishes to retain the distinction between mission *ad extra* and mission *ad intra*, however, I would argue that it can no longer be used meaningfully to discriminate between the church's missionary activity to the so-called "nations" (called mission *ad gentes*) and the church's mission in those countries with long-standing Christian roots (Europe and North America). Instead, I would argue, one does better to speak of mission *ad extra* and mission *ad intra* as referring, not to the geography or the historical circumstance of the faith, but to the reality of the church itself before the world. Thus mission *ad intra* would refer to the church's internal or "in-house" mission, its own self-evangelization and ministry unto its membership, while mission *ad extra* would refer to its mission outside and beyond its visible boundaries and membership. The former would be mission unto the church, the latter mission unto the world. I shall return to this later.

New Developments in Hermeneutics

Quite apart from the question of mission terminology, a second factor that has accentuated the need to re-vision the theology of mission (and hence the question of "being" a mission church in a new way) touches directly on the scriptural texts and the way these are interpreted. To raise the question of mission is to raise the question of hermeneutics, since the two issues are indissolubly conjoined. If it is true that the church came into being as a "speech-event," as a revelatory event of Jesus Christ, it is also true that the Christian church owes its ongoing presence in history to "a book," the scriptures of the New Testament. God's word was always associated with a book that had to be read in and to a community of faith. How that community interprets, reads or understands the scriptures shapes its mission just as decidedly as its understanding of mission surely conditions the way it reads and interprets the scriptural texts.

It would be difficult to exaggerate the importance of what can only be called the *basic reciprocity* between any Christian understanding of mission and the way a Christian community interprets the scriptures. Not only do mission and scripture condition and interpenetrate one another, but neither would really exist without the other. Hence we see that throughout history the vicissitudes of the one closely parallel the historical vicissitudes of the other. Failure to grasp this basic reciprocity, this essential "bond-in-being" between mission and biblical hermeneutics, is fraught with two dangers. To put mission so completely under the authoritative control and direction of the church's magisterium (where it effectively has been since the early seventeenth century) is to encapsulate the gospel and thus diminish much of its transforming and liberating power. Those in positions of ecclesiastical power and authority naturally tend to be critical of any movement that threatens to weaken their power.

They may resist important changes in the church by labeling them dangerous or unorthodox, as we saw, for example, when liberation theology first emerged or when feminists began calling for inclusive language in the church's liturgical texts. Then the overbearing concern in mission becomes one of control and orthodoxy. This of course stifles the "faithful imagination" of the church at the grass-roots level, and it certainly does little to encourage the transforming reading of scripture by the believers themselves, as we see taking place in Latin America.[14] Although Vatican II called for scripture to become the soul of the church, it is doubtful whether its aspiration will ever really succeed until the basic reciprocity between mission and hermeneutics is fully appreciated.

The opposite danger for mission is equally critical: to make scripture the principal defining moment of "being" church is to turn mission into an exclusively "in-house" religious affair, thus introducing a false dichotomy between faith and culture which in turn skews much of today's discussion about mission. For example, it too readily assumes that Christians today live their faith in two different, even contradictory, cultures: the ecclesiastical culture on the one hand and the popular North American culture on the other. What is not always appreciated is how these two cultures are actually *combined* (as they must be) in the consciousness of the laity. We must not assume, as is generally the case, that the two cultures are like two divorced, antithetical or metaphysically opposed entities. The real danger consists in trying to isolate a people's attitudes toward God, the church, or mission from their socio-cultural system. The development of religious faith in this country, as in any other, is intrinsically tied in with the cultural system within which it is contexualized and bodied forth. In this respect the church's challenge in North America is no different than anywhere else. Faith and culture are always inextricably bound to one another, and in their nuptial embrace they will always be seen as something of an "odd couple." The way one understands this union, however, is what ultimately determines how one perceives and defines mission. This will be the focus of Part Two in our study. Our purpose here is to draw attention primarily to the bewildering number of major changes that have taken place in hermeneutics since the beginning of the 1980s[15]—all of which have considerable bearing on how the bible is being read today and therefore on the expectations, assumptions and goals of mission. Charles Mabee states the bewildering confusion well:

> The term "crisis" appears throughout the literature of contemporary biblical scholarship. Since the demise of commonly accepted standards of interpretation...the entire field of biblical interpreta-

tion has exploded in myriad directions in the past decade. As a result, professors in the classroom stand in the same sort of isolation from the question of the meaning of the biblical text as does the minister before the congregation. The complexity of methodologies confronting the interpreter has caused the meaning of the text to recede from view, rather than become manifest.[16]

Among the many different, even opposite, theories and directions being suggested by scholars to interpret texts, including sacred scripture, the following are noteworthy:

—the hermeneutics of suspicion and retrieval [Paul Ricoeur]
—the socio-critical hermeneutics [Jurgen Habermas]
—the socio-pragmatic hermeneutics [Richard Rorty]
—the hermeneutics of liberation, with its varied distinctive strands:
    —Latin American [Gustavo Gutiérrez]
    —black American [James Cone]
    —South African black [Alan Boesak]
    —feminist [Rosemary Ruether]
—the literary approaches to hermeneutics, which place a firm emphasis on the role of the reader in the art of interpretation.[17]

The most recent document of the Vatican's Biblical Commission on the interpretation of the bible also surveys and assesses the numerous current modes of interpreting scripture. These include, among others, the historical-critical method and the rhetorical, narrative and semiotic analyses of the biblical text, as well as other modern approaches based on tradition: canonical criticism, recourse to ancient Jewish modes of interpretation and *Wirkungsgeschichte* (the study of the historical effects that biblical texts have had on the life of the Christian community). Approaches from diverse currents of modern life are also assessed, such as the liberationist and the feminist. This is followed by a discussion of a fundamentalist reading of the bible and the problems it creates.[18]

Taken together, these exegetical methods attempt to give us an objective exegesis of the bible, while taking seriously into account the incontrovertible subjective component of interpreting a text, biblical or otherwise. They also strive to safeguard against the danger of "reading into" a biblical text the meaning one wants to find in it. Nevertheless, however much these scientific tools are utilized by biblical scholars, they are not generally accessible to the average lay Christian who also has a unique responsibility and mission of interpreting the bible for his or her own culture and contemporary world. Since the bible itself is inherently hermeneutical, then logically each new generation of believers must have a say in the interpretation of the bible for their own times. Claude Geffré has long maintained that the whole of the New Testament can in fact be regarded as an act of interpretation and thus a task of equal importance for Christians today:

> There can be no living preaching today without a creative reinterpretation of Christianity. It is, in other words, not enough simply to "adapt" a traditional doctrine to contemporary attitudes. Our search for a new language of faith of necessity implies a reinterpretation of the content of that language. The task of reinterpretation involves a great risk and it can only be carried out by establishing a reciprocal correlation between the fundamental experience of the New Testament and the traditional faith of the Church and our contemporary human experience.[19]

Nor is Geffré alone in this line of theological reflection. Karl Rahner, Edward Schillebeeckx, Langdon Gilkey, David Tracy—and the list could doubtless be extended—have all attempted to bridge the yawning gap between the New Testament, Christian belief, and the conscious human experiences of men and women of today. Without exception, all are deeply concerned about the uncritical acceptance of beliefs which no longer "speak" to the reality of immediate, contemporary experience. In this regard, the work of Sandra M. Schneiders is of singular importance and merit, especially her interpretation of the New Testament as sacred scripture for women today.[20]

Biblical interpretation and mission also have this in common—that if immediate human experience is to be addressed in a meaningful way, they must both address the issue of *contingency* and *particularity*. Both are informed by a Christian vision, but this vision is mediated to Christians in and only through their situational, historical and existential particularity. With a pluralism previously unimagined in both today's church and world, mission will have to seriously take into account not only the diversity found in the public world, but also in the diverse publics within the church itself. And this is as it should be (and always has been), since the constitutive witness of our faith is not monolithic but pluralist. In the New Testament, one cannot identify Mark with John, nor Jude with James or Paul, nor Jerusalem with Corinth, or, again, Pauline theology with Johannine theology.[21]

Crisis in Religious Symbolism

Carl Jung was not the first to deplore the demise of Christian symbols, but he had good reason to express concern at the loss of their power and even death within large sections of the western world.[22] The erosion of the church's traditional symbols and symbolic rites (e.g., the sacraments) is certainly a further reason for a new utterance about mission. If Christianity is to survive in the postmodern world and retain its "core" identity and integrity, the Christian symbols, which go to the very heart of "being" a church with a mission, must somehow be recovered, revitalized and reappropriated; in a word: they must be "set free" in order to do what only living symbols can do for us.

It is not my intention to dwell here on the sociological factors that certainly contributed to the demise of the Christian symbols. Even Christian sensitivity to the symbolic can significantly diminish under certain social conditions and therefore requires constant nurturing, today possibly more than ever. Yet there is little the church can do to immunize itself against these "extraneous" social forces over which it no longer has commanding control or authority as it once may have had—very little, I say, short of becoming another Noah's ark, a church hermetically sealed off from the world and bent primarily on its own survival. Nor is it my intention for the moment to enter the debate about what may or may not be legitimately expected from the church's presence in the world.[23] Rather I merely wish to draw attention here to those ecclesial or "internal" areas over which the church does have a measure of "controlling" interest, and to that extent at least is also responsible for the demise and "degradation" of its religious symbols.

The survival of the church as a significant transforming and grace-full presence in today's society depends, as John Riches has correctly stated, "on its ability to adapt and change its symbolism to the new pattern of society; otherwise it will have a distorted view of God and the church and society."[24] This same challenge was voiced by Paul Tillich: "If the resurgence of religion would produce a new understanding of the symbols of the past and their relevance for our situation, instead of premature and deceptive answers, it would become a creative factor in our culture and a saving factor for many who live in estrangement, anxiety, and despair."[25] Has the church not neglected to "translate" and "ground" its symbols and symbolic rites in the actual structures of people's social existence, especially those like ours which are heavily conditioned by urban life and high technology? And is the "translation" of its symbols and ritual enactment not one of the main tasks of mission, whether in the younger local churches of Africa or right here in North America? One could argue that such a mission is even more urgently needed right here at home since African society still retains great sensitivity to rituals and symbolic action.[26] In our western civilization, the church's symbols are being edged out for want of a place to really take hold, but it is incumbent upon the church, not society, to find and drop just such an "anchor." If the Christian symbols speak to less and less people today, if the church's symbolic rites and sacraments no longer seem capable of "touching" the faithful at a depth sufficient to mobilize them in any real public or corporate sense, and if the young especially find them meaningless and quite irrelevant, then the church clearly does have a mission *ad intra*. This is especially true if we wish to continue to speak meaningfully of the church as a "sacrament of salvation," as Vatican II does, and hence as an eminently symbolic reality itself. There are at least two ecclesial or "internal" ways in which the church has been remiss in terms of its religious symbols and therefore ways that it might begin to salvage something of their original vitality, power and richness. Let us briefly take a look at these.

First, it must dispel the myth of urban irreligion, on the one hand, and, on the other, the idea that the artifacts of technology are less capable of mediating God's grace than nature, that a computer, for example, is not charged with as much of God's grandeur as "the birds of the air or the lilies of the field." Unlike the bubonic plague in late medieval Europe or the present-day AIDS infection, we can safely predict that cities and modern technology will be around well into the third millennium. With these two inescapable realities before it, the church can ill-afford to merely decry the depersonalizing aspects of city life or the dehumanizing aspects of modern technology. Much more is needed. Earthing the gospel in city-life and sacramentalizing some of the artifacts of modern technology means that the church will have to be more creative and imaginative in the kinds of questions it asks, without dogmatically presuming to know the answers to these questions, and certainly not before "consulting the faithful" on these matters— questions, I mean, like the following: *"How can we find God in the city?" "How can technology serve as a medium for a 'close encounter' with a transcendent God and hence become truly sacramental?" "How are we to unite modern science and technology to traditional Christian religion without losing our own identity as Catholics?"*

The covert distrust of the city and of everything connected with its ambiguity and artificiality has impeded the church's imaginative approach to urban ministry. Yet it is well to bear in mind that nearly half of the human race now lives in cities. Of the 2.6 billion human beings who will be born in the next twenty years, eighty-eight percent will be city-dwellers. By the year 2010, it is estimated that fifty-seven percent of the world's population will be living in cities. At present, there are some one hundred and twenty-five cities in the world with populations over one million. By the year 2000, there will be an estimated three hundred. Let us remember, too, that if the first scene in the bible takes place in a beautiful natural garden (Gn 2:8), the closing scene of salvation history takes place in a splendidly artificial city on high (Rev 21:10-27). It might be good also to keep in mind the fact that when the church first become missionary (in the *ad extra* sense) it was in the big cities that it found its first real home: Corinth, Rome, Jerusalem, Ephesus.[27] From the beginning, therefore, Christianity made its home in the bustling urban centers, not in rural villages where people lived off the earth and close to nature (and the word *pagan*, from the Latin *paganus*, literally meant a rural "country district"). God-in-the-city! Was that not the surprise discovery that the foot-dragging prophet Jonah made in the supposedly "godless" city of Nineveh?

Regarding the church and technology, James W. Heisig has stated the case succinctly yet better than most:

> The absence of a tradition of religious symbols to express the meaning of the relationship between people and their technology is one of the greatest challenges awaiting organized religions in the future. If the challenge is not taken up, symbols of the past will one day slip and fall from our hands, leaving only scattered shards where there were once whole vessels—like the lost religions of the ancient world, more fit for historians and archaeologists than for the human spirit.[28]

Langdon Gilkey is of the same opinion.[29] The question of the relation between the modern scientific and technological culture and the traditional religious tenets of the church remains one of the dominant challenges of our times.

Second, if religious symbols have to be constantly reset within the current structures of social existence in order to be truly effective, it is also true that symbols die as a result of too much magisterial dogmatism. The problem of dogmatism, in terms of the degradation of symbols, has been most penetratingly analyzed by the contemporary philosopher, Eric Voegelin.[30] Whenever the "teaching" church becomes overly zealous and intolerant, authoritative or dogmatic in its effort to safeguard "sound" doctrine, symbols lose their vitality and existential faith dries up into doctrinal belief. Then the faithful find themselves living in a church whose symbolic constructs no longer house or nourish their deepest feelings.

One reason for this is because whereas dogmatism has a very low tolerance for ambiguity, symbols cannot live without it. When functioning at their best, symbols give us a simultaneous experience of the most complex, contradictory, and even mutually exclusive feelings, and they do so moreover at the conscious and unconscious levels. To deprive symbols of their power to evoke a multiplicity of meanings simultaneously—their "multivocality" or "polysemic" character as it is sometimes called—is to deprive them of the very thing that gives them their richness and power. So for example, as a symbolic act, immersion in water can evoke destruction as well as purification, a sense of terror and renewal, death and life, cleansing and refreshment, etc. The church cannot hope to salvage the vitality of its symbols by being doctrinaire and reducing the meaning of its symbols to one "official" signification. When this happens, religious symbols degenerate into routine formulae; mystery and ambiguity are reduced to one dimension of meaning, and existential faith gives way to authoritative faith. Faith does have a cognitive element, but it can never be simply reduced to a propositional truth or truths. There is an infinite difference between the truth of faith and the conceptual formulation we use to express it. Even being a good teacher or producing a new official Catholic catechism is not enough. There exists a considerable difference moreover between that which is explicitly and officially taught by the magisterium and that which the average Christian in the church today actually believes.[31] If the church has favored *pedagogy* in the past, it must now become an even better *mystagogue* if its symbols are to survive in a postmodern world. The difference between the two approaches, as we shall see, is of vital importance when dealing with symbols and ritual enactment.

Moreover, symbols presuppose the acceptance of the unknown and openness to the unexpected, something that an overly dogmatic or authoritarian hierarchy is unlikely to countenance. As Ernest Skublics has judiciously warned, "Every pretense or even innocent conviction that we know everything the symbol means spells the death of the symbol."[32] We do not possess symbols, they possess us. Acceptance of the unknown, therefore, openness to the unexpected, "surrendering" to and letting oneself be "seduced" by a symbol, are the only favorable dispositions when being initiated into mystery. Any other controlling or manipulative intention, whether conscious or unconscious, hinders the life and proper functioning of symbols.[33] The reason for this, of course, is because symbols directly appeal to and actively engage—first and foremost—our religious imagination, not our intellect. A doctrinaire approach or bias, on the other hand, leaves little room for the free play of religious imagination, without which even Christian symbols degenerate and become atrophied. Thus a church contributes to the demise of its own symbols and symbolic rites when it fails to enlist the religious imagination of the faithful, when it fails to recognize their "faithful imagination" as a Christian's birthright, a baptismal gift, and therefore one that is eminently suited and open to the transcendent mystery of God and his word. By "faithful imagination," I mean, specifically, that imaginative dimension which not only adheres to faith *at certain times* or *on special occasions*, but is a constitutive element in every act of real theological faith, hope, and love. The implications of this for proclamation and mission are profound and far-reaching.

Crossing the Postmodern Divide

Today scientists are abandoning a Newtonian worldview that sees the universe as a collection of separate entities in a hierarchical order, in favor of a more fluid quantum worldview, one in which the basic unity of all creation is emphasized, and where relationships between entities are all-important because it is these relationships that create the structures of the universe, not vice versa. The rising sentiment that we are coming to the close not only of a century but of an era is a further reason why we need to re-vision mission. Although the sentiment has not yet become universal, the indications are too numerous to ignore and do in fact point to a major paradigm shift *from the modern to the postmodern*. When faith is viewed in this perspective, that is, within the historic process of passing from one era or epoch to another, how the Christian community negotiates this "betwixt-and-between" period in history becomes a crucial issue for mission. In such an axial or transitional period when the world and the church are both experiencing disjunction, the mission of creative reconstruction becomes especially important. Implicitly or explicitly, it becomes the shape of our contemporary "*Yes*" to God as we refashion the stuff of our lives and our faith into new possibilities. As a commitment that must be reappropriated time and again in the face of a future we cannot predict or control at will, our faith is always *in front of us*; it beckons us to walk into a "new" future with the "conviction of things unseen" (Heb 11:1). Only then can the Christian community seriously *re-vision* its sense of mission in today's world, and thus merit the name: "living faith."

Many serious authors are today concerned and writing about the church's mission in a new mode, one that strives not so much to predict a future as yet unborn, but to prepare the Christian community for mission in a rapidly changing world and in the face of a future that is already quite clearly in the throes of being born. To be sure, their work is tentative, limited and fallible. Yet the distinctive discourse of the majority of these authors is one of scanning, probing, discerning the signs of the times in view of repositioning and refocusing the mission of the church. This is creative faith at work. And behind these efforts one can even discern something of the Spirit which Paul describes as "groaning within us with sighs too deep for words" (Rom 8:26). With few exceptions, these authors would have us anticipate and face the new era, not as a "future shock," but like the progeny of Abraham and Sarah who "greeted them from afar" (Heb 11:13) or like the long-awaited bridegroom in the gospel parable who was eagerly anticipated by the wise virgins (Mt 25:1-12).

Walbert Bühlmann, in his book *With Eyes to See*, envisages mission very decidedly in terms of a future that is even now impinging upon us, as his subtitle makes perfectly clear: *Church and World in the Third Millennium*.[34] The substance of Bühlmann's work consists in drawing up a new decalogue based on the signs of the times, with concluding reflections on the new future. In a very real sense, Bühlmann has always boldly looked to the future as the titles of his two other major works attest: *Coming of the Third Church* and *The Church of the Future*. In the same perspective, one must also include the large-minded vision and important work of David Bosch, *Transforming Mission*, to which we referred earlier. While this major work has received favorable reviews and could well become a standard missiological text for some years to come (it has already been translated into French[35]), there are two shortcomings that I would like to signal out. I do so not to depreciate this fine study but to serve notice as to how the present study hopes to remedy these.

My first criticism concerns the way Bosch applies the notion of "paradigm" in Part 3, titled "Toward a Relevant Missiology." In this third and last section of the book (which comprises over one hundred and sixty pages), Bosch traces some thirteen emerging new trends in mission. No doubt many of these can indeed be discerned in various parts of the world church and as such can be justifiably counted as so many signal landmarks on the mission scene. What the author does not do, however, is draw these from any rigorous postmodern thinking or postmodern paradigm. Although labeled "postmodern," they are in effect but a somewhat arbitrary listing of elements already in vogue in one or other areas of the world church. While not without merit, such a listing does not constitute a paradigm (and certainly not a postmodern paradigm), nor can it really be called a typology of mission today in any strict sense. It is more an *enumeration* of various important elements of mission, with only the most nominal link with actual constructive postmodern thinking. Nowhere, except in a scant few pages (pp. 349-362), does Bosch define the word "postmodern" other than in its most negative sense, as a reaction *against* what he sees as the seven major characteristics of the enlightenment. It is unfortunate that Bosch apparently did not have available to him, for example, the excellent series on *constructive postmodern thought* published by the State University of New York Press of which David Griffin is editor.

A second shortcoming in this otherwise fine study, and which I hope to remedy, is the surprising lack of anything that approaches a mission spirituality. Such an absence is all the more conspicuous since one of the hallmarks of mission today (as well as of constructive postmodern thought) is surely the quest for an adequate new spirituality for our times. Already there is a growing consensus about the general profile and some of the basic elements of this mission spirituality. This will be the main focus in Part Four of this study.

2 | An Uneasy Dialogue in the American Catholic Church

In the preceding chapter, I have attempted to indicate some of the more general reasons why there is a need to re-vision mission. Here I would like to localize this need and its urgency by looking more closely at the church in the United States. I do so for two reasons: one personal, the other theological. It is in the North American cultural context that I feel most at home. Notwithstanding the fact that I was a missionary in southern Africa for fifteen years, it is from this particular local church in America that I grew up and returned to some sixteen years ago with a renewed sense of mission. It is also my theological conviction that missiology must be inductive rather than deductive, "from below," to use Karl Rahner's expression, rather than "from above"—that is to say, the conviction that it is "at home" and from within the context of one's local church that mission, like charity, must begin. If we are to construct a local theology of mission for North America, a task that is long overdue, then this is the only way to proceed.[1]

We have become so accustomed to think of mission as something that takes place abroad, away from home, in some distant and foreign land that it is difficult for most of us to think mission in any other perspective. Among American Catholics especially, who in the past have been very generous in supporting the so-called "foreign missions," such a conversion of mind and heart about mission as I will be suggesting in this study will not be easy. Real conversions never are. Yet the kingdom of God and becoming a mission church, although not to be equated or confused, do have at least one incontrovertible thing in common: they are both "within reach," both "at hand"—so close in fact that neither is ever further away from us than the person next door, the one to whom we suddenly become, one blessed day, an eighth sacrament: "a neighbor."[2] Mission must begin at home if it is ever to have any hope of reaching to the ends of the earth.

Only in this "homing" perspective, when reimagined within our own culture first, will the notion of "mission" be completely freed from paternalistic or guilt feelings that so often accompany our assistance to the poor and the oppressed of the world. Those of us who (quite accidentally) happen to be born and live in a country as rich and as affluent as America are prone to look upon the poor as the "wretched of the earth" instead of the "blessed ones" that Jesus saw and so named—a blessing in disguise to be sure, but an unsolicited grace nonetheless. As affluent Christians, our sense of mission must first of all be liberated and set free from its moorings of pity and guilt, and grounded more firmly in the simple yet astounding fact of just *being* Christian. Otherwise we will continue to equate mission with feeling sorry for others. Pity, of course, is but one of the many potent human emotions that the average person can and obviously does experience in the course of his or her everyday life, but mission cannot be so poorly grounded or so sorely restricted. The "preferential option for the poor" may well engender pity and compassion, but since this so often arises in America as a result of having been put on some guilt trip, much of our missionary compassion can be more properly called "reparation." And although reparation is clearly an important element in Christian life and mission, it can neither ground nor exhaust the full meaning and potential of being a missionary church.

Another prevailing misconception we have about mission in America is to think of it primarily, if not exclusively, as "giving" something to others; rarely do we imagine mission as "receiving" something we ourselves desperately need, initially from the poor closest to us. Our sense of mission must be informed with an inner disposition similar to the request made by the Roman centurion in Matthew's gospel (Mt 8:5-13) or that of the Syrophoenician woman in Mark (Mk 7:25-30), that is, something on the order of an earnest appeal for help. Failure to envisage mission as "reception" as well as "donation," as a reciprocal exchange and communion, means that we have either missed the whole point of the beatitudes or else have been terribly embarrassed by them. In many ways, this misconception of mission can be traced to a failure to attend to the voices, the experience, and the spiritual riches of the poor in our very midst, next door!

There are many historical reasons why we American Catholics have come to fuel our sense of mission with such high octane guilt or pity and generally think of mission as a unilateral proposition, a one-way street, if you will. Yet when we analyze the situation more closely we find that these and other misconceptions about mission are invariably conditioned by the more fundamental issue of the way Catholics live and experience their American culture.[3] What we are really faced with here is the question of "faith *and* culture," that is, being Catholic *and* American. In theory we may continue to think of these as two distinguishable realities (as though the one could be attended to independently of the other), but in real life this improbable "odd couple" conspires and gives us something quite indivisible, namely, our unique identity as *American Catholics*. It is the uniqueness of this "dual" identity that the present study will seek to address by proposing a new vision and model for integrating the "energy-charged" relationship between faith and culture.

The uneasy dialogue between being Catholic *and* American generally takes place at the undisclosed, pre-reflexive level of the believer's consciousness. This is not surprising since no credible local American theology of mission yet exists, nor does the new *Catechism of the Catholic Church* even address the important question of inculturation. In fact, the word "inculturation" does not even appear in the catechism's subject index, which comprises some forty-four otherwise impressive pages. Except for a few interested Catholic scholars, such a basic issue is rarely adverted to or discussed. Yet even hidden and left unattended, this "inner" dialogue between faith and culture is nevertheless very real, goes on all the time, and has an extraordinary, if silent, impact on the way Catholics perceive and live their faith in the American cultural context. My contention is that it is precisely this muted "inner" dialogue which takes place in the soul of most American Catholics, this abiding tension between one's culture and one's faith, that gives rise to and explains so much of the more visible and audible uneasiness at the surface level of church life in America. In order to better appreciate the dynamic and compelling interpenetration between "faith and culture," which we will consider at greater length later, we do well to stop here and review some of the more surface symptoms of uneasiness in the American Catholic Church.

American Catholics and the Vatican

The uneasy dialogue between Rome and American Catholics is obvious to everyone regardless of where one positions oneself in the church: to its right, left or center.[4] One of the most difficult areas of dialogue of course concerns the teaching role of the church, a role that has hitherto been regarded as belonging almost exclusively to the hierarchy, the magisterium. Hence the sharp dichotomy that still prevails between the "teaching church" and the "believing church" is something that goes against the grain of many American Catholics today. José Casanova states that

> as the lesson of American Catholicism indicates, the church will have to learn to let all the faithful participate in the constant elaboration and reformulation of its normative teachings and allow for different practical judgments as to how to interpret those normative teachings in concrete circumstances.[5]

The average Catholic rarely feels consulted on those issues of existential Christian importance about which they have informed opinions, with the hard evidence at hand of their own personal experience of "keeping" the faith in a complex world and (unless one is making a rash judgment here) with the living Spirit of their baptism still operative in their lives. As a result, while they continue to give outward signs of loyalty and due respect to the official "teachers" of their church, inwardly they are deciding *en masse* to follow their conscience in those matters wherein they feel competent to decide for themselves. An example: according to the 1992 Gallup Poll, eighty-one percent of American Catholics agreed that bishops should consult the laity so that the lay experience of sexuality can influence the development of church teachings (only fourteen percent disagreed; ten percent had no opinion).

Addressing the Catholic Press Association's annual meeting in Milwaukee in 1992, Archbishop Rembert Weakland publicly acknowledged what most American Catholics have known for quite some time. "As I travel around the country," the archbishop said, "I find a growing disaffection with Rome....It takes two forms. At times it is rather just [*sic*] an expression of indifference to what Rome says. People just do not find that it matters much to them. I find this attitude very pronounced in the academic circles but am always surprised to find it elsewhere as well at all cultural levels. In addition to this indifference, there is also a second group that shows much anger and some degree of animosity toward Rome."[6] In point of fact, the so-called "indifferent" American Catholics far outnumber the angry voices of discontent one hears in the church. Yet it should be remembered that *indifference* can be a very radical personal decision, a deliberate choice of insensibility toward the official teaching of Rome. As such therefore it should not be too quickly dismissed simply as a nonchalant attitude or unthinking distraction. Indifference toward directives from Rome, even when *outward* respect is still accorded to it, is conceivably a form of subjective detachment that is just as radical as that of the more vociferous forms of restlessness and public protest.

Such general indifference to the traditional teaching of the church is revealing in more ways than one. As a sign of religious pluralism within the church itself, this indifference obviously lends itself to a variety of different interpretations. Judging by the national polls that survey the religious attitudes of American Catholics, however, it is difficult not to conclude that what we are witnessing today in the United States as well as in Canada is nothing short of a "quiet but massive grass-roots revolution" among the Catholic faithful.[7] Without wishing to "rock the boat," as it were, or openly "buck the ecclesial system," a growing majority of American Catholics have now decided to follow their own conscience while remaining loyal to the Catholic faith as they perceive it. They appear to be doing so moreover without serious scruple or the need to ease their conscience in the confessional as was the case not so many years ago.

This is confirmed in the most recent *National Catholic Reporter/* Gallup Poll of May 1993, which shows that growing numbers of lay Catholics, especially among women and younger Catholics, are personally making up their own minds on matters of church practice and morality. Concerning this shift to greater self-reliance, Thomas Fox says: "The nation's Catholics are largely loyal to the faith as they perceive it, but increasingly at odds with institutional directives."[8] Among the major changes occurring between the 1987 and 1993 surveys, Fox reports the following:

- Only a minority of lay Catholics now think that bishops only should determine the morality of key questions of Catholic practice.
- A seventeen percent increase in Catholics saying, "You can be a good Catholic without obeying the church's teaching regarding abortion."
- A seventeen percent increase in Catholics saying, "The laity should have the right to participate in deciding how parish income should be spent."
- A seventeen percent decrease among Catholics saying, "It would be unacceptable if, because of the priest shortage, there would be no resident priest in the parish but only a lay administrator and visiting priests."

Such trends hold true, the survey reveals, even "for the most highly committed Catholics, those who go to mass at least once a week, who say the church is among the most important parts of their lives, and who say they would never leave the church." Jim Davidson of Purdue University, one of the sociologists who helped develop the survey, concludes: "An increasingly large number of people are unwilling to give the final say to the authorities in the church. A large number are saying they want the final say to be a joint decision on the part of church leaders and laypeople."[9] What appears from this and other data is that the so-called "indifference" of the Catholic laity in America may not be all that indifferent![10] Until there is real dialogue, it seems that American Catholics will continue to rely for guidance on the dictates of their conscience and a sense of their own lived experience of the faith. Evidence of this "quiet revolution" can be seen in the Vatican's concerns and attempts to curb such a trend.[11]

The Place and Role of Women in the Church

Another area of uneasiness (if one may be permitted a euphemism) is the question of women's concerns in the church. The frustration surrounding this issue was chillingly symbolized in the ten-year discussion within the National Conference of Catholic Bishops (NCCB) concerning the place and role of women in the church. Already frustrated with the second draft of the bishops' pastoral on women, Archbishop Weakland went on record as saying: "The whole issue of power and decision-making in the church and how they are, in our current thinking and legislation, related to orders is not mentioned. The question of whether this situation must be so is not even raised." Until this is done, Weakland feels, "there will be no credible treatment of women in the church. The gifts of women cannot be fully recognized if leadership roles have been tied into orders."[12] A third draft proposal was written, discussed and debated, as well as a fourth. In the end the bishops were more divided than ever on *what* to say to Catholic women and *how* to say it. At their annual meeting in November 1992, the bishops voted and in effect scrapped the whole idea of issuing a pastoral on women. Our North American culture gives so much attention to the rights of the person and the equality of women in society that what the church says—or indeed *fails* to say—about the place and role of women in the church appears disarmingly out of touch with contemporary life in America.

The ten-year odyssey of this failed pastoral, with its multiple drafts, debates and conflicting speech-modes between the progressive, moderate and conservative bishops, sadly reminds one of that telling biblical symbol of "linguistic" confusion and division, namely, the tower of Babel (Gn 11:1-9). And that project, as we know, also came to naught. It is curious and doubtless revealing that the American "teaching" church was so self-assured in telling the world how to become a more just soci-ety in its two major pastorals of the 1980s, *The Challenge of Peace* and *Economic Justice for All*; yet it was reduced to silence when it came to some fundamental issues of justice within its own ecclesial community. While its *ad extra* statements are generally assertive and self- confident, its *ad intra* directives seem woefully tentative. This is yet another indica-tion that a re-visioning of mission is necessary.

Within the "believing" church, however, Catholic women are not waiting to be told what they can or cannot do; they are moving ahead with their own agenda and are spurred on by ordinary Catholics, such as those in St. Joseph parish in Minnesota, for example, who publicly voiced their hopes for the church in these words: "We dream about a church where there will be lay representation at all decision making lev-els. We hope that the diaconate will be open to women. We dream about a church grown more whole because it has become balanced in its masculine and feminine spirituality and leadership."[13]

Such dreams on the part of ordinary parishioners are fueled and given theological weight by the growing number of distinguished women theologians in the church—a domain hitherto reserved for the clergy and those studying for the priesthood. Although still very much an uphill grind, many brilliant women theologians have already pene-trated, Trojan-horse fashion, well inside what was hitherto an all-male reserve and sanctuary, i.e., seminary education, diocesan tribunals, Catholic theologates and university theology faculties.[14] Some names? Mary Daly, Agnes Cunningham, Elisabeth Schüssler-Fiorenza, Rosemary Radford Ruether, Monika Hellwig, Rosemary Haughton, Sandra Schneiders, Lisa Cahill, Maria Harris, Margaret Farley, M. Shawn Copeland, Anne Carr, Isasi-Diaz, Anne Patrick—and the list could indeed go on! Some of the above represent visible minority communities, others have been president of the Catholic Theological Society of America, and many are in the process of actively plowing the feminist theological field. All are contributing new ways of thinking about classic theological ques-tions and reimagining God, creation, sexuality, church, ordained min-istry and other concepts from a woman's point of view. Needless to say, there is considerable resistance to feminist questions among traditional scholars, and the increasing number of highly competent women Catholic theologians is viewed by many as a threat rather than a blessing. Another source of contention in Catholic worship, of course, is the use of an authorized version of the bible that uses inclusive or gender-free language.

Being Catholic: A New Way of Belonging

Who is a "good Catholic" today? This question perhaps more than any other lies at the heart of much of the confusion and uneasiness in the domestic Catholic Church in America. There was a time not so long ago when the criteria for answering such a question seemed clear-cut and accepted by virtually everyone in the church. Besides certain beliefs, there were some specific ecclesial practices and responsibilities that gave reassuring visible identity to the American Catholic. Among these, "receiving" the sacraments of the church was by far the most indicative sign of a good Catholic. In the last twenty years, things have changed dramatically.

Today there are many different ways that Catholics understand their ecclesial identity.[15] The once-clear boundaries for assessing Catholic identity now seem problematic and less trustworthy, and to a growing number, they belong to another age. Already in 1989, for example, seventy percent of Catholics in the country believed that one could be a good Catholic without going to church every Sunday; sixty-eight percent said one could be a good Catholic without obeying the church's teaching regarding birth control. This has given rise to what sociologist Andrew Greeley has termed "the communal Catholics,"[16] and what Karl Rahner has described as "incomplete identification" with the institutional church. For Rahner, this means that a Catholic remains in contact with his or her church, continues to practice the faith in a certain way, never seriously thinks of separating himself or herself from the church at the manifest and social level, yet at the same time retains certain notable reservations toward the church.[17] José Casanova puts it this way:

> Implicitly at least, Catholics are saying that they are the people of God, that the church also belongs to them, not only to the hierarchy, that, irrespective of what the hierarchy says, they will not feel excommunicated from their church...and that ultimately they individually have the moral obligation to apply in conscience Catholic normative principles to their own personal situation.[18]

It is not my intention here to describe or analyze this newly perceived way of *being* Catholic in America, nor to speculate about the many contributing factors that may account for it. What is important to note is that any serious local theology of mission in America must address and re-vision new criteria for assessing the identity and faith quality of the *American Catholic*. The traditional criteria which hitherto defined ecclesial identity almost exclusively in terms of parish life and the sacraments served the immigrant church well in the past, but for many

Catholics today they no longer serve as sure guides and are no longer perceived as the only acceptable measure of valuation of genuine Catholic identity. While the "teaching" church still holds to the traditional criteria, the "believing" church gropes falteringly for new and more realistic criteria. It appears now that the emerging new criteria will seek to reflect three things with greater sensitivity: (1) the *particularity* of the American socio-cultural context, since being a Catholic in America is very different from being one in Chile, Zaire, Pakistan, or any other country for that matter; (2) the *faithful dissent* of a growing number of American Catholics and the *sensus fidelium* that is already starting to take noticeable form among them; (3) a new sense of *mission integration* (or spirituality) that will enable them to better integrate, rather than juxtapose, the *ad intra* and the *ad extra* dimensions of their Christian life. Indeed one of the conclusions of the NSRI is that, for a vast majority of Americans, religion is more of a private commitment than a shared experience. Until such a challenge is taken up, it is doubtful we will ever get a true "reading" of the Catholic faith as it is lived and experienced in the American cultural context, much less a true picture of its mission potential. What we will have instead is a continuous stream of questionable readings, not unlike those of a person's temperature taken with a faulty thermometer.

Unless the traditional criteria for establishing and judging Catholic religious identification are re-examined and modified, we can expect to see swell the number of those Catholics who are now spuriously labeled as "lapsed," "dissenting," "marginal," "seasonal," "dissatisfied," "alienated," or "communal." Change the present criteria ever so slightly and the entire ecclesial landscape changes, as does any judgment upon it. Criteria for ecclesial identity, though necessary, are never absolute nor are they ever absolutely reliable. Even the fifth century church father St. Augustine acknowledged that the criteria against which Christian identity is measured are relative and at times deceptive, as when he says: "Some seem to be inside [the church], who are in fact outside, while others seem to be outside who are in fact inside."[19]

It should come as no surprise therefore that the established and internalized criteria for ascertaining who is a "good" Christian (or Catholic) have changed in the course of the church's history, at times quite dramatically. As my colleague and good friend Robert Kress has amply demonstrated, one can read the entire Judaeo-Christian tradition as an ongoing debate about the criteria of the true worshiper of God (Jn 4:23), the true son of Abraham (Mt 3:9), the true Jew (Rom 2:27-29).[20] In the age of the martyrs, for example, when Christians had to publicly renounce their faith or be thrown to the lions, the question of who was a "good" Christian (and who was not) was clear-cut and uncompromisingly straightforward. Yet as Kress reminds us, the church went into a crisis not unlike our own today when the age of persecution ended and Christians were once again able to worship and profess their faith in the broad daylight of a more hospitable marketplace. What then were the new criteria for being a genuine Christian? And how did the church re-vision and come up with a set of new criteria more in keeping with its changed environment? In point of fact, we know that eventually the monk replaced the martyr: "The outer actions most frequently per-formed by them [monks] became the generally accepted criteria for the religious interests of not only all Catholics, but all human beings."[21]

Quite a number of monastic values (for instance, fasting and sexual denial) were gradually imposed by the church on the secular clergy and the whole of lay society. By the late middle ages these monastic values were formulated with such insistence by the mendicant friars that they became the accepted ideal criteria for following Christ "in the world." The evident changes we see taking place today regarding criteria for ecclesial identity are therefore neither unique nor unprecedented. As we take up the task of re-visioning new criteria for American Catholic identity, we might do well to recall that the first disciples of Jesus fol-lowed him primarily because he brought hope into their lives, and he was able to do this in a pre-eminent way by radically changing their entrenched notion of an Old Testament God and providing them with an entirely new, unprecedented way of envisaging God as "Abba." It is precisely this new vision of God that allowed the early primitive church to envisage its very own "down-to-earth" criteria, like the generous one we find in the epistle of James: "Pure, unspoiled religion, in the eyes of God our Father, is this: coming to the help of orphans and widows when they need it." (Jas 1:27).

The mission task of reformulating new criteria for Christian identity consists in "refounding" our special way of responding to Christ within our distinctive local American culture. Such a creative task consists in a return to the primordial Christian source of the New Testament faith in the God of Jesus Christ and the courage to accept as a blessing instead of a curse the fact that faith and culture are always inextricably inter-twined. At no time in its mission history has the church ever given itself new criteria for Christian identity independently of the socio-cultural context in which the faithful are called to live and exercise their mis-sion. In point of fact, it is only when the church falls unconditionally in love, "for better or for worse," with its host culture, as Jesus did his, that faith is quickened and becomes transforming for both the church itself (*ad intra*) as well as its social milieu (*ad extra*).

Clearly, there are some things in life that one must first get to know *before* one can really love them, such as a favorite author, city, or profession. There are other realities, however, that one must risk falling in love with first, warts and all, before one knows them in depth. It will be my contention throughout this study that the dual "gift" reality we call faith *and* culture is clearly of this order. Any talk of inculturation, therefore, must begin, continue, and end with an unconditional love for a people's culture. Whatever mistakes the church may have made in its missionary past, two in particular now appear in greater relief. The first mistake consists in thinking that it is possible to evangelize people without due regard for their cultural identity and the complex symbol system that gives them their unique identity in the first place—the mistake, in other words, of trying to address and convert individuals as though the culture of these individuals was somehow but an external and therefore expendable aspect of their being. With its call for the "evangelization of cultures," the church is clearly trying to avoid repeating such unwitting mistakes of the past, but as yet is still very unsure as to how to go about this new mission task.

The second mistake in mission, still prevalent today, consists in thinking that evangelizing a culture can be carried out by selecting those elements in a culture that "appear" compatible with the gospel message and rejecting the others as secular, worldly, un-Christian, ungodly, or otherwise unacceptable. The basic mistake here is due to a faulty notion of culture, namely, to think of culture as though it were a loose collection of variegated marbles (values) and that one could arbitrarily select some and discard others. Such a misguided view of culture, as we shall see, is tantamount to a mortal vivisection of a culture. John Coleman is quite right: "A moralistic reading of cultural traits all too often stakes out easy contrasts between good points and bad points in a culture as if one could rather handily have one without the other, to separate the wheat from the chaff, the sheep from the goats."[22] If anything, culture should be viewed more like an indivisible spider's web wherein every strand hangs together and forms a *whole* filigree of meaning. This precludes the "pick-and-choose" approach to culture. Either one accepts the total constellation of culture texts, values, and symbols—the *total* package deal, as it were—or else one must desist from trying to evangelize a culture in anything but a most superficial way, the very thing Pope Paul VI warned us against.[23]

The real missionary genius of Matteo Ricci was precisely his initially unqualified and wholehearted acceptance of the Chinese culture *as a whole*; his was far from the typical preemptive selection or piecemeal approach that was common in the sixteenth century. Herein lay the source of his difficulties with Rome. In many respects the American Catholic Church is being criticized today for having done precisely what Ricci and his companions were attempting to do in China, namely, embrace wholeheartedly and unstintingly the culture in which they came to live and call "home." There are many parallels that could be drawn between the Jesuit experience in China and the Catholic experience in America.

From the onset, like Ricci, American Catholics loved their country and deeply cherished the socio-cultural values they found: equality under the law, the due process of the courts, the right to vote, and the freedom of speech, press and assembly. And like Ricci in China, American Catholics did not come to America through the "back door," as it were, sheepishly and unsure of their faith convictions. While paying all due respect to the civil authorities and allegiance to the flag, they strove to make their presence felt by competing with their Protestant neighbors in the arduous task of being accepted and competing honorably for a rightful place in the American cultural landscape. In this sense, contrary to what many critics say, the church in America can serve as a model for that first essential phase of what today we call "inculturation."

In this process, again not unlike Ricci, American Catholics came under the suspicion and misjudgments of Rome, as in the "Syllabus of Errors" issued by Pope Pius IX in 1864.[24] Curiously, Rome seems always to have been uneasy about the freedom and sense of democracy that American Catholics have come to cherish.[25] Even today, one cannot avoid the impression that Rome will not allow the Catholic Church in this country to develop in such a way that it would reflect the American genius. What can be emphasized here, however, is that, having finally "come home," the time has perhaps now come to seriously consider how it will negotiate yet another phase in the inculturation process, and how it might begin to articulate for itself a genuine local American theology. But more on this later.

Still an Immigrant Church?

It has almost become a commonplace to observe that in the last two or three generations Catholics in this country have gone from feeling like "outsiders" to "insiders" in America. Demographic and sociological data would seem to support this observation. Roman Catholics today represent over twenty-one percent of the total U.S. population (or 26.2 percent of all those who consider themselves Christians), thus constituting the largest religious denomination in the country. Three-fourths of the Catholic population now belong to the middle class and since the 1950s have rapidly moved into professional, managerial and administrative occupations. "White Catholics are now very much a part of the established American middle class and upper-class. When one looks only at white Catholics, it appears that a social revolution has occurred since the 1950s. They have become better educated and socially and economically more integrated into suburban society."[26] There are even those who speculate, like the conservative Protestant theologian Richard John Neuhaus, that "the Catholic moment" is at hand, meaning that the Catholic Church can and should now become the lead church "in the culture-forming task of constructing a religiously informed public philosophy for the American experiment in ordered liberty."[27]

While Neuhaus' reading of the Catholic Church in America may be understandable from a conservative point of view, it remains wishful thinking for two remarkable reasons. *First*, there is no indication that American Catholics *want* their church to assume such a public role in American society, much less become the official moral conscience of the nation. If anything, data from recent surveys indicate that they do not want their church leaders to assume such a role. Moreover, there are good reasons why the church should not take up such a conservative agenda.[28] While acknowledging the right and competence of the church to speak out on public issues, the Catholic bishops themselves are very modest in their concrete public policy recommendations. As José Casanova sees it:

> It was the very reticence of the bishops to present authoritative Catholic solutions to contemporary societal problems that was most significant [in the bishops' public speeches]. What the bishops did was to present the Catholic normative tradition as the basis for public debate. They did not claim to know the answers, a claim which de facto would tend to preclude any public debate, leaving room only for partisan mobilization.[29]

Even were Neuhaus' "Catholic Moment" something more than a wistful dream, and notwithstanding the Vatican's encouragement to dream on, the local American Catholic Church still lacks the kind of mission consciousness that would be necessary to pull it off. As Joe Holland grimly sees it, "The modern religious crisis...is its fearful retreat into the comfortable womb of community, where there is no outward mission, and where the retreating community inevitably begins to die—as if a fetus from within chose its own abortion."[30]

Second, such wishful thinking overlooks another difficulty. Just when Catholics are beginning to feel "at home" in America and quite comfortable with their hard-earned "insider" status, millions of Latin American and Asian-Pacific immigrants began swelling their ranks to a point where the distinction between insiders and outsiders is becoming a real problem *within* the Catholic Church itself. This means that the Catholic population is now made up of insiders as well as outsiders, an unprecedented feature that is already emerging as a major source of internal confusion and alienation in the church. In his pioneering study of Hispanic-Americans, *The Second Wave*, Allan Deck describes the situation this way:

> At this moment in time, consequently, the U.S. Catholic Church is schizophrenic, caught between two identities. One is the achievement of the mainstreaming process; the other is the result of a new migration that shows no sign of abating. This migration will transform that Church by the next century into a predominantly Hispanic American institution just as today it is predominantly Irish American.[31]

According to figures reported by the U.S. Census Bureau in 1990, the nation's Hispanic population alone totaled 22.4 million. If undocumented Hispanics are included, then the number could be as high as twenty-five million. And even if only eighty percent of these are baptized Catholics, as some estimates have it, this means that Hispanics represent over one-third of the Catholic population in the country. Perhaps even more important is the fact that the age profile of the Hispanic population is very young: fifty-four percent are twenty-five years of age or younger. All of this makes Allan Deck's forecast seem plausible, namely, that the Hispanics could well become the majority of U.S. Catholics sometime early in the twenty-first century.[32] The formidable religious and cultural challenges such a prospect raises for the Catholic Church in America are amply dealt with by Joseph P. Fitzpatrick in his book *One Church Many Cultures*.[33] However, while it is true that Hispanics are an important and growing constituency for the Catholic Church, it should also be noted that their impact varies geographically. As the NSRI figures clearly indicate, nationwide they comprise less than two percent of the Catholic populations of the midwestern and New England states.[34]

This dramatic shift within the Catholic population, with all the inherent cultural and counter-cultural religious issues involved, is yet another reason why a local American theology of mission is so urgently needed. The construction of such a theology is unlikely, however, until the more fundamental issue of "inculturation" is directly addressed and envisaged as an urgent mission priority in the context of American culture. While the literature devoted to this topic is impressive, there is still considerable confusion as to what inculturating faith actually involves, and even more confusion as to how, in practical terms, it can be translated into an effective pastoral program and applied specifically to our American culture.

It is to this major challenge, the heart of our study, that we now turn our attention.

PART TWO

Inculturation: A New Challenge

3 | Re-Visioning Inculturation

How one interprets the conjunctive adverb "and" in the now popular expression "Faith *and* Culture" determines to a large extent everything that follows. It not only reveals the way one envisages and defines the mission of the church in the world, but it also predetermines the outlook and conclusions one arrives at about the notion of inculturation. The word "inculturation" is one of those key words we spoke of earlier, as having angelic power to awaken and fire the staid imagination of the church at a given time in its history. It is a word that suddenly appeared in the church's discourse, unannounced yet charged with potent meaning, and like all such "visitations" from on high, it has kept theologians busy ever since.

The word itself made its first appearance in 1959, during the twenty-ninth Week of Missiology in Louvain, but was initially used as being virtually synonymous with the word "adaptation."[1] The word had been coined, however, and would soon have theologians wrestling to uncover its deeper meaning and true nature. It was introduced by the Jesuit superior-general at the synod of bishops in Rome in 1977 and further clarified by French Dominican theologian Yves Congar, who, in a note to Monsignor Coffy, described it as follows: "Inculturation means that Christianity, the faith, must be sown like a seed in...a certain socio-cultural human space, wherein it must find its own proper expression from that culture itself."[2] The word was used for the first time in a papal document by John Paul II in 1979.[3] Since then it has become one of the most pivotal points of discussion among scholars in mission studies. It has, in effect, become central to the grammar of the postconciliar church to describe the interdependence and proper relation between faith and cultures.

Despite the vast literature on the subject, there still exists considerable confusion and lack of clarity about the actual process of inculturation and what it *really* entails. This can be seen, for example, in Stephen

Bevans' appreciable attempt to "classify" the many methodological approaches to inculturation,[4] as well as in Robert Schreiter's masterful overview of the current literature on the subject.[5] Although progress has been made in clarifying some of the issues surrounding the methodology and praxis of inculturation, discussion still has a long way to go. As yet there is no general agreement on the symbolic nature of culture, nor on the manner in which the process of inculturation is to be conceived and carried out. Still less attention has been given to what inculturation means or might entail for the Catholic Church in the American cultural context, which is one of the reasons, I submit, why attempts to construct a truly *local* American theology are found wanting and still very rare.

What follows is an attempt to shed further light on some of these crucial issues by, *first*, pointing out some of the questionable assumptions in the current literature on inculturation and, *second*, by proposing a "root metaphor" for re-visioning the relation between faith and culture. I use the word "re-vision" advisedly here, as will become apparent, (a) to emphasize the neglected yet fundamental role of theological imagination in our deliberations about inculturation, and (b) to propose a constructive alternative view of inculturation that is irreducibly metaphorical.

Questionable Approaches and Assumptions

The first questionable assumption in much of the current literature is that the pastoral praxis of inculturation is primarily if not exclusively of concern only for the young churches in the non-western world. Any talk or discussion about inculturation almost invariably conjures up the mission agenda and task of those local churches in what we have traditionally called "mission countries." To be sure, this is where the proverbial shoe pinches most noticeably, where the traditional cultural values and customs are so patently at odds with the imposed Roman rite and with so much of the canonical legislation of the Roman curia. In these countries the liturgy, the piety, the architecture and the ecclesiastical art were all imported from the west, as well as the theology. It is not surprising therefore that it was initially in these countries that discussion about inculturation first started and has hitherto received the most attention and serious consideration. Understandably, one of the major topics of discussion at the recent African bishops' synod in Rome was precisely the urgent need and challenge to inculturate the gospel in African cultures. This also explains why so much of the best literature on inculturation still comes from local theologians in Africa, Asia, and Latin America.

Somewhat belatedly, European and North American scholars have entered the discussion and debate, but by and large they continue to view the process of inculturation more as a mission priority of the church in Africa and Asia than a serious missionary challenge for the church in western Europe and the United States.[6] The assumption behind this bias seems to be that the Christian faith is *already* incultu-rated in those countries which were evangelized centuries ago and where the church has had an appreciable influence in shaping the his-tory and culture of these countries. The missionary urgency of "incul-turating" the Christian faith in the western world is rarely addressed because inculturation is often misconstrued with the degree to which a local church assimilated and became securely entrenched in its cultural milieu. It will be my contention throughout this study that the task of inculturating the faith can no longer be viewed as a missionary chal-lenge of relevance only or even primarily for the churches of the non-western world, that henceforth it must be seen as a mission imperative even for the Catholic Church in America. One should not assume that the ubiquitous presence of the church in a country like the United States, however long-standing and prominent, is a sign or guarantee that the Christian faith has indeed already been inculturated. Nor should one think that just because the Catholic Church is well-established and respected among American institutions, the high demands of incultu-rating the faith in our culture have already been met. Inculturation of faith and ecclesial assimilation in a country are two different things. As we shall see, the criteria for judging the degree of inculturation that is necessary in a given country cannot be predicated on the basis of how long the Christian faith has been present to that people or how well-ensconced the institutional church may be in the public life and social fabric of a given culture. In fact, many of the unresolved problems sig-naled out in the previous chapter would indicate just the opposite: that the Christian faith has yet to be really inculturated in America.

As evidence of this first questionable assumption about inculturation, one has only to review Pope John Paul's speeches to Catholics liv-ing in modern, democratic societies like the United States and Canada. To be sure, the question of the relation between culture *and* faith is repeatedly taken up by the pope in these addresses, a theme that is clearly one of the hallmarks of his pontificate.[7] However, two character-istics stand out in this pope's reflections on North American culture. There is, first, a strong emphasis on the brokenness of our contempo-rary culture, as though our culture were simply synonymous with the negative features of individualistic and utilitarian modernity, and thus with little or no reference to the positive aspects of our political culture. Gregory Baum put it well: "During his Canadian visit John Paul II recognized and admired the various cultural traditions, but said very little of Anglo-American culture....We have been told many times in Vatican declarations that the various cultures of the world are great human treasures and that in some way at least they can be integrated into Catholicism, but no Vatican document has so far extended this benevolence to the Anglo-American ethical political culture."[8]

The second characteristic of John Paul's reflections is a conspicuous absence of any real summons to inculturate the faith in North America. Generally speaking, inculturation is presumed to be a *fait accompli* in societies such as ours, and hence the missionary task enjoined upon us is not one of *inculturation*, but one of *evangelizing* our secular culture. And the tacit (though questionable) assumption here, as Schreiter points out, is "a people's ability to change their culture at will, and concomitantly the role of the Church in directing these changes."[9] Inculturation of the faith and evangelization of culture, though not unrelated, are two very different mission objectives, each with its own merit, its distinct strategy and praxis, as well as its own unique complexity. My contention is that both missions—inculturating faith and evangelizing cultures—are incumbent on all local churches, regardless of their historical, cultural, or geographical situation. Faith offers a critique of culture, and faith seeks to incarnate itself in cultural forms— but not in that order!

A second cause of confusion surrounding the pastoral praxis of inculturation is the failure, in many instances, to seriously honor the important distinction between "adaptation" and "inculturation." The latest instruction issued jointly by the Congregation for Divine Worship and the Discipline of the Sacraments entitled *The Roman Liturgy and Inculturation* is a case in point. While recognizing in its preliminary observations that "the expression 'adaptation,' taken from missionary terminology, could lead one to think of a somewhat transitory and external nature," and that "the term 'inculturation' is a better expression to designate a double movement," the Roman document then goes on to use the term "adaptation" (or the verb "adapt") no less than twenty-five times.[10] It does so moreover interchangeably with the expression "inculturation," almost as though the two were synonymous, thereby threatening to devalue and neutralize the notion of inculturation as a mere superficial accommodation. This is certainly not what Pope Paul VI had in mind when he spoke of the yawning divide between the gospel and culture in our modern world and the need to bridge this gap "not in a purely decorative way as it were by applying a thin veneer, but in a vital way, in depth and right to [the] very roots" of a culture.[11]

The real process of inculturation, as we shall see in a later chapter, does not begin with the external manifestations or visible "signs" of a culture, as does mere accommodation and adaptation. Rather it will first try to seek out and fathom the deepest level of a culture, that dynamic inner "core" of a culture where its primordial myths and mobilizing symbols fuel the "collective unconscious" of a people and give rise to a peculiar constellation or "cluster" of cultural values. This "family" of cultural values, generated and governed at the deepest essential core of a culture, is then in turn made manifest and bodied forth in the observable discrete and non-discrete semiotic "signs" at the surface level of that culture. In the semiotic study and analysis of culture, these are called "culture texts."[12] Were we to compare culture to a floating iceberg, as we shall, nine-tenths of which lies deeply hidden beneath the surface of the water, we would not be wrong in saying that adaptation deals primarily with the observable "top" one-tenth of culture's reality, whereas the pastoral praxis of inculturation has much more to do with the deeper, hidden, and more pervasive levels of a culture. We will return to this more at length in a later chapter when we analyze the notion of "culture." Suffice to say here that until and unless the gospel and the core mobilizing symbols of a culture are directly exposed to one another in what can only be described as a gratuitous grace of encounter and genuine dialogue *between equals*, there can be no genuine inculturation, only accommodation or adaptation.

To put it differently, I would say that the practice of adaptation is *from above*, whereas the process of inculturation is *from below*, and that adaptation invariably proceeds from the *outside inward*, while inculturation proceeds from *inside a culture outward*. Failure to recognize this has led to many ill-conceived pastoral and liturgical experiments under the misguided semblance and name of inculturation, often to the dismay and utter bewilderment of the Christian community. Whenever such a strong adverse communal reaction takes place, it is generally a sign that precipitous adaptations were introduced before genuine inculturation could take place. The precipitous and dramatic changes that took place in the Catholic mass and liturgy immediately following the Second Vatican Council are a case in point: many changes were introduced in view of *adapting* the liturgy to modern times, but unfortunately this was undertaken before any serious consideration was given to the much more demanding task of *inculturating* the liturgy. With hindsight, we now realize that this was like putting the proverbial "cart before the horse." Judicious adaptations, we now know, should only be made after a serious, in-depth process of inculturation has been effectively undertaken...not before! Whenever the practice of adaptation precedes the process of inculturation, the results are sure to be disappointing and superficial. Moreover, the existing gap between faith and culture will not have been lessened.

Much of the current debate about inculturation is badly skewed from the start because of yet another questionable assumption: the need to have either faith or culture play the *dominant role* in the process. This invariably gives rise to an either-or proposition and thus to two unsatisfactory approaches to the praxis of inculturation. On the one hand, there are those who emphasize the autonomy, transcendence, and sovereign power of the gospel over any culture, and hence attribute a paramount role to the gospel and its alleged capacity to purify, transform, ennoble and save from destruction any culture in which faith is inculturated. If one were to think in terms of H. Richard Niebuhr's classic typology in *Christ and Culture*, this first approach would no doubt compare somewhat favorably with Niebuhr's fifth type: "Christ the transformer of culture" (or what he calls the "conversionist" Christian answer).[13] On the other hand, there are those who put much greater emphasis on the dynamic of culture in which even the gospel is involved. For genuine inculturation to take place, they argue, a more dialectical approach between gospel and culture is needed: "one in which the presentation of the gospel is gradually disengaged from its previous embeddedness and is allowed to take on new forms consonant with the new cultural setting."[14]

Robert Schreiter is quite right in maintaining that while the above two approaches have their respective merits and valid insights, they cannot be seen as an either-or proposition—the reason being as follows, according to Schreiter:

> Each affirms an important point: the transcendence of the gospel and the complexity of human cultures. And each position acknowledges the validity of the other's concerns. But neither position has been able to answer the objection of the other: just how does the first position assure that its approach to inculturation is not a form of cultural domination? How does it answer the objection that much so-called Christianization has really been a Westernization? And when will the second position articulate criteria that will assure that close identification with culture does not end in a false inculturation of the gospel?[15]

By his own admission, Schreiter doubts that satisfying answers can be given to these issues, and yet he attempts in the same *Concilium* article to indicate how one might go about mediating between these two positions. His reflections and suggested approach, however, are somewhat problematic in the way he initially sets forth and defines the issues at stake. One's starting point, it should be remembered, invariably determines one's approach to inculturation. Schreiter starts from (and in my view remains within) a questionable, if not false, theological dilemma: *either* the inculturation of faith *or* an identification with culture! A variation of this would be to ask the question: "Where is the appropriate place to begin: with the gospel message or the culture?" In either case, to begin from such a problematic starting point—however many distinctions and theological nuances one may advance in order to resolve the dilemma—will not, in the end, provide the church with a clear, reliable, missionary praxis of inculturation. Nor would everyone agree that the two positions in question, as set out by Schreiter, are indeed reconcilable. Moreover, there can be no question of "identifying" faith and culture, however close one defines the relationship between them and however dominant a role one ascribes to the dynamic of the cultural context. I know of no scholar in mission studies who regards or treats culture and faith as being so fused and identified as to become indistinctive. In the categories employed by Niebuhr, such a theological "melt down" would be tantamount to a "Christ of culture" position—the view in which all tension between faith and culture is virtually removed and, in Niebuhr's own words, "Christ is identified with what men conceive to be their finest ideals, their noblest institutions, and their best philosophy."[16] However, such a view can hardly be misconstrued with the position of those theologians who give a preponderant role to culture in the praxis of inculturating faith.

A New Metaphorical Approach

As we said at the onset, how one envisages the coupling of "faith *and* culture" will invariably determine how one views and defines inculturation. Our purpose here therefore is not to describe all the difficulties that presently swirl around the question of inculturation, but rather to suggest a "root metaphor" that can help us to re-vision the faith-culture relationship. Before naming and elaborating on this radical metaphor, however, a preliminary remark is called for. In my metaphorical approach to inculturation, I am using metaphor in the sense that Ricoeur analyzes and speaks of it as an "impertinent predication," that is, the result of an intentional contradiction at one level of discourse *for the sake of the emergence of a new meaning at another level.*[17] Another way of putting this is to insist that a metaphor is first of all a clash of meanings embedded in language, through which new meaning emerges. It is not, as so often viewed, a mere poetic and rhetorical figure of speech, a sort of window dressing as it were, designed to make one's speaking or writing more colorful but which provides no new information or new insights. On the contrary, metaphors have the ability to disclose hitherto hidden or largely ignored aspects of things.

Root metaphors not only provide new and exciting insight, but they also have the power to bring about a profound reorganization of our thinking on an issue such as inculturation. They are able to do this because of a twofold dynamic: *first,* by drawing our attention to the proportional similitude between two realities (in this case between inculturation *and* marriage), and, *second,* by provoking something of a "mental jolt" in us through the very impertinent nature of the comparison. It is precisely the metaphor's "impertinence" that affords us, at yet another level of theological discourse, an even deeper insight into the relation. For metaphors to function properly, both elements must be present. It is to this dual metaphoric function that we now turn our attention.

(a) Metaphor as Proportional Likeness

The root metaphor that I am suggesting for the coupling of faith and culture is that of a *marriage* or *nuptial union,* symbol of the loving union of man and woman. The Christian tradition of marriage as a metaphor is extensive, very rich, and, above all, illuminating in the many diverse ways it has been applied. Throughout history, the conjugal metaphor has been used time and again to foster a sense of mystery and give deeper insight into those sacred unions of a most spiritual order. On the other hand, with its intimate love-making and communing, the married state is also one of the most down-to-earth, normal, and frequent forms of union. It would be hard to find anything more human than the conjugal union, more spontaneously natural, or more immediately derived from nature itself. And yet, as Saint Paul reminds us, it is also a profoundly sublime mystery. The evocative and revelatory power of marriage as a master symbol or metaphor is celebrated in almost every known religious tradition. In Judaism, rabbis have extolled the covenant at Sinai as the marriage of Yahweh and Israel.[18] The Torah is the marriage contract, Moses is a friend of the bridegroom and Yahweh comes to Israel as a bridegroom to his bride. First captured in the prophetic literature, particularly in the book of Hosea, marriage as metaphor would be later expressed by Saint Paul in his letter to the Ephesians (5:31-32).

The church fathers also regarded the Song of Songs as singing of conjugal love and thus symbolic of the union between Christ and his church, as well as that of the soul with its God. Origen calls Christ the "spouse of the soul," John Chrysostom compares baptism to spiritual marriage, and even eucharistic communion was presented in the patristic period through the metaphor of spiritual marriage. In an excellent and well-documented study, Jean Leclercq has brought to light the extensive use of conjugal union as metaphor in such classic twelfth century writers as Bernard of Clairvaux, Richard and Hugh of St. Victor, Pope Innocent III, and many others.[19] As early as the fourth century, the Synod of Elvira speaks of the consecration of virgins as a spiritual marriage, and as Jean Gaudemet has shown in his illuminating study of canonical collections and decretals, the symbolism of marriage was also seen as applying to a bishop with his diocese.[20] Nor was the extensive use and application of the nuptial union as metaphor a purely poetic or edifying device; Jean Gaudemet shows how such representations had far-reaching liturgical and canonical implications.

We do well to pause here for a moment and listen to the way Robert Bellarmine uses nuptial imagery to describe the union between God and humanity and how strikingly he brings out the historic/anagogic pairing between the incarnation and a typical marriage. The following text, quoted at some length purposely, is a commentary by Robert Bellarmine on the parable of the wedding feast in Matthew: "The kingdom of God may be compared to a king who gave a wedding banquet for his son" (Mt 22:1).

> The king is God the Father; the son is the Word of God; the marriage is the Incarnation; and the bride is human nature. Most appropriately, indeed, is the Incarnation likened to a marriage. First, before a marriage is contracted, there is an *engagement period*: hence the declaration of divine love, celebrated by the wise Solomon in his nuptial poem, the Song of Songs, and the solemn promise made by God to the patriarchs and the prophets that the nuptials would take place. A marriage also requires *mutual consent*: this took place when God, through the angel Gabriel, voiced his Son's intention to Mary, and she, the mother of the bride-to-be [humanity], answered for her daughter: "Behold the handmaid of the Lord; let it be with me according to your word" (Lk 1:38). The marriage is thereafter *consummated*, whereby in all truth the two become one flesh—two natures so intimately united in one person that, unlike other marriages, not even death itself could long separate them. Once a marriage takes place, *the couple hold everything in common*: what had hitherto belonged to the Word—his unique titles, honors, and special privileges—are now bestowed on his bride; and

similarly everything that belonged to human nature—its needs, aspi-rations, weaknesses and sufferings—is assumed by the bridegroom. Even more, a certain familiarity, a definite relationship, begins to exist between the relatives and friends of each: that happy inter-course between earth and heaven is what we call the "communion of saints." And finally, the usual *ends of marriage* are also apparent in the Incarnation....Rightly, therefore, is this union called a mar-riage which the King of kings made for his divine Son.[21]

Clearly, then, in applying the marital "root metaphor" to the union between faith and culture, we are not only in good company, but also well within the best Christian tradition. If we open ourselves up theo-logically to this metaphor of conjugal love as applying to the union between faith and culture—warm up to it as it were, let it fuel our Christian imagination and seduce us, as all symbols must if they are to be fruitful—we will discover a new way of reimagining and thinking about inculturation.

As in marriage, so in the coupling of faith and culture: it is first and foremost a "profound mystery" and as such must be initially regarded not as a problem but as a grace, a divine "happening," before which one stands in awe, reverence and wonder. Such a contemplative stance, as Abraham Heschel reminds us, "is a sense for the transcendence, for the reference everywhere to mystery beyond all things. It enables us to perceive in the world intimations of the divine."[22] Is it not curious and strange that in most of the current literature on inculturation there is little or no suggestion that what we are really confronted with here is not so much a *problem* to be solved as a *mystery* into which one must be initiated? Even before questioning it or speculating about it, must we not praise, wonder and marvel at the divinely appointed communion between faith and culture? at the way this divine covenant, as in mar-riage, symbolizes God's faithful, focused, and intense love for humanity in its constitutive cultural dimension and diversity? at the mutual propensity that attracts them to one another to form an indissoluble union? as though faith and culture were but "the two hands of God" in dealing with us human beings?

If the *first* important insight gained from our marital root metaphor is the intuition that a sense of deep mystery must preside over any and all discussion about inculturation, a *second* one with equally far-reach-ing implications is that inculturation, like marriage, is a process—or bet-ter, an *on going journey*. Basing his analysis on data selected from a series of extensive interviews with couples about their marriage, Mark Johnson has shown how this same metaphoric system of meaning underlies the experience of marriage. I quote him at some length since his analysis is most pertinent to our discussion about inculturation.

> Our very experience and understanding of marriage is metaphorical, and the language we use to talk about marriage is just one manifestation of the underlying metaphors. For instance, the MARRIAGE IS AN ONGOING JOURNEY metaphor, which is a specific case of the LONG-TERM PURPOSEFUL ACTIVITIES ARE JOURNEYS metaphor, is the conceptual structure behind ordinary conventional expressions, such as "We've *just started out* in our marriage," "They've *come a long way* in their sense of marital responsibilities," "She thinks its been all *uphill* with her husband these last few months," "They're just *spinning their wheels* and *going nowhere fast*," "I'm afraid their marriage is a *dead end*," "Who knows, maybe they'll get *back on track* after all." The language we use concerning marriage is so heavily conventionalized that much of it does not seem obviously metaphorical. But we could not understand this language without presupposing the metaphorical systems from which that language is generated. Such systematic metaphors reach deep down into our *experience* and *understanding* of marriage, and so they involve consequences for *actions* in our daily lives. These consequences might include goals for the marriage, expectations for oneself and one's spouse, criteria for evaluating the health or success of the marriage, and the range of (morally) permissible responses and actions sanctioned or suggested by the underlying metaphorical mapping.[23]

To view the process of inculturation in any terms other than those of an adventure and journey in faith is to minimize both the need and the conditions of genuine inculturation. As in marriage, there are stages or "seasons" in the *praxis* of inculturation that must be recognized, ritualized and celebrated throughout the process. The reader is thus invited to envisage the process of inculturation not unlike the way we now conceive and implement the Rite of Christian Initiation of Adults (RCIA), that is, as an extended process having various interconnecting "liminal" stages, each with its own appropriate rituals.[24] A more detailed schema for mapping the various stages of inculturation as a metaphoric journey will be the subject of the next chapter.

(b) Metaphor as Impertinent Predication

The truly disclosive nature of our metaphor, however, becomes especially apparent and insightful if the metaphor in question is also perceived as an impertinent predication. That is to say, if the metaphor initially strikes us as most apposite and fitting, it should also appear, upon further reflection, as a somewhat disconcerting comparison, an impertinent and unseemly likening. To affirm that faith and culture can be compared in some respect to a marital union is quite reasonable and not too difficult to accept. Yet the metaphor yields even greater insight into the nature of the relation between faith and culture when it is also perceived as inappropriate and out of character. In the cultural context such as that of the United States, where one half of all the nuptial unions end in divorce, the impertinence of our designated metaphor becomes immediately apparent.

How can the breakdown of so many marriages in the United States warrant the use of the nuptial union as a root metaphor and model for the inculturating mission of the church in today's society? Does this high divorce rate not render our root metaphor inappropriate and presumptuous—perhaps even "null and void" in its applicability to the process of inculturation? Divorce almost always seems to bring a deep sense of failure and sometimes an overwhelming load of guilt. It invariably leaves in its wake some feeling of pain and anger and sadness. And if we consider that millions of Catholics in the United States avoid the church because of failed marriages, how then can one realistically contend that the tenuous bond of marriage is an apt or appropriate metaphor to describe the coupling of faith and culture? We touch here upon the truly evocative nature of all metaphoric discourse as Ricoeur construes it. According to him, a metaphor is not meant to simply illustrate an otherwise obvious point; it is meant to make us think more deeply and more imaginatively. Being the result of an intentional contradiction, an "impertinent predication" as Ricoeur has it, metaphors are designed to evoke in us the urge to go beyond our conventional way of thinking, beyond the security of our immediate expectations, in order to gain deeper insight into that which is being "metaphorized."

In similar fashion John Dominic Crossan speaks of the impertinent character of Jesus' own parabolic imagination. "The surface function of parable," he says, "is to create contradiction within a given situation of complacent security but, even more unnervingly, to challenge the fundamental principle of reconciliation by making us aware of the fact that *we made up* the reconciliation."[25] Like parables, metaphors are meant to deliberately shock and intentionally raise questions, thus undermining the structure of our conventional expectations in order to initiate us into the deeper mystery of God's "ways" which are very seldom our own. We see this, for example, in the way Jesus himself cast his central message in the *kingdom-of-God* metaphor, an "impertinent" metaphor if ever there was one. Not only did Jesus adamantly refuse to be made king himself, but when he spoke of God's rule and kingdom, this had scarcely anything in common with the actual kingdoms then in existence. Nor do the connotations of royalty and kingship sit very well with our contemporary American mindset of a free and democratic society. But more on this later.

What the impertinent character of our marriage metaphor suggests and points to, then, is that as in any marriage, things can and often do go wrong in the process of inculturation—sometimes terribly wrong. Correspondence is never easy or perfect between "faith" and "culture." There are always blocks and points of tension: blocks such as unwarranted fears and compensatory aggression or withdrawal; blocks such as indifference, misunderstanding and betrayal, which can result in one (or both) of the partners having to live in a wounded condition. We should expect no less vulnerability in the nuptial union between faith and culture than is clearly in evidence in Christ's union with his bride, the church, or with God's marriage covenant with Israel.

Our suggested metaphorical approach, I will argue, helps us to better understand the challenge and high demands of integrating faith and culture in a modern society such as ours. The missionary implications of this will become clearer as we go along, but already it should be clear that culture must not be seen as a mere extraneous benefit to Christian faith, but rather as an integral element of faith itself, that is, integral to our baptismal ability to assent and respond to God's word. What follows is a preliminary list of some other pastoral insights and correctives that our root metaphor would seem to suggest:

1. Instead of speaking of "evangelizing cultures," which is not a very happy expression since it strongly connotes a *unilateral* approach to mission, we are suddenly made aware of the *reciprocity* that is involved in any marriage, and our metaphor would have us speak of evangelizing, not cultures as such, but rather the *union* that is being forged between faith and culture, whether this be in the individual lives of the Christians themselves or in the society at large. Such a shift in focus changes the mission agenda of the church considerably and redefines the challenge of evangelization in terms of dialogue and "marriage counseling" rather than of confrontation and perpetual antagonism.

2. Instead of asking *who* plays the dominant role in the process and mission of inculturation—the gospel or culture?—our nuptial metaphor would remind us that there should be no dominant part-

ner in a marriage—only *equal partners*. Should one find difficulty in
starting from such an "impertinent" premise of equality, one need
only contemplate the kenotic "way" the Word of God embraced
human equality to become "like us in all things, except sin."

3. The marital root metaphor offers yet another advantage: it suggests an *in-depth relationship* and not merely a superficial association or a casual collaborative partnership. Thus instead of
   regarding inculturation as a "pick-and-choose" process whereby
   the church selectively opts for some aspects of a culture (while
   rejecting others it deems incompatible with its gospel), inculturation presupposes an initial unconditional assent and acceptance
   of a culture—warts and all!—and seeks the deepest possible co-
   penetration ("*commixtio*"[26]) between faith and culture. Being married, as woman *or* man, means that differences and shortcomings,
   whatever their effect, are accepted and respected. Conjugal love is
   a mutual donation of the whole person, not just the more attractive or favored qualities of the partner. Spouses no longer exist as
   separate entities but are interdependent, and their union creates
   possibilities for interaction and growth that were not available to
   the individuals separately. Only if so envisaged can we legitimately
   entertain the real prospect of a "new heaven and a new earth."

4. The question of autonomy in any such union must also be interpreted in an *inclusive* rather than in an *exclusive* sense. Instead of
   unduly trying to safeguard the autonomy and transcendence of the
   gospel over culture, our conjugal metaphor would remind us that,
   as in the state of marriage, both partners (faith and culture) have
   and must retain their respective autonomy, integrity and freedom.
   However deep their communion, faith and culture never become so
   fused or identified as to lose their respective identity and autonomy.

5. Marriage as metaphor also has the advantage of including an *affective dimension* in any future theology of inculturation. As we indicated earlier, the inculturation process begins, continues and ends
   with the surprise of love. Instead of constructing a theology of
   inculturation which only professional theologians can understand, our metaphorical approach, with its more pedestrian,
   "earthy" dimension and its rootedness in conjugal love, will yield a
   theology whose distinctive thrust can be more readily grasped by
   the laity and not just by the specialists in mission studies. It will
   make generous allowance for the *sensus fidelium*, the inspired felt
   needs, impulses and inclinations of the faithful at the local church

level. In short, such a theology will speak directly *to* them instead of *for* them or on their behalf.

Before turning our attention to the successive stages in the actual process of inculturation (as we shall in the next chapter), it is important to be clear about the kind of *reciprocity* we are dealing with when we speak of faith and culture as a marital union. Between husband and wife there exists a basic bond-in-being, a "reciprocity of conjugal existence," as it is sometimes called. In the marriage covenant, therefore, "being" and "being related to one's spouse" are but two essentially interdependent or reciprocal features of the same reality: the nuptial union. We call this reciprocity "basic" or "primordial" because it defines the essence of what it means when two individuals begin to exist *as* a married couple. We can illustrate this with an example taken from common experience, namely, the basic reciprocity that defines the terms "mother" and "daughter" (or "father" and "son"). In either case, there is no priority of the parental relationship (being or becoming a "father" or "mother") over the filial terms "son" and/or "daughter"—nor do these filial terms have priority over the fact of becoming a "parent" (mother or father). To put it more simply, Mr. Jones never existed *as* a "father" until little Jimmy, his first-born, started to exist *as* his father's "son." They are, in the strictest sense, reciprocal terms of existence.

So it is with the basic reciprocity that exists between faith *and* culture: the one cannot be adequately defined without an essential reference to the other (and vice versa). It is just as inconceivable to define what faith is, without including in its very definition a primordial reference to the cultural nature of being human, as it is to imagine that one could define culture without a similar reference to faith. The two realities, though distinct, are profoundly reciprocal and hence "connatural." In another age and using another metaphor, the church fathers would put it this way: "The world without the church is like a body without a soul, but the church without the world is like a soul without a body." In short, faith and culture were "made for each other" in the wild "imaginings" of a creative and loving God.

The bible itself is the best illustration of the bond-in-being between culture and faith. As John Paul II told the biblical commission in 1979, "The Mesopotamian cultures, those of Egypt, Canaan, Persia, the Hellenic culture and, for the New Testament, Greco-Roman culture and that of late Judaism, *served, day by day, for the revelation of God's ineffable mystery of salvation.*"[27] Again, in this vein, he said that "the synthesis between culture and faith is not only a requirement of culture, but also of faith."[28] On this point the Latin American bishops were equally

unequivocal in their final 1979 Puebla document: "The essential core
of a culture lies in the way in which a people affirms or rejects a religious tie with God."[29]

Elsewhere, in describing the relationship between the church and
the world, I argued that the world not only brings certain "auxiliary"
benefits to the church (as *Gaudium et Spes* n. 44 clearly recognizes), but
that it performs a vital, ongoing, fourfold function *in* the church, without which the church would not exist—at least not as the "incarnational"
church we know it to be.[30] Similarly, I would argue here that culture
functions in a similar manner in Christian faith, something that will
become more readily apparent as we turn our attention now to the various stages in the process of inculturation.

4 | Mapping the Process of Inculturation

My purpose in the preceding chapter was to show how inculturation might be approached and understood metaphorically, with special reference to the "root metaphor" of marriage. We call marriage a "root metaphor" because from it grow many shoots which, taken as a whole, constitute an entire system or way of looking at things, including inculturation. Even without much prior explanation, the reader will no doubt agree with Andrew Ortony's contention that the use of such a metaphor has three distinct advantages: (a) it is *compact*, in the sense that our metaphor can transfer chunks of experience from a well-known context (marriage) to a less-well-known context (inculturation); (b) it is *vivid*, in the sense that it conjures up the "full-blooded experience" of marriage and is therefore more memorable precisely because of its greater imagery or concreteness; (c) it is *inexpressible*, in that our marriage metaphor carries with it, as all metaphors do, a "surplus of meaning" never encoded in language; it harbors a "mystery" and a symbolic dimension more profound than human words can express.[1] Even St. Thomas Aquinas, in a remarkable and little known text, says that *"theology ought to be expressed in a manner that is metaphorical, that is, symbolic or parabolique."*[2]

In this chapter I propose to map out the salient phases in the actual process of inculturation. Much has been written about the nature of inculturation, and of the theoretical machinery required to account for it, but so far little has been done to show how inculturation *works*. How does the process begin? How does it evolve? And through what stages of growth and/or decline does it pass? For this we need some sort of structure. My contention here is that the marriage metaphor provides us with just such a structure. Like the story of any marriage, the process of inculturation is more than a succession of haphazard events or isolated experiments; it is an unfolding process, a synthesis of parts in a unified whole, a story whose structure, as Aristotle was first to note, "has a

53

beginning, middle, and an end" (*Poetics* 50b). This narrative structure, when applied to marriage and the process of inculturation, would basically consist in the following schema: it typically begins at some point in time, moves through a series of more or less connected intermediate stages, and ends with some culminating event. Ricoeur's description of the structure that underlies prototypical stories is noteworthy: "To follow a story," he says, "is to move forward in the midst of contingencies and peripeteia under the guidance of an expectation that finds its fulfillment in the 'conclusion' of the story....It gives the story an 'end point,' which, in turn, furnishes the point of view from which the story can be perceived as forming a whole. To understand the story is to understand how and why the successive episodes led to the conclusion."[3]

The story of every marriage has a beginning, a middle and an end; it also has certain thresholds or liminal indicators that mark one's progress along the way. When viewed as a journey, our marriage metaphor would suggest the following three-phase structure:

1. The phase of courtship and acceptability
2. The phase of ratification
3. The phase of establishment

As we walk through each of these three phases, we will point out the significant correlations between how two people fall in love, get married, and live "for better, for worse" their conjugal union on the one hand, and on the other the coupling of faith and culture. In other words, the above threefold structure provides us with a "model," a "developmental image" which enables us to view and interpret inculturation as an organic *process* similar to the one suggested by our marriage metaphor. While marriage does have a contractual and therefore juridical dimension, as we shall see, marriage is above all *un projet de vie*, as the French would say, an ongoing vital project that one embarks upon and pursues through various phases of development (or disintegration). As we walk through these phases, however, we should bear in mind that ours is a metaphoric journey and therefore not one that is strictly bound by chronological time. Nor is our model predicated on the concrete details or existential variables that different individuals bring to their nuptial union.

In a pluralistic society such as that of the United States, moreover, one must assume that there are many cultural variations and sub-cultural differences in the way people understand marriage itself. Not everyone views marriage the same way or in the same light; not everyone attaches the same importance or value to marriage; and clearly, no two marriages are lived out in the same manner. Depending on the individuals undertaking the journey, the marriage covenant can and does in fact take in many variables and different shades of meaning and emphasis. These differences, however, whether personal or ethnic, religious or civil, need not detain us here since they do not invalidate our "model" structure as such. Whatever individual or social variables may exist with regards to marriage in the United States, the basic story line of every marriage is the same: they all have a beginning, a middle, and an end.

What *is* important, however, is that the reader make generous appeal to his or her imagination in what follows. Since our approach to inculturation is *metaphorical*, the role of the imagination becomes crucial. Imagination is our natural inborn faculty for transcendence, and the word "transcendence" literally means "to cross over," "to go beyond." The reader is thus being challenged to go beyond a purely rational way of thinking and assume a more imaginative mindset. Only then will our myths, symbols, metaphors and parables really "speak" to us and move us to deeper insights. The imagination is the one genuine means by which the disparate or contradictory elements between "marriage" and "inculturation" can be held in tension long enough to yield some new insight and creative knowledge. To interpret a "root metaphor" literally instead of imaginatively, therefore, is to violate the metaphor and rob it of its unique power to engender *new* insights and *new* meaning. Failure to honor its "impertinent predication," that intentional clash of meanings we spoke of earlier, is to defuse and discharge the metaphor. On the other hand, if we can tolerate the creative tension that metaphors put on our habitual way of thinking, there is every chance that it will yield something new.

(1) The Phase of Courtship and Acceptability

The voice of my beloved!
   Look, he comes,
leaping upon the mountains,
   bounding over the hills....
I am my beloved's,
   and his desire is for me.
Come, my beloved,
   let us go forth in the fields,
   and lodge in the villages;
let us go out early in the vineyards,
   and see whether the vines have budded,

whether the grape blossoms have opened
and the pomegranates are in bloom.
There I will give you my love.
(Song of Songs 2:8; 7:10-12)

Like the process of inculturation, marriage begins with love, a romantic, sometimes passionate love, an almost "blind" yet conscious mutual attraction between two individuals. Why the romance begins in the first place is always something of an enigma. The chemistry of falling in love, especially in its first flush, is always a mystery, and since this mystery remains veiled even after many outer veils have disappeared, the question invariably arises: What does *this* person and *that* particular individual "see" in each other? Why did these two unlikely individuals happen to fall in love? When did it all begin and why? Did it happen just by chance, did some inner predisposition trigger the romance, or was it, as we say of other unexplainable happenings, an "act of God"? Perhaps none of these possibilities can be ruled out, but the truly interesting thing about it is that falling in love always comes as a mutual surprise, an unexpected wonder and sudden discovery.

Similarly, answers as to how and why Christian faith and American culture have come together in mutual fascination and romance have been variously advanced by sociologists, historians and other experts. But while their explanations all have certain value and undoubted credibility, the romantic coupling of faith and culture in the United States remains something of a mystery. Indeed even the best social analysts are still at a loss to explain adequately why Americans (as a people) continue to give, even today, such great public importance to their religious faith and beliefs in an otherwise highly industrialized, modern, secular society. Hence the best way to approach the mystery of inculturation, at the onset, is with an attitude of rejoicing, wonder and gratitude. In its initial phase, inculturation, like love, is first and foremost a rejoicing over the existence of the "other," a deep mutual desire that the beloved *be* rather than *not* be.

Perhaps the best way to understand the first phase in the process of inculturation is to read it in the light of the biblical love song quoted above. To recognize the first signs of inculturation is to recognize the first signs of romantic love between faith and culture. When we see signs of acceptance and joyful recognition of everything faith and culture desire to be for each another, when they love one another—"warts and all," as the saying goes—then we can safely assume that each has been seduced by the other and that the process of inculturation has indeed begun. The process of inculturation begins, not with threats, admonitions or moral judgments, but with seduction, the kind of seduction Jeremiah experienced and voiced: "You seduced me, O Lord, and I let myself be seduced" (Jer 20:7). Once seduced, lovers become *fascinated* with one another; they tend to pay attention to one another even when they perhaps should be involved in other activities. Such fascination is the basis for idealizing the other, a phenomenon often noted in romantic love and so typical of the way Americans generally try to love. As Arthur Schlesinger Jr. has pointed out: "Only the Americans have attempted on a large scale the singular experiment of trying to incorporate romantic love into the staid and stolid framework of marriage and family."[4]

Catholics in America and elsewhere have on occasion seen their church make efforts to become more seductive and more attractive in the eyes of the world and the world of cultures. Its seductive demeanor and voice, for example, were clearly in evidence at Vatican II. In many ways, *Gaudium et Spes*, the Constitution on the Church in the Modern World, reads like the biblical love poem, the Song of Songs. In his opening speech at the second session of the council, Pope Paul VI was beautiful and equally seductive: "The world should know," he said, "that the church constantly looks at her, sincerely admires her, and sincerely intends not to dominate but to serve, not to despise her but to increase her dignity, not to condemn her, but to bring her comfort and salvation." The language of love can hardly be more explicit. The many visits of John Paul II to countries around the world must also be seen and interpreted in this "courtship" tradition, as so many loving advances not only to the local Catholic communities around the world, but also to the hosting cultures.

It should be remembered, however, that the process of inculturation does not begin when Rome speaks or the pope visits; it begins when the *local church* commits itself unequivocally (meaning: without a hundred-and-one prior reservations or caveats) to having a love affair with the *local culture* it wishes to court and in which it seeks to live and move and find its being. The practical implications of this first phase of inculturation (courtship and mutual acceptability) are quite numerous and far-reaching. I indicate the following by way of illustration:

- It takes two to tango, as the expression has it, and the coupling of faith and culture is no exception. Since the church cannot, unilaterally and on its own, make inculturation happen, it must make renewed efforts to make itself more beautiful, more enticing, more seductive, and, for it, that can only mean living and manifesting the beatitudes more convincingly.

- The church must also try to know its local culture better and more deeply, instead of judging American culture merely on the basis of what it sees being played out on the "surface" level of society. It can at least begin to celebrate, ritualize and rejoice in those fundamental American cultural values that it itself has already found to be so attractive. (More on this later in a chapter on "culture.")

- Instead of appreciating a local culture principally for its serviceability and the ecclesial benefits it might hope to derive from it (a *bonum utile*, as the ancients would say), the church would do well to look upon culture as a graced reality worthy of honor in and of itself (as a *bonum honestum*).

- In this first phase of the inculturation process, as in the first flush of true love, the church must put aside its neurotic fear of ambiguity and syncretism, as well as its insistence on excessive purity in both moral and doctrinal matters. A church that begins with a low tolerance of ambiguity does not plan to inculturate the gospel very deeply. (More on this later in Chapter 10).

- And since inculturation is above all a local grass-roots affair, the church must learn to put more than its customary faint-hearted trust in the *sensus fidelium*, the inspired baptismal instinct of the faithful and the lived experience of the Catholic laity.[5]

(2) The Phase of Ratification

> *I, N., take you, N., for my lawful spouse,*
> *to have and to hold, from this day forward,*
> *for better, for worse, for richer, for poorer,*
> *in sickness and in health, until death do us part.*
> (Marriage Rite of Consent)

When two individuals publicly pledge their troth before an unforeseeable future, they are in fact making a public statement about their *hope* in a future together. At this point they embark on the second phase of their journey. The rise from the first phase of inculturation to the second, from courtship to public commitment, marks a new register of intimacy. Whereas courtship sets the partners *face-to-face*, public commitment places them *side-by-side* and prepares them to shoulder one another in their striving for a future they must create and bring about jointly. What we call wedded hope is a hope that prevails in love. As

Saint Paul says, "love hopes all things" (1 Cor 13:7). Hopeful partners are so intimately united that the one cannot let the other down without at the same time betraying himself or herself and thus breaking the very commitment on which the other partner has come to rely. When I say to a loved one, "You can count on me," I do not restrict the "you" to just a certain aspect of his or her being; I embrace the partner in his or her entire being. The hope of wedded love is neither selective nor parsimonious; it is an all-embracing, all-or-nothing affair.

When this new state of affairs is reached, the partners then seek to go public and to have their hope ratified through some form of social ritual, whether religious or civil. In our western culture and church, this is deemed to occur in the mutual consent which each partner freely and publicly bestows on and accepts from the other. The church has always valued rituals of this sort because they serve to establish a vital contact with the source of life, both human and divine. For a Christian, the institution of wedded love is seen as signifying and sharing in the mystery of Christ's loving union with his bride, the church. In fact, it is tied so closely to life that we call marriage a sacrament. Yet "to designate a special area of human life as sacramental is not to change it into something else, but to acknowledge and celebrate its existing sacred status." As David Thomas rightly says, "Christian sacraments are not actions that launder a dirty world, but are gestures of gratitude to God for establishing this world as bathed in grace through creation and the forgiveness of sin."[6]

In this second phase of inculturation, this coming together of faith and culture in wedded hope, we are dealing with much more than that intermittent and sometimes capricious relationship we call companionship, helpfulness, and obligingness; it is a more permanent engagement, one in which the two partners resolve to sustain one another and are at each other's abiding and resourceful disposal. Over and above the determination of common interest and reasonable expectation, they will come to discover one another as unique subjects, equal in dignity and equally transcendent. They do not draw their hope from each other's human resourcefulness, gifts or talents, as though somehow reading the future in these. It is not the possibilities in the other partner that engender this kind of hope; rather it is this kind of hope that creates new possibilities—the possibility of a new heaven and a new earth. This second phase in the inculturation journey, then, can rightly be regarded as a form of ritual play—a playing with imaginative yet very real possibilities. If the coupling of culture and faith does not engender such play, does not release such wild re-visionings of the way the world might spin or could possibly dance to another tune, then one can be quite sure that this second phase in the inculturation process has not yet been attained.

The reader may well ask at this point: By what sign or signs will we know that this special moment has come? When can we be sure that our faith and our culture are ready to ratify their mutual consent and resolve to face an uncertain future together, instead of separately? As invited guests, when do we come to the wedding feast? Is it when one's religion becomes the official religion of the state? Or when Catholics become the largest religious denomination in the United States?[7] Or is it perhaps when the church is given charitable exemptions and other largess from the welfare state? Or perhaps when our church leaders give public support to a particular political party or candidate?[8] None of the above suggestions, of course, serve as reliable criteria for knowing when faith and culture have entered this second phase of the incultura-tion process. Nor does an official government policy establishing the separation of church and state, as in the United States, necessarily pre-clude such a ratification. All the above instances, while certainly not neglible or unimportant, are but "surface" occurrences that in and of themselves neither promote nor hinder inculturation. As we shall see, inculturation does not begin at the veneer surface of either culture or faith, but deep within the "core" realities of both.

Much as we long for external signs which might suggest to us that a wedding feast is being prepared, as Christians we must be able to read those small, subtle and often inconspicuous signals that tell us the king-dom of God is near and at hand. Though subtle, these signals can be all around us yet we fail to discern in them the long-awaited invitation: "Come, for all is ready." The gospel is replete with such invitations that go unheeded, as the parable of the great feast would remind us. We look for invitational "signs," but perhaps signs are not what we should be looking for. Since one of the distinguishing marks of faith is "the conviction of things *we cannot see*," as the author of Hebrews describes it (Heb 11:1) or, as St. Paul says, "we walk by faith, not by sight" (2 Cor 5:7), perhaps we need more discerning eyes and the more penetrating vision of the mystic. Karl Rahner was surely right when he said that "the Christian of the future will be a mystic or he will not exist at all."[9] The mystic is one who can see beyond what meets the eye and is there-fore not too disturbed by the absence of conspicuous signs.

Should we insist, in good faith, on having some messianic sign over and above those already given to us in the "signs of the times," perhaps the prophet Hosea can help us. There we read: "I will take you for my wife forever; I will take you for my wife in righteousness and in justice, in steadfast love, and in mercy" (Hos 2:21). Here the invitational nuptial signs are righteousness, justice, kindness and mercy. Wherever we see a concrete manifestation of these, either at the behest of our culture or our faith, then maybe it's time to start celebrating. In sum, the invitation, "Come, for all is ready" is extended when faith and culture, as "one flesh," can love and be compassionate without having a reason to do so, thus transcending the category of necessity, utility and contingency—a love therefore which stems from sheer joy and gratuitousness. "Where love rejoices, there is festivity" (*Ubi caritas gaudet, ibi est festivitas*).[10]

Jürgen Moltmann has aptly called this "*the Messianic Intermezzo*," by which he means that festal joy of love that transcends the air-tight distinction between a *holy* day of obligation and an *ordinary* working day.[11] He explains:

> The love that serves our neighbor without having any personal axe to grind is joy. It is the feast of the new life. Here no special festal times and periods of leisure are required. Wherever it comes into being there is the sabbath, God's sabbatical year, the messianic era. To preach the gospel of the kingdom to the poor, to heal the sick, to receive the despised, free prisoners, and eat and drink with the hungry is the feast of Christ in the history of God's dealings with the world.[12]

Thus the "signs" we are looking for could well turn out to be none other than the signs of God's kingdom—a kingdom, we must not forget, which can be as small as a tiny mustard seed at the onset yet ever so promising (Mt 13:31). To the extent that the wedded love of faith and culture signals the "in-breaking" of God's kingdom, a vigilant church might wish to heed the following:

- A church that is missionary "in its very essence" and seeks to inculturate the gospel message will avoid equating faith with religious expediency and see it more in terms of the ability to read the signs of God's kingdom in its local cultural environment.

- It must abandon the tacit assumption that grace would no longer be "divine grace" if God were to become too free or too reckless with it, if he gave it away too liberally, too lavishly. The church will be more cautious about putting limits on the workings of the Spirit and more mindful of the magnanimity of Jesus' own words: "I came that they may have life, and have it abundantly" (Jn 10:10).

- Knowing that praise generally precedes faith, that we learn to sing before we believe, the church can also strive to be more creative in appreciating the "sacramental connection" between its own liturgy and the cultural life of a given society, between its own symbol system and the mobilizing symbols that gave rise to culture.

· And knowing that the Spirit always precedes it and gets there first, the church can encourage its faithful to make all possible haste to be at those unexpected places where the Spirit might already be "hovering over" the integration of faith and culture. The moral is: "Keep your eyes open, for you know not the day or the hour" (Mt 25:13).

(3) The Phase of Establishment

> *What we call the beginning is often the end*
> *And to make an end is to make a beginning.*
> *The end is where we start from.*
>   (T.S. Eliot, "Little Gidding"[13])

There can be little doubt that the second phase in the marriage journey that we have just described marks an "end" as well as a "beginning." On the one hand it brings closure to the period of courtship and on the other it inaugurates wedded life, with all its work and woe, its elements of joys and pains, it successes and its disappointments. Real as the couple's love may be on their wedding day, it is still a hope, an ideal; it has yet to be tested in the crucible of daily life and domesticity. Here in America, we attach considerable importance to the actual wedding celebration: the engraved invitations, the bridal showers and stag parties, the expensive gown and floral decorations, the liturgy and exchange of vows, and the costly reception that follows. Such emphasis, though exaggerated and costly, is not altogether misguided. *First*, because one could argue, as Harvey Cox convincingly has in his book *The Feast of Fools*, that one of the essential ingredients of genuine festivity is conscious excess: "We always over 'overdo it,' and we do so on purpose."[14]

Second, and perhaps more important, is the fact that marriage is one of the few privileged instances when the laity can exercise their public priestly role in the sacramentalization of God's love, since on this occasion *they* are the principal celebrants who actually confer the sacrament of marriage on one another. Surely, and if for no other reason, this infrequent opportunity given to the laity in the church calls for rejoicing and a certain excess. The point we wish to make here, however, is that when all the wedding festivities and honeymoon are over, living together as man and wife begins in earnest. As T.S. Eliot put it, "And to make an end is to make a beginning. The end is where we start from."

If the nature of married life is love, why must one work so hard at it? If love is the complete receiving and giving back of all we are, why is it that things go wrong in married life—often terribly wrong? The most agonizing decision in a marriage relationship that isn't working must surely be: Can our marriage be saved? Should it be saved? When is it time to call it quits? Sociologist Diane Vaughan has researched the various stages couples go through as they move toward separation.[15] She found that some of the signs that a relationship is heading for a breakdown include: when both partners start keeping more secrets from each other; when they start complaining more or displaying discontent in subtle ways; when they are no longer capable of playing together; when they start looking outside the relationship for trust, intimacy and love; when both partners start to feel they are walking on eggshells or constantly trying to improve things that never seem to get better—in sum, when one or both partners feel unloved, unappreciated and lonely in marriage.

Every marriage has its proverbial "ups and downs," to be sure, but given the high divorce rate in the United States and the fact that even those marriages which survive the difficult first years do not necessarily make it in the long run, the reader may well ask how our marriage root metaphor can possibly serve as a "model" for inculturating faith in a culture. The question is a valid one, especially if we consider the basic reasons why people get divorced, like sexual and physical abuse, alcoholism, infidelity and monetary disputes. What, then, in this crucial third phase of our "story," can married life teach us about inculturation? What new insight does our marriage metaphor give us about the "coming together" and integration of faith and culture in the United States? Much of what follows will be an attempt to answer this question.

It is precisely at this very juncture in our story that the "impertinent predication" of our metaphor becomes helpful. Its theopoetic "fire" potential to spark new insight into the process of inculturation lies in its ability to evoke, not unmitigated bliss or certain success in married life, but rather the very *ambiguity* inherent in all such relationships. If the nuptial union has been extolled as a sign of God's loving union with humanity, or Christ's union with his bride, the church, our metaphor also "epiphanizes" for us the fragility, precariousness, and vulnerability of any such relationship, including the divinely intended union between faith and culture. Things do go wrong even in the most sacred partnerships—and the more sacred the union, so it seems, the more ambiguous. Thus what our root metaphor is challenging us to do here

is re-examine our basic *intolerance of ambiguity*, both in our human relationships as well as in our "close encounters" and union with God. The
theological basis for admitting ambiguity in our life of faith will be
developed more fully in a later chapter; here, however, if only in a preliminary way, we wish to indicate why this "impertinent" ambiguity is
something we must all learn to live with, instead of too hastily turning
our backs on it.

Our root metaphor is realistic: it asserts the fact that there is "objective sinfulness" in all of us. We all belong to a world shot through with
many layers of structural injustice and inequality. What is more, as
Pope John Paul reminds us in his apostolic letter *The Jubilee of the Year
2000*, we are all members of a church in which there has been grave
"objective sinfulness" over the centuries and right up to the present day.
Yet our marriage metaphor is realistic in yet another way: it also asserts
that there is "objective grace" in the lives of all of us, as well as in the
church. Thus the inherent ambiguity in life, even in the most sacred
union and in our redeemed human condition. Our impertinent
metaphor would have us recognize and accept this fact, namely, that
grace and sin are never far removed from one another. In fact, good
and evil can never be completely dissociated in real life (or even, so it
seems, in the life hereafter). Paradoxically, there seems to exist between
them a strange kinship, not altogether unlike that which exists between
the sun and the moon.

In the mythology of nature, the sun and the moon are never simply
portrayed as distinct realities but also as complementary: night is as necessary as the day, and in a certain sense it is good that moonlight is not
as bright or luminous as sunshine. There is an obvious cosmic kinship
between the *radiating* light of the sun and the pale *reflected* light of the
moon. This strange symbiosis or kinship between good and evil is
depicted in various ways in the bible. In the biblical narrative of salvation history, good and evil, though clearly distinguishable, are invariably
portrayed as being quite inseparable. They seem to condition one
another reciprocally, as it were, as though the good can only be adequately defined or portrayed in its radical difference from evil. In the
bible, for example, this strange, ambiguous kinship is often "typified" in
the relationship between rival siblings: between the hairy Esau and the
clever Jacob (Gn 27:11, 16); or between Leah with the weak eyes and the
beautiful Rachel (Gn 29:16-17). Sibling rivalry is also shown to exist
between twins disputing precedence in their mother's womb, like Jacob
and Esau (Gn 25:24-26), or Perez and Zerah, the sons of the incestuous
Tamar (Gn 38:27-30). More often than not, the brothers are hostile to
one another from the very beginning, and it is usually the "good" char-

acter, like Jacob, who is banished from home before he can return, a rich and blessed individual. Sometimes the roles are reversed and it is the "prodigal son" who returns home, celebrated and feasted (Lk 15:11-32).

Ambiguity is the challenge our marriage metaphor brings to the complacent normalcy of our accepted ways of thinking about inculturation. Its disconcerting wisdom of "two in one flesh" can be summed up this way: Like marriage, the integration of faith and culture is at once utterly awesome and awesomely normal in its ambiguity. Marriage is great in that the partners search for perfect happiness together, but ambiguous in that, without ever ceasing to search, they know that they can never approach perfect happiness. So it is also in the process of inculturation. The only way to express this wisdom adequately is, of course, through metaphor; a metaphor which does not prove the contrary but which can maintain the paradox in creative tension. If the goal sought in the inculturation process is a deeper co-penetration and union between faith and culture, such a union cannot be brought about by absorption, by one of the partners being dominated by or dissolved into the other. In marriage, as in the inculturation process, the surrender or loss of personal identity and autonomy is both ruinous and pathological. However deeply conjoined, neither Christian faith nor local American culture must lose its uniqueness or its integrity.

Moreover, when we speak of faith in the context of inculturation, whether we envisage it as a gift from God, a likely marriage partner for culture, or simply as the doctrinal teaching or catechism of the church, faith is always subjectively received, held, and expressed by living individuals and local communities. In this sense it is true that there can be no Christian faith outside the world of human experience and culture. Faith is always endorsed and appropriated as an experienced reality, both personally and culturally. Some degree of awareness invariably goes along with this subjective appropriation, but were this awareness more fully mined, articulated, and celebrated, we would have the makings of a genuine *local* theology, something that does not yet exist in North America as it does in Africa, Asia and Latin America. Although one cannot identify faith with the awareness of it, it is nevertheless impossible to separate one from the other. It is precisely this fundamental *inseparability* of the divine and the human that signifies and makes credible, humanly speaking, the real catholicity of the church.

If marriage is rightly described as participating in the creative power of God, so too with inculturation: the interpenetration of faith and culture should evince—or better, "epiphanize"—something of God's rule and kingdom here on earth. If inculturated faith means anything, it surely means that what God has effectively begun to bring about in the world is made even more perceptible and manifest when faith and culture no longer confront each other as strangers, but as creative co-partners as in a nuptial union. Creativity here means that "joint" willingness of both faith and culture to envisage new ways of living and facing the future together—God's future!

In his book, *The Mission of the Church*, Edward Schillebeeckx has shown in what sense the church can be called "sacrament of the world" (*sacramentum mundi*).[16] By this he means that the church makes visible, more tangible, more readily discernible to the world what God's saving grace is already in fact bringing about in the world and in the lives of men and women everywhere in the world. Lest this active presence and forgiving proximity of God in the world be left hidden, undisclosed, or too elusive, the church is rightly called the "sacrament of the world." The church shows the world what it truly is and what it can truly become by virtue of God's gift of grace already operative within it. Our nuptial root metaphor, however, would have us go one theological step farther, and it does this by reversing the polar equation.

What our nuptial metaphor suggests here—and indeed suggests very strongly—is that we regard culture as the "sacrament of the church" (*sacramentum ecclesiae*). Without culture, the church's faith would not be able to declare itself, would not be able to show its face, let alone reveal to the world its own true face and reality. Whether in the individual believer or in the community of believers, culture is what gives faith its "flesh," its human face, its grammar, and in so doing offers faith the real possibility of being "encountered," "translated," "interpreted," "ritualized," and so effectively communicated to others. In other words, culture gives Christian faith the real possibility of emerging from its hidden baptismal depth and moving into the broad daylight of public profession, witness, and song; it enables faith to "surface," as it were, to express itself completely and manifestly for what it really is, whether this be in creedal or catechism form, in theological or encyclical form, in ritual or sacramental form. Without culture, faith alone would be mute; it would be condemned to remain hidden, a precious but mysteriously undisclosed gift from God. It would exist like a hidden vein of rough, uncut diamonds in the bowels of the earth.

Yet another point is important in this central consideration: the church is also "catholic." From where does this fundamental defining quality derive? What exactly gives our faith and our church its catholicity? Is it a self-appointed title, or perhaps an inherent self-induced quality that stems from the catholicity of the faith of which the church is a veiled, but complete embodiment? Or does it come from some other source? Yves Congar, the eminent French Dominican theologian, says that the catholicity of the church—that intrinsic, universal capacity for unity—is derived from a *dual* source: (a) the risen Lord who actively brings all things more perfectly together in himself and unto God, on the one hand, in conjunction with (b) the world and the virtually infinite resources of human nature and cultures.[17] It is in this dynamic participatory sense that culture, together with the risen Christ, gives the church and its faith the *real possibility* of being catholic, that is, of courting, embracing and becoming deeply wedded to the plurality of local cultures around the world.

We must not understand this to mean that the world and its many races and cultures are merely the "stuff" or passive material out of which the church gains its catholicity, as it might be said, for example, of a sculptor who hews a piece of wood or marble to produce a statue. World cultures offer *real* possibilities to the church, real in the sense that these possibilities are dynamic, pro-active invitations to see and behold what has not yet been seen or discovered, whether in the church's own "deposit" of revealed truth or in the cosmic certainty of the world's truth that it has indeed already been redeemed by Christ. Cultures must therefore be read as so many "formal" invitations that cultures incessantly send.out to the church, each carrying the embossed entreaty: R.S.V.P. The efficient grace inherent in these cultural offers of "catholicity" lies in their power to entice and seduce the church, as in courtship, with the prospect of an eventual nuptial union between faith and culture that might proclaim—just possibly and more convincingly—the coming of God's reign.

5 | Theological Foundations

In this chapter, the strictly theological section of this study, I wish to examine the theology underlying the process of inculturation and to show how such a theology can only be articulated on the basis of a proper understanding of the incarnation. In particular, my aim will be to show how the marriage root metaphor we have been considering brings several important theological correctives to the way the mystery of the incarnation has hitherto been applied to the principle of inculturation. My contention is that, far from harboring any serious inadequacies or drawbacks, as Aylward Shorter contends,[1] incarnation terminology remains the best—indeed the only adequate—terminology with which to develop a theology of inculturation. The principal of incarnation underlying the whole process of inculturation states that all communication between God and us human beings follows the pattern of the incarnation. The "God-made-man" means that the divine word becomes human word, divine love human love, divine power human power. This does not mean that it ceases to be divine, but it does mean that God now communicates with us through the natural realities and constitutive social structures of this world, including culture, into which he has incarnated his revelation and salvation. Incarnation means the human is henceforth irrevocably defined in terms of the divine and the divine is henceforth inescapably expressed in the human.

Clearly, one of the advantages of our metaphorical approach is that it quickens the current discussion with theological imagination. It is for lack of theological imagination that attempts thus far to elaborate a theology of inculturation have generally been either tentative or improbable. Without theological imagination, or what is sometimes referred to as *theopoeisis*, attempts to model the process of inculturation on the mystery of the incarnation often succumb to the temptation of rationalism. This can be seen, for example, in a persistent inability to abandon the traditional western style of theologizing and its classical categories.

Christology in particular has generally been strong in the practice of treating reason (not imagination) as the basis of belief and theological wisdom.[2] Aylward Shorter's attempt to develop a theology of inculturation is a case in point. Typically, when he examines inculturation Christologically, he distinguishes and hence develops his theology of inculturation "from the standpoints of the Creation, the Incarnation and the Paschal Mystery," as though these represented *three* distinct Christian mysteries.[3] The multiplicity of mysteries and the separatist approach which this entails are reminiscent of the conventional scholastic treatises: *De deo creatore, De verbo incarnato, De gratia*, etc. Having opted for a fragmentary approach, Shorter is then obliged—again typically—to conclude his theological study with a last minute disclaimer, namely, that the aforementioned standpoints are "not contradictory or mutually exclusive in themselves."[4] Despite this disclaimer, the primordial unity of the Christian mystery is clearly lost sight of and it becomes difficult to see how the mysteries of Christianity, in the plural, are really intrinsically connected.[5] Without such an understanding, any attempt to develop a theology of inculturation will be deficient. The master symbol of marriage, on the other hand, corrects this deficiency precisely because it is an inclusive rather than a separatist metaphor. By letting our theological imagination be saturated with nuptial imagery that is affective, inclusive, moving, and wise, it is possible to effect a deeper and theologically more accurate *rapprochement* between the mystery of incarnation and the process of inculturation.

A second temptation that besets those who would attempt an alignment between inculturation and incarnation without sufficient theological imagination is the sin of extrinsicism. By that I mean the serious mistake of reducing the "God-became-man" mystery to a purely external model or pattern to be imitated in the process of inculturating faith, an exercise therefore that would only touch a culture superficially, from without, but with no real power to embrace it from within. Evidence of this can be seen whenever the dialogue between the gospel and culture is naively modeled on Jesus' own personal enculturation as a first century Jew from Galilee, that is, the way he himself assumed and identified with the cultural symbols and values of his Palestinian communities. The reason why such an approach is critically flawed is twofold. First, while the process of enculturation entails some formal teaching and learning, it is largely an informal, and even a deeply unconscious, experience. We become inserted in our native culture without being fully aware of it, early in life and uncritically, even before becoming expressly aware of its dynamic and make-up. This holds true for everyone, including the growing and maturing boy Jesus. Moreover, our four gospels are virtually silent about Jesus' early life, and the only thing we know about his personal enculturation has to be gleaned from his public ministry. Such a brief time frame and the spotty historical evidence which the gospels do provide about Jesus' insertion into his culture do not yield sufficiently clear guidelines for inculturating faith. Second, and perhaps more important, to view the reality of the historical Jesus primarily as an external model to be imitated is but a half-truth of what the church has consistently and unequivocally proclaimed about Jesus Christ. Christian tradition has always attributed a *dual* dynamic function to the incarnate Son of God. In the words of T.W. Manson, this tradition can be summarized as follows: "The living Christ is there to lead the way for all who are prepared to follow him. More than that, the strength to follow is there too. The living Christ still has two hands, one to point the way, and the other held out to help us along."[6] The fathers of the church had another, more succinct, way of expressing the same idea, the same dual function of the living Christ: they used the short formula "*sacramentum et exemplum*."

It is beyond the scope of this study to outline the history of how these two key words came to be theologically connected in Christian tradition, especially since this history is so very rich and unbroken. For our purpose, we need only highlight some of the major representatives of this tradition. St. Augustine was the first to use and systematically elaborate on the formula "*sacramentum et exemplum*." He did so, moreover, as a felicitous way of expressing the dual remedial function of the incarnation. For him, this was important since the redemption wrought by Christ must be seen not only as affecting man's external behavior (*exemplo exterioris hominis*), but also as touching the depths of his being (*sacramento interioris hominis*).[7] The short formula was later taken up by St. Leo the Great who developed it further and gave it even greater importance in his own theology of the incarnation.[8] Toward the end of his life, in what must be considered the clearest and most mature expression of his thinking, St. Leo will say: "The all-powerful physician prepared a dual remedy (*duplex remedium*) for us, on the one hand his grace (*sacramentum*), and on the other his example (*exemplum*): with the first, he was giving us divine assistance, and with the second, he was eliciting our human cooperation."[9] This idea comes up again and again in the sermons of St. Leo, and the formula "*sacramentum et exemplum*" is one of the major organizing principles of his whole theology.

In the twelfth century, Saint Bernard of Clairvaux will also have recourse to the now well-established formula, especially in his attempt to safeguard against the excesses of "exemplarism." The defects of a bare "exemplarist" interpretation of the redeeming work of Christ have of course often been pointed out, but perhaps never more succinctly than by St. Bernard in his *Treatise Against the Errors of Abelard*.[10] Elsewhere, in his *Treatise Concerning Grace and Free Will*, Bernard will say: "In truth, we need the help (*adjutorium*) of him whose example (*exemplum*) we are incited to imitate."[11] And to his fellow monks, he says, "And this same man [Jesus] is the all-powerful God whose way of life heals me, whose support is my strength....Because he is man I strive to imitate him; because of his divine power I lean upon him."[12]

Clearly then, the dual Christological function expressed in the short formula "*sacramentum et exemplum*," which is derived directly from the mystery of the incarnation and soundly embedded in Christian tradition, must be taken into account when constructing a theology of inculturation. If not, such a theology will be deficient and sorely impoverished; conceivably, it will be found wanting for at least one or more of the following reasons:

- It fails to do justice to the deeper meaning and mystery of the incarnation, especially as a "continuing" and "redemptive" reality even unto the present day, as we shall see. It would thus have to settle for a much weaker, perhaps spurious, theological foundation. (A case in point: those who would ground the theology of inculturation on Justin's notion that the spermatic Logos or seed-bearing Word had been implanted in the heart of every human culture.[13])

- It deprives the process of inculturation of its intrinsic sacred character by failing to envisage inculturating faith as a real *sacramentum*, that is, a human gesture, ritual, or process that is transparent and charged with divine power and presence. Instead, the process of inculturation is depreciated to little more than a tactical pastoral endeavor on the part of the church in an effort to "adapt" or "adjust" to a changing world. (A good example of this: the 1994 Vatican document, *The Roman Liturgy and Inculturation*.)

- It fails to adequately explain, as it surely must, how inculturating faith involves genuine contemporaneity with the risen Christ, and how the risen body and humanity that Christ continues to assume even now in his glorified state does not terminate or bring closure to the incarnation, but prolongs and gives it even greater human density. Failing this, such a theology would unavoidably reduce the risen body and humanity of Christ to little more than a decorative trophy, the incarnation to but a memorial of some past event, and

inculturation to a mere ecclesial exercise with little or no gospel imperative behind it.

- It fails to validate and draw upon, as from a genuine *locus theologi-
cus*, the rich Christian tradition that views the incarnation as a
marriage between heaven and earth and therein discovers new creative inspiration and insight for celebrating inculturation as the
ongoing nuptial union between gospel and culture.

In order therefore to avoid the perils of rationalism and the dangers
of extrinsicism, let us now consider the possibility of a more integrated
theology of inculturation, one in which the present-day task of inculturating faith is clearly perceived as a direct, ongoing result of Christ's
"redemptive" and "continuing" incarnation, a theology also wherein
incarnation/resurrection/redemption are viewed as a single Christian
mystery.

Incarnation as Redemption

First thesis: Theologically, the incarnation should not be perceived as
a mere prelude to redemption, a "launch pad" as it were which enabled
Jesus to then begin redeeming the world, but must be seen as the theological "hard core" of redemption itself. In other words, *redemption is
incarnation*. The principal agent or cause behind Jesus' capacity to
redeem—in everything he does, endures or suffers—is precisely the very
dynamic of his being "incarnate."

Today, when we speak or think of redemption, we automatically
think of the principal redemptive act by which the incarnate Word
saved the world, his passion and death on the cross. This tradition of
correlating redemption with the sacrificial death of Jesus is of course
both venerable and patently orthodox. What is often overlooked and
recent scholarly studies reveal, however, is that in an earlier age the
fathers of the church spoke of a dynamic interrelationship between
redemption and incarnation. Not only did they consider these two
terms as being synonymous and hence interchangeable, but in an even
deeper sense they regarded the mystery of the incarnation as the
dynamic principle that gives redemptive value to *all* the actions of
Christ. For them, redemption was the direct, immediate result or consequence of the incarnation.

Having lost sight of the inherent reciprocity between incarnation and
redemption, theologians developed a doctrine of redemption quite
independently of incarnation. One of the heated debates in the middle

ages was whether or not the incarnation could be called redemptive in the strict sense of the word. By and large emphasis was placed on the redemptive *motive* of the incarnation rather than on its intrinsic redemptive nature, as though the Son of God became incarnate in order to *then* save the world. The ensuing debates saw theologians sadly pitting the Latin fathers against the Greek fathers, and in their polemics unwittingly did something of an injustice to both traditions. In reality, and notwithstanding the real difference of outlook and mentality between the two, on this point at least there is substantial agreement among the fathers: the term "redemption" covers a much broader and more extensive reality than what we generally understand by it today when we distinguish or separate it from the term "incarnation." A closer look at the theology of Pope Leo the Great, the acknowledged champion of orthodoxy in the Latin west, will confirm our thesis.

Incarnation and redemption were never conceived by Leo as separate mysteries but as one and the same great mystery of the "God-made-man." As Marie-Bernard de Soos points out in his excellent study of Leo's theology: "In the person of Christ, incarnation and redemption are profoundly united; they are in fact but two sides of the same reality, two facets of the same phenomenon."[14] In the Leonine sense, the term "redemption" is used to describe, not an isolated episode in the life of Jesus Christ, as we shall see, but the earthly mission of Jesus in all its variegated amplitude, including everything he experienced, did, or endured during his lifetime. Moreover, Leo sees the redeeming quality of Jesus' life as stemming directly from the fact of his "in-carnation." We see this, for example, in the way he attributes the destruction of sin in the world to the birth of Jesus as well as his passion,[15] or, again, in the way he calls Christmas "the day of our salvation," "the mystery of human restoration."[16] Behind everything that Jesus will do, experience or suffer from this point on, for St. Leo the principal cause or efficient agent of redemption lies ultimately in the enduring *union* of two natures in the personal being of Jesus Christ. Since divinity and humanity are indissolubly wedded in the incarnate Word, everything he does or endures becomes redemptive, including his passion and death on the cross. One may speculate about what Jesus might have died of had he not been crucified on the cross: would it have been of prostate cancer, a heart attack, an accident, or simply old age? The point of course is that he would have died, being like us in all things except sin. How he did *in fact* die on the cross remains of singular revelatory importance, but that he took on our human nature, lived and died *for us*, is of even greater theological importance.

With the incarnation, therefore, a new and utterly unique "state" of affairs is attained in the human condition. And it is precisely this new state in life that our marriage metaphor evokes and would keep before us in constructing a theology of inculturation. As we saw earlier, marriage is much more than simply the celebration of a wedding ceremony on a given day, although that is where it all begins; rather it constitutes a new and abiding "state" in life, a new "way" of life, one in which everything that follows is changed and deeply conditioned. Not only are the destinies of the married couple henceforth irrevocably bound up with each other, but the benefits that accrue to one of the partners redounds on the other. This wonderful exchange, which is so compellingly evoked in our marriage metaphor, is a central and recurring theme in Leo's theology of the incarnation. Time and again he parallels the descent of God with the elevation of humanity: *creatoris descensio, creaturae provectio* (the descent of the Creator=the elevation of the creature).[17] "He wanted to give us what was his," Leo tells us, "and heal in himself what was in us."[18] The first antiphon for Vespers on the octave of Christmas depicts this exchange in the following way: "O admirable exchange! The Creator of the human race has become man, born of a virgin; we have been made sharers in the divinity of Christ who shared in our humanity."[19] In sum: the saving remedy or redemption that Jesus brings to the world is made efficacious and truly remedial precisely because of the incarnation and always by virtue of it.

*   *   *

If we accept the fact that there is indeed an intrinsic connection between the mystery of the incarnation and redemption, then its implications for constructing a theology of inculturation would appear profound and far-reaching. The more obvious of these may be summed up as follows:

- The process of inculturation, like the mystery of the incarnation itself on which it is grafted, is *inherently redemptive* and should not be viewed simply as a pastoral strategy in view of better adapting the gospel message to a people's culture.

- In the same way that redemption came about through the union of divinity *and* humanity in Jesus Christ (and not solely through his divinity), similarly it is the *union* of gospel and culture that is salvific and transforming, not the gospel in and of itself alone or as somehow existing apart from and independently of culture.

- Inculturation, as in marriage, must be seen as a *reciprocal exchange* between gospel and culture, failing which neither would be affected or enriched by the other. What each brings to the other is of the very essence of inculturation as *sacramentum*.

Incarnation as Ongoing Reality

Second thesis: The incarnation is not simply an initial act or episode in the life of Jesus Christ, a *fait accompli* as it were, but is an abiding, dynamic operative throughout his entire life and mission, and indeed even today as he continues to assume his glorified body and humanity.

It has always been the firm conviction of Christian faith that the Son of God united himself in a most radical way to humanity. The absolutely radical nature of this union explains why the incarnation has so often been described in nuptial terms and imagery. The nuptial union remains one of the most intimate, life-generating unions one can humanly conceive or imagine. For all its precariousness, high risk, weakness and human frailty, marriage remains one of our better and more evocative symbols of everything that God has revealed himself to be for us, and indeed everything that he wants us to be for him. This master symbol embraces a whole cluster of metaphors expressing freely chosen love, intimacy, cohabitation, fecundity, the commixture of blissful sharing and painful drudgery, all centering about the supreme idea of a sacred space: a home, a *"chez soi."*[20] And each of these multifarious facets of the master symbol can give us new insight into the way faith and culture are to be conjoined and integrated. As the symbolic summation of what has been revealed to us in Jesus Christ, our marriage metaphor not only evokes a human reality that is charged with empowering divine grace (marriage *is* a sacrament!), but also the idea of an ongoing relationship, a new state in life, one that is not easily terminated, dissolved or broken up.

If the incarnation is to serve as the theological basis for the process of inculturation, it is important to view it as a *continuing* reality and not merely as the initial act whereby the Word of God assumed a human nature. On this point again, St. Leo and the fathers of the church were very explicit. Their notion of a continuing incarnation is embodied in the patristic principle: *"What is not assumed is not healed."*[21] In the mind of the fathers, the idea was that Jesus had to experience ("take on") everything that constitutes human existence (with the exception of sin), and in so doing was able to radically restore and heal our human nature through the concrete forms which his life assumed. As his life unfolded, Jesus continued to experience and so "incarnate" all aspects of human life, including all the joys and tribulations that typically make up human existence—"the good, the bad, and the ugly." As St. Leo says: "He healed the infirmities of our human weakness by experiencing them *in* himself."[22] Restoring humanity through humanity is the way Leo puts it: *in hominem renovans*. He is not asserting merely that redemption has been wrought in Jesus Christ, but that it has been wrought *by a human being* and therefore in a manner immanent to humanity itself. This principle of "interiority" is central to Leo's theology of the incarnation, and he makes bold to say that in Jesus Christ the restoration of our fallen nature came about, not from the outside as though from God, but from within human nature as though from man.[23] Elsewhere, speaking of the way Jesus overcame the temptations of the devil in the desert, Leo says that he did us a great honor by defeating the enemy as a man, and not in his divine capacity.[24] To paraphrase Leo, we could say that Christ made it possible for us human creatures to say in all truth: "We were responsible for bringing about our own downfall in the first place; but now we can take legitimate pride and credit for having fixed things up and made them even better."

Such is the realism of Christ's nuptial solidarity with humanity: as in marriage, the two partners become one flesh and journey together. Everything in the life of Jesus becomes remedial, according to this view, precisely because it is seen as a continuous dynamic "taking on" of real human experiences and passions, from the time of his birth in a manger to his death on the cross. We find this dynamic notion of a "continuing" incarnation beautifully expressed in the following text of Cyril of Alexandria:

> By his own death, the Savior abolished death. In the same way therefore that death would not have been abolished had he not died, similarly it must be said of all the other infirmities of the flesh. If he had not experienced fear, human nature would never have been without fear; if he had not experienced sadness, nature would never have been without sorrow; if he had not experienced what it means to be deeply troubled, we would never be free of anxiety. And so it is with all the other human passions that he experienced: these were alive and real in Christ, not to dominate him as they do us, but to be tamed by the power of the Word who dwells in the flesh and who transforms nature into something better.[25]

This notion of a "continuing" incarnation, with its strong emphasis on the "connaturality" between Christ and what is typically experienced in life by every human being, is clearly evident in St. Irenaeus, especially in connection with his notion of "recapitulation," which he borrowed from the apostle Paul and developed significantly. For Irenaeus, God draws his creation on to perfection gradually in an ever-present, progressive and creative action, with time and history being the measure and record of this sequential progress. And he does this through the incarnate Word who "recapitulates" or "takes up again" in himself (assumes) all aspects of the human condition, including the biological stages of growth and development: "He passed through every stage of life," Irenaeus says, "restoring communion with God."[26] Elsewhere, he elaborates more fully:

> Therefore he passed through every age, being first made an infant unto infants, to sanctify infants; among little ones, a little one, to sanctify such as are of that same age, being made to them an example both of piety and righteousness and obedience; among youth, a youth, becoming a pattern to youths and sanctifying them in the Lord. Thus also he was an elder among elders, in order to be a perfect master in all things, not in setting forth the truth only, but in age also, sanctifying the elder persons as well and becoming an example for them too. Lastly he came even unto death, that he might be *the first born from the dead, having himself the preeminence in all things*, the Prince of Life, the first of all, and going before all.[27]

Irenaeus also makes it clear that Jesus assumed the socio-historical dimension of being truly human. For him, a person's individual history would be incomplete were it not "enfleshed" in the history of the individual's family, group, or tribe—and indeed in the history of humankind as such. In biblical times, of course, such historical relationships were thought of as being somehow inscribed in the flesh and blood of the individual and transmitted by birth. Hence the Jewish custom of recording lengthy genealogies, an example of which we find in Matthew 1:1-16 and Luke 3:23-38. Irenaeus exploits Jesus' genealogy to demonstrate how our Lord "has summed up in himself all nations dispersed from Adam downwards, and all languages and generations of men."[28] For Irenaeus, it was important not only to establish the nature of Jesus' humanity in the abstract, but to show how Jesus was truly born in the flesh and thus assumed its historical realities, namely, the fact of being born into a particular lineage, a particular culture, at a particular time and place in history.

With the fathers of the church, therefore, we should not think of the incarnation as a once-upon-a-time occurrence in the life of Jesus, but as a dynamic, ever-present reality that spans his entire life. It is equally important to realize that just as the incarnation does not cease with the actual birth of Jesus, so we must not think of the incarnation as somehow coming to an end with his death on the cross. On the contrary, it continues to be a most dynamic reality even as Christ assumes his glorified human being and body. As French theologian M.-D. Chenu reminded us years ago, "The incarnation of God was not accomplished once-for-all in some remote corner of Judea; it continues still, it is still operative everywhere; and anything that would not come under its sphere of influence in man and, through man, in our strained and wonderful world, would in fact fall back in its own misery and the redemption of the world would thus be a failure. If God becomes incarnate to divinize us humans, he must assume *everything*, from top to bottom in human nature; otherwise what is not assumed would not be redeemed or divinized."[29]

Nor can it be said that the resurrection of Christ withdrew him from the humanity that he had assumed and in-carnated during his earthly life and ministry—as though once he had completed the work of redemption, there was little reason for the existence of Christ's bodiliness. The resurrection in no way makes his individual humanity into something less human, less real. By being taken up into the glory of God, Christ's human nature did not become an expendable accessory; rather it took its rightfully appointed place "at the right hand of the Father" and so gained its full human maturity and unsuspected dignity. In other words, the human nature that Christ assumed in the incarnation, along with its constitutive solidarity that binds him to the rest of humanity, is maintained in all its integrity and authenticity even in Christ's state of risen glory. Only in this way is it possible to maintain that the Christian dogma of the resurrection of the body is more than just a figure of speech, that God does indeed have a *real* human face and body, and that with the resurrection human life "is changed, not destroyed or taken away."

Even today, in his eternal now, Christ continues to actively assume his glorified body and humanity. If he were not, he would be little more than a memory, a paradigmatic figure of the past, like Buddha, Socrates, or Gandhi, whose words and deeds, life and death, are still compelling examples to follow, but only as figures or voices out of the past. Contemporaneity with the risen Lord, on the other hand, is of the very essence of saving grace; it alone gives sacramental meaning and real presence to Christ's words: "I am with you always." Talk of divine grace would be meaningless babble if Christ were not even now becoming in-carnate. The truth and reality of grace (whether "sacramental," "sanctifying," or otherwise) consist precisely in the fact that the risen Lord continues to assume our human nature and, through this abiding solidarity with the things of the earth and the human family, remains thrillingly alive and present to every generation throughout time. All the benefits that accrue to us through the Christ-event derive now from a unique and fundamental Christian mystery, namely, *the ongoing incarnation of the risen Lord*. Edward Schillebeeckx says it well: "Redemption turns its face towards us in Christ's glorified bodiliness."[30]

To think or speak of God as having human form and qualities is of course one of the salient features of the Old Testament. Anyone who reads the bible must be impressed by the frequency with which the Old Testament writers ascribe human attributes to God. God is said to have hands, feet, eyes, ears, mouth, face, head, heart. He uses these faculties to see, hear, speak, etc. Yahweh's hands create, shape, punish, liberate. God can walk, stroll, advance, sit, and withdraw. He gets angry, sleeps, relents, changes his mind, remembers, and is jealous. This eminently anthropomorphic way of depicting God in the Old Testament sought to express the fundamental religious belief of the Hebrew community. It celebrates their lively faith in a *living* and *personal* God (in ironic contrast to those dead idols, ridiculed in Psalm 115, "who have mouths, but cannot speak, and eyes, but cannot see"). Yahweh is a living God who communicates and remains everlastingly "in touch" with his people. He is the God of Abraham, Isaac, and Jacob, all of whom had close personal encounters with him. Such anthropomorphic God-talk was justified in the Old Testament on the grounds that man and woman were created in the image of God (Gn 1:26), but it remained nevertheless anthropomorphic speech.[31]

With the New Testament, things change dramatically: the incarnation of Jesus Christ marks an absolute end to all anthropomorphic speech or talk about God. In Christ, human attributes can now in the strictest sense be predicated of God. The God who previously had only been *spoken of* in human terms now really *becomes* human. Henceforth Christian faith will rest on the preposterous claim and testimony of the first disciples: "We have heard him, we have seen him with our eyes, we have looked upon him, and our hands have touched him" (1 Jn 1:1). The incarnational fact that God's "hand" is now in all truth the real hand of one particular fellow human being—Jesus of Nazareth—makes the hand of every other fellow human being something absolutely and utterly new—something divine! something holy! something sacramental! "When you did it to one of the least of these brethren of mine, you did it to me" (Mt 25:40). This is not just a moral injunction or exhortation wrapped in some felicitous figure of speech. With the incarnate Son of God, it now becomes a blessed (and frightening) reality! The fact that God's "face" is now a real human face, his "word" a truly audible human word, and his "heart" a real beating heart, makes every human gesture and every human being a "sacrament" (in the fullest, most divinely empowering sense of the term). It is precisely because of Christ's continuing incarnation, the primordial sacrament, that there now exists a sacramental quality inherent in our *being* or *becoming* "neighbor" to someone in need, as portrayed in the parable of the good Samaritan. One can even say that the sacrament of the "neighbor" is *always* valid and efficacious (*opus operatum*, as classical theology would put it), that is to say, its grace-full efficacy does not depend on the individual's subjective disposition or awareness, as Matthew's depiction of the last judgment makes abundantly clear (Mt 25:31-45).

It follows from this central Christian mystery, also, that the radical, ontological solidarity which the risen Christ has with every human being in virtue of his continuing incarnation does not simply apply to the individual person in a restricted, isolated or monadic sense; it must include everything that constitutes "being human" in the deepest and fullest sense, everything that is essential in defining what it means to be a real human being. Now this obviously includes that social fabric, web, or matrix we call human "culture." Culture not only conditions our external behavior to a greater or lesser degree, but it goes to the very core of the personal human subject and indeed defines "being human" just as radically as does, say, rationality and human sexuality. A person's culture is not just an external accretion or extrinsic additive to human nature, something to be prized and valued perhaps, but not strictly essential—as it might be said, for example, about getting rich, educated, or "ahead" in life. Today culture is seen as an essential constituent of being human since the very *identity* of a person hinges vitally on his or her native culture.[32] Culture therefore is not a luxury, but a human necessity; it is not something a person can live or do without, since everything in us is conceived, develops, and flourishes—or dies—in and through our social culture, including our perception of God and our life of faith.

Just as human sexuality or rationality is of the very nature of being human, so too is human culture: we are essentially cultural beings since culture enters into our ontological (not accidental) definition as social human beings. This explains why the systematic domination, oppression, or denial of a people's culture is at long last beginning to be seen for what it really is: not just an historical or political "mistake," but a "crime" against humanity. It is criminal precisely because it violates the autonomy of human personhood and the social cultural matrix which sustains and nourishes it. This explains, also, why the plight of untold immigrants and refugees who are forced out of their country and culture is so appallingly inhuman: to be forced to give up one's cultural identity—for whatever reason—is to become a "non-person," an "invisible people."

Thus when we speak of Christ's continuing incarnation and his concomitant ontological solidarity with the human family, this includes the
cultural dimension of being human and therefore the cultures of the
world. To think otherwise, I submit, one would be guilty of a modern-
day version of an old heresy, namely, Nestorianism. The heresy of
Nestorius consisted essentially in this: although he sought to preserve a
close union between Christ's divinity and humanity, he was only able to
admit a "moral" union of the Logos with humanity, not a real hypostatic
union. The propositions of a mitigated version of this heresy today
might read something like the following:

- Since his resurrection, the solidarity that Christ now enjoys with
  the human family here on earth is a "moral" or "mystical" union,
  and no longer one that refers immediately to or is contingent upon
  his having a human nature and body as was the case when he was
  on earth.

- One therefore cannot say, without serious reservation or remis-
  sion, that the risen Lord is *ontologically* united with humanity here
  on earth, nor does his now glorified individual humanity have any
  bearing upon or connection with the cultures of the world today
  (as it perhaps did when Jesus was on earth—but even that is doubtful since the gospels are silent on this specific issue).

- Nor can it be said that the particular culture into which the Son of
  God historically became incarnate is part of the content of divine
  revelation. It is merely the cultural "context" in which God chose to
  reveal himself, the "medium" as it were, but not the "message."
  Human culture cannot add anything to divine revelation since the
  one is human, the other divine.

The above three propositions, though written with a touch of humor,
do reflect, I feel, something of the deep, unspoken assumptions that lie
behind much of today's discussion on these issues—in particular: (1) the
failure to fully appreciate the indivisible interrelationship between incarnation and resurrection, (2) the scant awareness in North America of
the need to inculturate the faith and give more than a cameo role to culture in the discourse and task of evangelization, and (3) the curious
absence of any serious consideration given to the inherent and abiding
connection between culture and Christ's risen humanity.

There are no doubt many factors that could explain why Christ's glorified individual humanity has not figured prominently in attempts to
develop a theology of inculturation. One of these, certainly, is the fact

that Catholic tradition has never laid down any view concerning the nature of the link between the risen body of Christ and his earthly body. This is not surprising for two reasons: first and foremost, the resurrection is an object of faith, not of scientific knowledge, and, second, the gospel narratives do not shed any light on what *actually happened* to the dead body of Jesus. Basically, the New Testament simply declares that the risen Christ is the same as Jesus of Nazareth, but a Jesus who is now entirely transformed and fulfilled in glory. Another factor is that Christ's individual glorified humanity was overshadowed, if not totally eclipsed, by the prominence given to the doctrine of the church as the "mystical body" of Christ. Since contemporaneity with the risen Lord seemed more than sufficiently mediated through the visible church and its sacraments, and since the church moreover had clearly received a mandate from the Lord to "continue" his work and mission here on earth, Christ's glorified body became something of a residual (not to say redundant) theological category. Moreover, the difference between a body that is "mystical" (as applied to the church) and one that is "glorified" (as in the risen Lord) is admittedly open to confusion and misrepresentation. We see this expressed in Simone Weil's *Letter to a Priest* when she says: "Everything has proceeded as though in the course of time no longer Jesus, but the church, had come to be regarded as being God incarnate on this earth."[33]

*   *   *

If the foregoing is accepted as a valid interpretation of the incarnation, then several important implications follow for constructing a theology of inculturation. The result of the redeeming incarnation, as an enduring heavenly reality, is that Jesus Christ is the head of created humanity. He is this, moreover, through his personal insertion of himself into our human condition and history, and the subsequent glorification by God of his individual humanity. While the latter has made Jesus disappear from the visible horizon of our life here on earth, we can and do speak of an earthly prolongation of Christ's bodiliness in the visible church. The church is quite rightly called the "sacrament of the risen Christ" because Christ continues to make his glorified bodiliness visibly present to and for us earthbound creatures in the sacraments of the church.[34]

But this is not all; we do not have the whole picture of Christ's union and radical solidarity with humanity when we view the church as the earthly sacrament of Christ in heaven, but only half the picture. There is also another non-ecclesial bond-in-being between the glorified Christ

and our earthly, as-yet-unglorified humanity, namely, his ontological solidarity with the cultures of the world. If the one earthly prolongation of
Christ's bodiliness is called the "mystical body" of the Lord, the second
one, properly understood, might well be called his "cultural body."
Vatican II made reference to a similar solidarity when it stated that "by
his incarnation the Son of God has united himself in some fashion with
every man" (*Gaudium et Spes*, no. 22), and the whole of humanity to himself. Cardinal Paul Poupard, the president of the Pontifical Council for
Culture, has put it better and more explicitly than most when he says: "If
Christ the Redeemer has accomplished the work of salvation of ALL MEN
AND ALL OF MAN, HE ALSO SAVED HUMAN CULTURE, that fundamental manifestation of man as an individual, as a community, a people, and a
nation."[35] If it is true that Christ continues to assume his glorified
humanity in all its "constitutive constants" and integrity, a nuptial knot
that can nevermore be undone binds him to humanity—not to humanity
as might be conceived *in abstracto*, but to humanity concretely constituted
as a "family of cultures."

In what is perhaps his most significant contribution to a theology of
inculturation, Edward Schillebeeckx, in his major work, *Christ: The
Experience of Jesus as Lord*, has delineated six anthropological constants
that constitute being human. And insofar as these form a synthesis, he
says, human culture is an irreducible autonomous reality.[36] It is also
clear from what we have said that Christ's ongoing and redeeming
incarnation (which cannot be reduced or restricted to the sacramental
"visibility" of the church) embraces everything that permanently constitutes humanity, and this includes human culture. The concrete particularity of the culture into which the Son of God was inserted, its
historical and geographical limitations, as well as its singular peculiarity,
are now *transcended* in the risen Christ who, through the glorification
by God of his individual humanity, is now wedded and ontologically
united to *every* culture of the world. In the same way that Christ is the
"Lord of history," so is he also the "Lord of human cultures." What this
means is that the risen Christ is ontologically present to and for every
human culture; it also means that every culture, in its visible and in-
depth reality, is a means of immediate encounter with the glorified
bodiliness of Christ. If I wish to hear and encounter Jesus Christ, I must
find him "enfleshed" in my culture, failing which I would never recognize or know him intimately. On this point, Schillebeeckx is very clear:
"Only in concrete particularity can the gospel be the revelation of the
universality of salvation from God, because men and women are cultural
beings with their own particular cultures and can only be reached as
human beings in them."[37]

Just as we speak of the church as the "mystical body" of Christ, therefore, so too must we speak of the "cultural body" of Christ—*the two being indivisibly interrelated.* In other words, if the church is a sacrament to and for the world (*sacramentum mundi*), as it unquestionably wants to be, it is also true that human culture is a sacrament to and for the church (*sacramentum ecclesiae*). The theological justification for this assertion of course is that the sacramental nature of the church, by virtue of its very sacramentality, must embrace all the human realities and cultures of the world and not simply the material elements such as bread, water, wine and oil, with which it confects its own "domestic" sacraments. Were this not so, the church would cease to be an effective sacrament to the world. The nuptial root metaphor not only points and speaks to the espousal of Jesus Christ and humanity, as we have seen, but also to the indissoluble union that exists between faith and culture, on the one hand, and between the church and the world, on the other.

We must remember also that culture is not just something which is added to or acquired by our nature as human beings, but the vital site of our identity and of the way we perceive and communicate with others. *My culture* is the universe received and made particular for me in time and space; it is constituted by the various relationships which define me profoundly as a human individual in the midst of the universe. This means that a twofold dimension is included in the notion of culture: (1) it is a direct relationship with the universe and (2) it is a structure of human continuance. This defining dual dimension is precisely what makes culture a sacrament to and for the church. For without it, the "catholicity" of the church would be unthinkable and without theological foundation, as would be also the possibility of "transmitting" Christian faith from one generation to another or from one culture to another. The gospel message is open to all cultures, but its actual power to be "cross-cultural" derives from the social and cultural laws of the world. It is in this sense that culture is a sacrament to and for the church. While it is true that the gospel is not bound to one culture, it is also true that "the gospel" has never existed above or outside any culture, as though one could strip it down and neatly isolate it from the particular culture in which it is already embedded and acclimatized. The same holds true for the faith of the believing community. As Schillebeeckx says: "Human beings are subjects of faith, but they are also cultural—cultural beings. So the specific culture in which believers live, that *on which* Christian faith is in fact modeled, is at the same time the culture *through which* this faith is assimilated in a living way and finally that *in which* it is experienced concretely by men and women living here and now."[38]

It follows from the above, also, that the task of evangelization consists not only in the process of inculturating *faith*, but also and concomitantly in the process of inculturating *the church*. Although the expression "inculturation of the church" is admittedly still rare, it has already found its way into an official church document, the final document of the Fourth General Conference of the Latin American Episcopate held in Santo Domingo in 1992. Among the pastoral resolutions this general conference called itself to, after having spoken of inculturation as "an imperative of the discipleship of Jesus," we read: "[To] promote within the indigenous peoples their own native cultural values by means of an **inculturation of the church** so as to embody God's reign more fully."[39] The implications of this new expression have still to be worked out, but already it should be clear that there cannot be a true inculturation of the gospel anywhere without a concomitant inculturation of the church which proclaims and celebrates that same gospel.

In summary: Nowhere is the primacy of God's love asserted more realistically and universally than in the redemptive incarnation that even today unites all people to Christ in a radical bond of solidarity, a state of "original grace" that touches and affects all peoples from within their very own culture. In Christ the cultural order is abundantly infused with grace. Unseen and unspoken, this extra-ecclesial reality of Christ's "I am with you" is silently at home in the heart of every human culture—not merely as a small "seed" that must somehow be painstakingly discovered and nurtured, but as "superabundant" grace so characteristic of the incarnation itself.

PART THREE

Culture Revisited: A New Approach

6 | Culture Revisited: Some Misconceptions

In order to appreciate more fully just what is involved in the coupling of faith and culture, in this section of our study we will focus our attention on human culture and the way inculturating the faith in American culture might proceed. What is culture? With what words can we describe it? To what may we compare it? Already in 1952, some one hundred and sixty-four existing definitions of culture were inventoried by A.L. Kroeber and Clyde Kluckhohn. Twentieth century writer A. Lawrence Lowell put it well when he compared the attempt to define culture with "trying to seize the air in the hand, when one finds that it is everywhere except within one's grasp." With such an array of definitions, descriptions and theories of culture, there is probably no more comprehensive a word in the English language than the word "culture." Yet, unnerving as the prospect may first appear, a better understanding of the meaning of culture is a prerequisite to any serious attempt to construct a theology of inculturation. While there yet may be differences concerning the meaning of culture, there can be no doubt that the study of cultural phenomena is of central importance for the social sciences as well as for mission studies. Since the concept of culture has a lengthy history of its own, it may be useful to give a brief overview of the way "culture" has been conceived in the past and some of the misconceptions about culture that still prevail today. In the next chapter, I will propose a model for understanding culture that should enable the church to inculturate its faith more deeply in American culture.[1]

What Is Culture?

The word "culture" derives its semantic origin from the Latin *cultura*, which initially referred to the cultivation of the soil and then by extension to the cultivation of the mind and spirit, as when Cicero speaks of "culture of the soul" (*cultura animi*) and identifies it with philosophy and

89

learning generally. The word "culture" itself, however, only gained currency in European thought in the second half of the eighteenth century, and the so-called *classical* conception which emerged was generally identified with the process of intellectual and spiritual development and closely associated with the progressive character of the modern era. Behind this notion of culture was the assumption of continuous improvement as a conscious goal or ideal, together with the idea of uninterrupted progress associated with the European enlightenment. This conception of culture was therefore steeped in the unbounded optimism of humanity's mounting capacity to understand and hence control the "laws" of its own development. For Condorcet, no less than for Thomas Paine and Thomas Jefferson after him, cultural development was continuous and the canon against which they appraised cultures was deemed absolute. What they did not see of course was the ethnocentric bias of their conception of culture. Hence it was confidently predicted that savagery, barbarism and underdevelopment generally were bound to recede before the advance of western knowledge and the diffusion of scientific and technological "know-how."

With the appearance of the discipline of anthropology in the late nineteenth century and stemming in large part from the ethnographic descriptions of non-European cultures, a major shift in the conception of culture took place. The names of Gustav Klemm, E.B. Tylor, and later Malinowski are associated with this new *descriptive* conception of culture. Tylor's definition remains classic:

> Culture or civilization, taken in its wide ethnographic sense, is that complex whole which includes knowledge, belief, art, morals, law, custom, and any other capabilities and habits acquired by man as a member of society. The condition of culture among the various societies of mankind, in so far as it is capable of being investigated on general principles, is a subject apt for the study of laws of human thought and action.[2]

Two things are noteworthy in this definition. *First* is the idea that culture, however else it might be conceived, is non-selective in the sense that it embraces all aspects of human life in a given society: its values, beliefs, customs, forms of knowledge and art, etc. It is no longer an "elitist" concept of the educated but one that applies to every individual and to all peoples. *Second*, this all-inclusive descriptive conception of culture is said to form a "complex whole." Any given culture, according to this view, represents a complex of interrelated and interdependent constituents, each of which shares with the others certain distinctive characteristics. Culture is now seen as an integral whole or configuration.

Interestingly, when Vatican II defines culture, it will do so very much in keeping with Tylor's descriptive conception.[3] This marks something of a milestone in that church leaders and anthropologists now concurred in their way of viewing culture. Although this conception of culture prevailed in the emerging scientific discipline concerned with analysis, classification and comparison of the inherent elements in a given culture, it did have its limitations. Much of its value and utility is lost, as anthropologists and others have shown, because it does not provide us with a ready instrument or operative tool for analyzing culture. It is useful in classifying and comparing cultural phenomena (akin to the way botanists classify flora and fauna), but it offers no insight into or interpretation of the deeper meaning of these cultural phenomena. Moreover, the all-inclusive scope of this descriptive conception of culture remains superficially vague since it is virtually co-extensive with human nature itself. As such, therefore, it does not have the kind of precision that would enable either the social scientist or the missionary to gain deeper insight into a given culture. Herein lies its greatest weakness and no doubt one of the reasons why the evangelization of cultures has not always been conducted, as Paul VI complained, "in a vital way, in depth and right to the very roots" of a culture.[4] The descriptive conception of culture we find in *Gaudium et Spes* is of little value in terms of knowing how to proceed with the praxis of inculturation or what a theology of inculturation might actually entail. The more metaphysical understanding of culture adumbrated by Pope John Paul II in his discourses is clearly more insightful in this regard but, again, it provides us with a vision and not an instrument or means for analyzing culture. In his 1980 address to the executive council of UNESCO, he says, for instance: "The essential meaning of culture consists....in the fact that it is characteristic of human life as such. Man lives an entirely human life only due to culture....Man cannot live without culture... Culture is that which makes man become ever more human."[5] (Parenthetically, it is interesting to note that Vatican II also ascribes to Jesus Christ a similar humanizing role: "Whoever follows after Christ, the perfect man, becomes himself more human."[6])

Yet another important shift in our understanding of culture came about with the realization that symbols play a crucial role in culture. This new *symbolic* conception of culture, associated initially with the name of Leslie A. White, who observed that all human behavior originates in the use of symbols,[7] would be refined and further developed by such notable scholars as Clifford Geertz, Mary Douglas, Victor Turner, and Robert Schreiter. This major shift away from a purely descriptive approach to a symbolic approach to culture was marked by a growing concern with questions of meaning, symbolism and interpretation (the very concerns, in fact, that have always preoccupied the church in its own religious tradition).

At the outset of his work, Geertz makes his position quite clear: "Believing, with Max Weber, that man is an animal suspended in webs of significance he himself has spun, I take culture to be those webs, and the analysis of it to be therefore not an experimental science in search of law but an interpretive one in search of meaning."[8] Culture, he says, is "a stratified hierarchy of meaningful structures." When we analyze a culture, therefore, we are in effect engaged in unraveling layers upon layers of meaning embodied in symbolic forms. These patterns of meaning, by virtue of which individuals communicate and are able to live out their lives with others, are inherited from the past and are therefore *already meaningful* (consciously or unconsciously) for these same individuals. Making himself quite clear, Geertz says: "The culture concept to which I adhere...denotes an historically transmitted pattern of meanings embodied in symbols, a system of inherited conceptions expressed in symbolic forms by means of which men communicate, perpetuate, and develop their knowledge about and attitudes toward life."[9] There are of course some methodological problems in Geertz's work, but these need not detain us here since it is his basic insight, and not his actual methodology, that offers us a solid starting point from which to elaborate a new method of analyzing cultures.

One of the most disquieting aspects of the church's dealing with culture in the past—and indeed even with cultures today—is its tendency to appraise a culture or its parts largely (sometimes exclusively) on the basis of what "meets the eye," that is, on the outer, epidermal surface of a culture. It has not always paid sufficient heed to the deeper "invisible" strata of culture, the dynamic myths and mobilizing symbols that burn like a fiery furnace within it. This is unfortunate since it is precisely from these lower-level strata, I will argue, that the true pattern of meaning and symbolism of culture emerge and can be interpreted. A classic example: missionaries from western cultures have tried to eliminate polygyny in societies where they found it *before* uncovering the deeper meaning and symbolic import of such a custom; nor were they even aware that their censure could drastically affect (possibly for the worse) the functioning of that culture as a "complex whole."[10] Most missionary mistakes in the past can be traced to this lack of awareness, that all aspects of a culture (economic, political, social, religious, etc.) have an inherent tendency to function as an interrelated whole. Herein also lies the key to any realistic hope of evangelizing a culture. If the praxis of inculturating faith is to be more than a superficial and highly selective undertaking, then a deeper, more organic appreciation of culture is needed. On the other hand, our instrument for analyzing a culture must not be so complicated or so professionally "elitist" that ordinary Christians and pastors in the field cannot avail themselves of its benefits.

The reader will have surmised already no doubt that my approach to cultural analysis assumes that culture is a unified, symbolic, and stratographic human reality which prompts a people to perceive, behave, judge, value and interact in a certain characteristic manner. Before outlining my model of culture, however, there are several misconceptions of culture that must first be addressed.

Structure and Interaction

A first misconception of culture can be seen in those theories that move away from (or reject) a unified conception of culture to one that proposes a "duality of culture," such as the one advanced by British sociologist Anthony Giddens[11] and Margaret S. Archer.[12] Those who espouse this theory suggest that a sharp conceptual distinction must be made between "structure" and "interaction" and that these must be analyzed at two independently separate levels. The structural dimension, according to this view, consists in the systemic factors or constants that define the enduring components of a culture and that provide meaning for the participants: those cultural symbols and values that are fundamental to members of that culture. Interaction, on the other hand, refers to the free, spontaneous communication that *de facto* takes place between individuals within the culture framework. This "double-vision" perspective arises, I submit, from an *a priori* misconception of the nature and dynamic function of cultural solidarity.

In her critique of what she calls the "myth of cultural integration," Archer argues that the long-held anthropological "doctrine" of the unity of culture fails to recognize or account for the recurring inconsistencies within every culture, the inherent differences that can and do exist in every population, and the unpredictable volatility of human behavior. What such a view in fact fails to recognize is that culture, properly understood, is not a straitjacket that would supposedly guarantee uniform behavior or interaction in a given society. Culture simply does not function for its members in this way—nor indeed has it ever. It does not oblige people to act in a given way, nor does it predetermine how they will interact with others in the kind of "deterministic" way we see in a beehive colony. Cultural solidarity, at its best, merely *prompts* people to act or react in a certain way but it does not eliminate the responsibility and freedom of individual choice characteristic of human behavior. We should also keep in mind that the "cultural system" exists prior to any active personal interaction on the part of the individuals in that culture. It exists as a pre-given solidarity or "bond-in-being" between individuals even before they meet and interact with others.

The distinguishing characteristic of this cultural solidarity, this "being-together-with-others," is that it is forever challenging and inducing a personal subject to take an active stand or position in the face of others. The dynamic nature of culture discloses itself precisely when members of that culture engage in active interaction. *It is not the interaction itself, but the inducement to respond that constitutes culture*. It is a collective inner summons that elicits from the individual a free personal response in the face of others. Since people are united in cultural solidarity, they inescapably "implicate" one another in everything they say, will, or do. Inescapably, I say, because we cannot live as human subjects outside culture nor are we ever born outside a specific culture. It is precisely this unavoidable involvement in the lives, beliefs, and actions of others that "evokes" a reaction in people, who are thereby pressed into giving a personal response of either agreement or disagreement. In short, cultural solidarity "prompts" me to continuously redefine myself and my personal beliefs in the light of what others say, do, and believe. Thus the study or analysis of active interaction between people, independently of the cultural matrix or ambience from which it arises and from whose inner promptings it is never spared, is to misconstrue the nature of human interpersonal relations generally, and the dynamic character of culture reality in particular.

If cultural solidarity beckons and induces us to interact with others in a certain way, it does this not only by giving us a particular "slant" or "outlook" on life (the English term "worldview" is a bit too inflated, too grandiose, in my opinion), but also by giving us a sense of self-identity as a people, without which our interactions with others would scarcely be those of an autonomous personal subject. The inestimable value of culture, as inducement and inner summons, lies precisely in the fact that *it constantly prompts us to overcome the self-destructive possibility of remaining neutral in the face of others*. Culture, in the last analysis, is what "saves" us *from* ourselves *for* others. It is, one might say, an inner invitation to respond to others, a suasive R.S.V.P. Neutrality (or indifference) in the face of others is not only humanly self-destructive, but from a Christian perspective it also stands against everything that would hasten the coming of God's reign here on earth. Thus while culture must not be identified with the actual way people order their lives and interact with others, neither can it be divorced from the dynamic tension between personal freedom and the cultural summons to respond in a certain way. For between these two there exists a subtle but profound interplay. Therefore if we are to understand how culture functions ("works"), we must avoid making a cleavage or divide between what culturally "prompts" individuals to act in a certain way, on the one hand, and how these same individuals do in fact choose to act, on the other. To do so would be like trying to master the laws of physics quite independently of and without any reference whatsoever to the science of mathematics. Such a "separatist" approach, though conceptually tidy and perhaps appealing, is just as deleterious for the social sciences as it is for theology, as when incarnation/redemption/resurrection are envisaged as three distinct Christian mysteries. Maintaining clear conceptual distinctions is one thing; getting to the heart of human reality is something else.

Technology and Culture

Another source of confusion about culture has to do with the prevalence of modern technology. The term "culture" has become encrusted and overlaid with many things that are not intrinsically cultural even though they may have originated historically in one cultural zone of the world instead of another. Modern technology is certainly one of these. Culture is *not* the outgrowth and proliferation of twentieth century technology we see all around us, in whatever hemisphere or country we may live in. Because the scientific revolution took place in seventeenth century Europe and is massively fueled today by the industrial "super-powers" of the world, this does not mean that the technologies themselves are intrinsic to some cultures and not to others. It is more appropriate and certainly more realistic today to speak of the impact of technology on human culture than it is to speak of culture's impact or imprint on the technologies that have now settled over most cultures of the world.

Technology has long since acquired a life and momentum of its own, quite independently of the western countries or cultures that opened Pandora's scientific box in the seventeenth century or that continue to reap enormous benefits and power from it still. As Reinhard Rurup put it: "Modern industrial technology emerged under specific historical conditions and in response to needs one can assume existed; yet over the course of time this technology became increasingly independent of such social conditions, to the extent that it is now obeying no laws but those of its own development. Technology...progresses on its own power after an initial takeoff phase."[13] Technology is *not* culture, it is supra-cultural. What faces us today is the homogenization of human cultures, including the United States, through modern technology. Today, Nigerians, like other people, are hardly more Americanized in their lifestyle than they are Japanned or common-marketed. What this means is that now that technology has been ushered in and let loose on the global scene, it not only has gained a cross-cultural momentum, but has even become autonomous, with a supra-cultural status and life of its own.

No one has addressed this issue more thoughtfully or more thoroughly than Langdon Winner in his *Autonomous Technology* and his *Democracy in a Technological Society*. Winner begins by debunking a set of presuppositions that have hitherto supported the myth that we have control and mastery over technology. They are, in the words of Winner:

—*that men know best what they themselves have made;*
—*that the things men make are under their firm control;*
—*that technology is essentially neutral, a means to an end; the benefit or harm it brings depends on how men use it.*[14]

While these three propositions may seem conspicuously reasonable, Winner shows how they are no longer valid. The loss of mastery manifests itself, he says, in a decline of our ability to know, to judge, or to control our technical means. His basic argument is that the technologies that have been invented to satisfy our material needs have now developed, in size, complexity, and costliness, to the point where they now determine and dictate our conception of the needs themselves. Moreover, those people who must rely for their very existence upon technological systems they do not understand or control, Winner argues, "are not at liberty to change those systems in any way whatsoever."[15]

The notion of autonomous technology and its self-generating, self-sustaining advance has been addressed by philosophers, sociologists, anthropologists, and economists. Jacques Ellul's position of course is well known. One of his basic insights concerning the exponential growth and autonomy of technology is that the modern technological system constitutes a single artificial complex of interlocking components so mutually dependent on one another that we now must view it as one encompassing environment. The point is that this "environment" does not feed off or depend whatsoever on the cultural norms and values of a people for its sustenance, growth, and orientation. It is autonomous in the sense also that it is *culture-free*. Not only has the modern technological system become emancipated from human culture, rising and "floating" above it so to speak, but it now manipulates the very cultural processes it ostensibly claims to serve.

"Technological systems," Winner says, "impose a permanent, rigid, and irreversible imprint" on the lives and cultures of a people.[16] Winner's judicious choice of adjectives is significant. What is especially noteworthy for us is that these three adjectives describe the antithetical characteristics of culture, *qua* culture. If there is one thing that scholars agree on, it is the indisputable fact that human cultures are not rigid, but inherently plastic and flexible; that cultures are not irreversible, but surprisingly open and subject to change, both from within as well as from external contacts and transfers from other cultures. As for a culture's permanence or staying power, it is all too apparent from the history of cultural domination, suppression, and alienation through "deculturation" that culture is, like all things *truly* human, most vulnerable in the face of coercion and oppression. Under such conditions, culture either lives guiltily in disguised form or dies under the heavy hand of repression.

Ideology and Culture

Let me introduce a third misconception of culture—by far more subtle but also widespread—with a typical example. The context of my illustration is taken from a book about the growing number of Hispanics in the United States and the challenge this presents to the Catholic Church in America. In his Foreword to this book, Virgil Elizondo states the following:

> It is the ministers of evangelization who come from the North American cultural reality who first of all need to be evangelized in relation to *the materialism, individualism and hedonism of North American culture*. To the degree that we neglect to evangelize North American culture, we will never truly evangelize the Hispanics in this country. Rather, *we will impose the values of North American culture* in the name of the gospel.[17]

This text illustrates well, I think, the unfortunate tendency to equate ideologies with fundamental cultural values. I will argue that not only must we clearly distinguish between the really *inherent values* of a culture on the one hand and ideologies on the other, but that failure to do so is one of the major reasons why inculturating faith is stymied in North America and why, so misconstrued, the important task of evangelizing our culture that Elizondo otherwise rightly calls for is well-nigh impossible. Not only are culture's real fundamental values sorely maligned and distorted when equated with the various and sundry "isms" of ideologies, but culture itself is made the scapegoat for every conceivable ill that is visited upon humanity. It then becomes virtually impossible to perceive culture—any culture—as being redeemable (let alone evangelized); it also explains why culture is often regarded as a most unlikely marriage partner for faith. I would argue that although ideologies can and do enter cultural structures, they are not *constitutive* of culture as fundamental values are; they are more like viral infections that weaken or distort a culture, but which do not belong to its essential nature.

How often have we not heard our American cultural values defined or equated with terms such as "relativism," "materialism," "individualism," "consumerism," "social Darwinism," "hedonism," "narcissism," etc. etc. Even the term "culture" itself has become a facile "catchword" for just about every imaginable social ill or irritant. One sees this, for example, in the loosely extensive use of the term "culture" in recent book titles: "The Culture of Narcissism," "The Culture of Poverty," "The Culture of Inequality," "The Corporate Culture," "The Culture of Complaint," and "The Culture of Disbelief," to mention but a few titles in our bookstores and libraries. Ironically, those who would identify culture with ideology seem naively unaware that their own imputations are ideological and biased. It also says a lot about the way culture has been made the scapegoat for any and all evil that still lurks in the human heart. Those who do define culture so negatively forget that, by definition, an ideology sets itself up as a *total* system by willfully or uncritically ignoring culture reality as a whole and in depth. They select one or other aspect of social life, usually data in connection with the more practical matters of socio-political action, and absolutize it to such an extent that it becomes in its turn an ideology and hence an erroneous interpretation of a culture, *qua* culture.

Take, for example, the "totalizing" label with which Stephen Carter has branded American law and politics: "The Culture of Disbelief."[18] While it may appear that our political and legal systems treat religious devotion and discourse with indifference—and indeed an indifference that to many may appear as a trivialization or disdainful neglect of religion—nowhere are the religious rights of believers better protected or guaranteed than in America. Nor is there anything *inherent* in our secular culture that would prevent a citizen from taking his or her religion seriously, as Stephen Carter and other "virtuecrats" would have us believe. In the end, the importance of religion stands or declines, not on the laws we pass or the politicians we elect, but on the lives we lead.

But even that, the actual religious *lives* we lead, cannot be the only criterion for establishing the existence of religious belief or disbelief, since it is a verifiable fact that we don't always succeed in putting into practice what we *truly* believe. Clearly, one may disagree over the role and place of religion in government, or the extent to which any religion can legitimately set itself up as the "moral conscience" of a nation; but to willfully equate two significant cultural domains (law and politics) with a "culture" of disbelief not only flies in the face of a host of other empirical data about America's religious distinctiveness,[19] but it becomes in turn a religious ideology of its own making.

While Stephen Carter has amassed an impressive number of raw "facts" to make his claim, nowhere does he prove or demonstrate that any or all these have had a *de facto* adverse effect on the actual religious belief and devotion of American citizens. Herein lies its greatest flaw and the first clue that Carter's account is ideological in nature. What effect the laws we enact have on the religious devotion is much more difficult to establish than Carter would have his readers believe. Carter mobilizes "meaning" in subtle and surreptitious ways without establishing a real connection between his raw data and the deleterious religious effect this supposedly has on the religious devotion of America's believers. This flaw is serious because it cannot be assumed that the laws and politics of a government will have, by virtue of these specific enactments, a given result or effect on the individual citizens in the course of their everyday religious beliefs (or disbeliefs). It cannot be assumed that the populace will, by the very fact that certain ordinances are decreed, be impelled to believe or disbelieve any more or less than they already do. In fact, a case could be made that historically the faith of Christians has always fared quite well in both non-Christian "pagan" cultures (as in the Greco-Roman world of St. Paul) or in times of outright religious oppression (as in Nero's Rome or in Poland under the communist regime). So the fact that American culture is commonly portrayed as "hedonistic," "materialistic," "narcissistic," etc., not only stereotypes our total cultural experience, but it grossly misconstrues the constitutive "core" values of American culture. It so confuses culture and ideology that the two become indistinguishable. In short, every ideology, even a religious one, deals with some aspects of life in a given society and then stolidly proclaims these as the fundamental determinants of that culture. While this may appear to be true in the outer, more visible layer (semiotic domains) of a culture, it does not describe the real "national character" or cultural "soul" of the American people—nor indeed what this people most deeply aspires to *as* a people.

This is what John B. Thompson has called ideology *as dissimulation*.[20]

By this he means one of the ways ideology can and does operate, namely, through the figurative use of language, by which a thing is designated, not by its own name, but by the name of something else, although there is no necessary connection between the term and that to which one may be referring. This ideological technique, Thompson observes, "may dissimulate social relations by confusing or inverting the relations between collectivities and their parts," while the referent in the latter "may be positively or negatively valued by association with something else."[21]

During the cold war era and before the fall of the Berlin Wall, it will be remembered, we had grown accustomed to equate Russian culture with Soviet communism. In hindsight and to the amazement of virtually everyone in the western world, we now see more clearly that the lead-like mantel of communism which had settled over Russian society was not intrinsically cultural, but rather an ideology that was imposed upon the Russian people and their culture. Ideologies always masquerade under the guise of authentic cultural values; that is why they operate so effectively, if deceptively. When unmasked, however, they are seen for what they really are: surreptitious, "intruders" in a culture, wolves in sheep's clothing as it were. In short, ideologies do not *belong* to a culture by birthright, but by insidious subterfuge. In the same way that it was erroneous (and short-sighted) to equate Russian culture with its former ideological overlay of Soviet communism, so too is it wrong to equate American culture with capital*ism*, or, for that matter, with any other "ism." A safe and practical rule of thumb in these matters for those who would seek to analyze a culture deeply in order to inculturate faith may be formulated as follows: If the attribute in question supports the suffix "ism," there is every reason to believe it is not an inherent cultural value, but a crustaceous ideology that must be carefully distinguished from culture itself.

The above rule of thumb holds true, moreover, regardless of the way a particular ideology may have crept into or circulates within a culture, whether it be as a fully developed theory or as an unreflexive attitude of mind, or as an arbitrary and voluntaristic mood. The point is that ideologies are not constitutive components of a culture, even though they co-exist and find a "home" in a culture.

The Church and Ideology

Just as ideologies adhere to culture like a cancerous growth but are distinct from its fundamental and constitutive values, so too they can and sometimes do exist in the church, even though Christianity itself is not an ideology. Karl Rahner has shown why Christianity is not an ideology, but this is not the place to examine the arguments he advances to make his claim. What interests us here, apart from the errors that characterize all ideologies, is the way an ideology can in fact find its way even into the church, not as a constitutive element of its nature, but as an ideological adhesion that can cling to its being and at times even contaminate its gospel message.

In this connection, Rahner describes one such ideology (the ideology of "transmanence") to which, he says, church leaders are particularly susceptible. He describes this ideology as follows:

> In this kind of ideology what is ultimate, infinite and pervasive of all spheres of reality is absolutized (or better still: totalized) in such a way that the penultimate and finite, the things always given and assumed in immediate experience, are not given their due and are overlooked. If anything, they are manipulated by the projections from that absolute vision of the mind.[22]

There are several theological factors that can conspire to create a climate in which this kind of ideology can develop and thrive in the church.[23] Among these, of course, there is the question of truth, or more accurately the way one envisages and approaches truth. A typical example of this was the condemnation of Galileo. The ideology of transmanence in this case involves the apparent contradiction between religious truth and the truth of science. How the church reacts to any such apparent contradiction is where we get an indication of the presence or absence of ideology. In Galileo's case, it failed to heed what Galileo had observed in the skies and insisted on its own doctrinaire position, its own "absolute vision" of the truth. Rather than critically re-examine its own hitherto "orthodox" teaching concerning the truth about the solar system in the light of the astronomer's new findings, the church absolutized its position and in the end resorted to the power of ecclesiastical censure. Whenever the church believes it possesses absolute and incontrovertible truth and accordingly forecloses all further dialogue or discussion on the matter, it is not unreasonable to suspect the presence of an ideological mindset. The Vatican's stolid stance against any open discussion or dialogue today concerning the ordination of women would appear to be tainted with a similar ideology. Whatever the theological merits of the case, premature foreclosure of debate and discussion on an issue is always at best a dubious pastoral solution, and at worse an ideological controlling device.

One also detects a certain ideological posturing in the way some church officials have dismissed the notion of inculturation altogether. Cardinal Ratzinger is quite right when he says that "the height of a culture is revealed in its openness, in its capacity to give and to receive, in its power to develop, to allow itself to be refined and thereby to become more in accord with the truth, in accord with being human."[24] Ratzinger also makes the point that "faith itself is culture." What is more problematic and difficult to accept, however, is Ratzinger's logic and reasons for rejecting the notion of inculturation, as when he says:

> For inculturation presumes that a faith stripped of culture is transplanted into a religiously indifferent culture whereby two subjects, formally unknown to each other, meet and fuse. But such a notion is first of all artificial and unrealistic, for with the exception of modern technological civilization, there is no such thing as faith devoid of culture or culture devoid of faith. It is above all difficult to envisage how two organisms, foreign to each other, should all of a sudden become a viable whole in a transplantation which stunts both of them.[25]

Several things should be noted. *First*, faith and the cultures of the world, however conceived, cannot be said to constitute "two foreign organisms," as Ratzinger alleges, since both ultimately stem from the same creative hand of God, and it must be assumed, theologically, that what God creates with one hand is not "totally foreign" to the other but must be intrinsically related in some divinely appointed way. *Second*, inculturation, as I have tried to show in this study, does not "mutilate" or "stunt" either faith or the host culture; we envisage it rather as a *nuptial union* in which both partners retain their autonomy as well as their integrity. *Third*, while faith can be understood as the *gestalt* (Ratzinger's term) peculiar to the living Christian community, it refers us, first and foremost, to the *person* of Jesus Christ. And the Jesus of *my* faith, like that of all Christians, is the incarnate Jesus who was enfleshed, lived and proclaimed the kingdom of God in one very specific human culture, which is not *my* culture but which imposed on Jesus all the limitations that my culture imposes on me. Moreover, unlike his disciples, Jesus never lived or ventured outside his own cultural world. Hence the need for a creative reinterpretation of Jesus' fundamental experience and message. The question therefore becomes: How can the Christian faith, first experienced and symbolically articulated in an ancient culture quite foreign to mine, meaningfully inform human existence in today's culture?

Behind the cardinal's reasoning there also seems to be a subtle identification of Christian faith with the "culture" which is the Church of Rome, as though the one were inexorably and necessarily bound to the other. Clearly, the church does have a living tradition into which every baptized Catholic is incorporated and from whose source all Catholics live their faith, consciously or unconsciously. Yet to equate this living Christian tradition with the cultural reality we refer to when we speak of world cultures is to use the term "culture" in an improper and misleading way.

Far more constructive and enlightening in this regard is the instruction of the Pontifical Biblical Commission on "The Interpretation of the Bible in the Church," which states:

> The theological foundation of inculturation is the conviction of faith that the word of God transcends the cultures in which it has found expression and has the capability of being spread in other cultures, in such a way as to be able to reach all human beings in the cultural context in which they live. This conviction springs from the Bible itself....This is not, as is clear, a one-way process: it involves "mutual enrichment." On the one hand, the treasures contained in diverse cultures allow the word of God to produce new fruits and, on the other hand, the light of the word allows for a certain selectivity with respect to what cultures have to offer....The word of God is, in effect, a seed, which extracts from the earth in which it is planted the elements which are useful for its growth and fruitfulness.[26]

Another theological factor that can and does invite ideology into the church is when official interpreters of Christian tradition fail to view statements of faith as a structured hierarchy of truths (*hierarchia veritatum*). By this is meant a structured unity in which the secondary or peripheral aspects of one's confession of faith are related to the central or core mysteries of the faith, thus forming a great creedal whole. Within the framework of this whole, and depending on their more or less direct relation to the core Christian mystery, these secondary truths are relativized.[27] This is how Karl Rahner personally envisages for himself the "hierarchy" of Christian truths:

> For me, the true and unique heart of Christianity and its message is the communication which God really makes of himself to his created beings, in his most authentic reality and glory. It is to profess that most improbable of truths, namely, that God himself, in all his reality and infinite glory, his holiness, his freedom and his love, can truly come to us without any reduction on his part, into

the very midst of our existence as creatures. In the face of this, whatever else Christianity offers or demands from us *is provisional and of secondary consequence.*[28]

What this means, in pastoral, catechetical and theological terms, is that the "truths" of our Christian faith do not form separate disconnected clumps, representing independent doctrines clustered together like marbles in a flaxen bag. Rather they are all connected and form a hierarchy of truths. If followed inward they all point to a common reductionist source—ultimately to the heart of Jesus Christ and the central mystery of the Most Holy Trinity. When this hierarchy of truths is overlooked and all revealed truths are said to claim our Christian and intellectual adherence in the same way and to the same degree, then uniformity, rather than communion, becomes the overriding pastoral norm. This not only militates against the prospects of any serious in-depth inculturation of the faith; but it then becomes possible to absolutize any doctrinal statement, even though the truth of the statement is several removes in the "hierarchy of truths" from the heart or core of the gospel message. It is difficult to say that such a state of affairs, in and of itself, is the result of ideological thinking, but it is no less difficult to dismiss the claim that it is. This is especially true since Vatican II, in its Decree on Ecumenism, made explicit reference to the notion of "hierarchy" of truths: "When comparing doctrines with one another, they (Catholic theologians) should remember that in Catholic doctrine there exists an order or "hierarchy" of truths, since they vary in their relation to the foundation of the Catholic faith" (2,11).

7 | A Model for Analysis of Culture (1)

In keeping with our metaphorical approach, I will be suggesting "images" of culture to the reader instead of "definitions," descriptive models for analyzing culture rather than abstract theories. My appeal to the reader's imagination is deliberate and purposive: the roots of every culture run deep into the dark ground of a people's dreams and originating experience when they first became aware of being a *distinct* or *peculiar* people, and this "founding" experience is initially shaped and accompanied more by images and social imagination than by abstract ideas. Indeed the role of social imagination is not only determinative in the "birthing" and formation process of a culture, but also for the interpretation and analysis of that culture. Contemporary mission studies on inculturation have not yet adequately addressed this question of social imagination and its hermeneutical role in understanding culture. It is this deficiency that the present study seeks to redress.

The relationship between metaphor and imagination should already be apparent in the way we have thus far envisaged inculturation as a nuptial union between faith and culture. My purpose here is to go a step farther and articulate a more imaginative approach to culture itself. If successful, this should enable us to explore the implications of inculturating faith more deeply in a culture than has hitherto seemed possible. Informing the construction of my model for analyzing culture are three sources from which I have drawn insight, and it is well to acknowledge these at the outset, if only to help situate the reader more comfortably within my model. The first of these is David Bryant's book *Faith and the Play of Imagination*. The issue at the heart of this work is the nature of the imagination which he describes as "the power of taking something as something by means of meaningful forms, which are rooted in our history and have the power to disclose truths about life in the world. Creative imagination arises out of the openness of these forms both to

105

new experiences and to new and illuminating combinations of forms."[1] Without theological imagination there can be no inculturation.

My model for analyzing culture also owes much to Robert Schreiter's excellent work *Constructing Local Theologies*, in which he emphasizes the sign-making or symbolic nature of culture. However, Schreiter's approach to culture is not without its problems, since, by his own admission, the purely semiotic approach "is so complex to use that it would be beyond the reach of most practitioners."[2] My principal aim in this study has been precisely to construct a model for analysis that is practicable, more readily accessible, and at the same time does justice to the sacred union between faith and culture. And, finally, my model is constructed very much in the perspective of the systems theory in science and psychology, with its rich and promising perspectives on wholeness and interrelatedness.[3] Accordingly, my model for interpreting culture is one that views culture in its basic unity, an *orderly whole*, with interrelated "layers" of meaning.

Clearly, one of the advantages of using images rather than abstract concepts is that it more closely respects and safeguards the organic unity of culture. A pictorial image or root paradigm, like culture itself, is a configuration of a complex whole which is qualitatively unique and quite different from a mere aggregate or collection of separate entities. Thus, for example, one might aptly compare culture to a live oak tree, which sinks its invisible roots into the deep dark ground from which it originates and is nourished, and from its solid massive trunk many limbs branch out on all sides, each having its own characteristics, yet never severed from its life-supporting trunk.[4] Thus, as we said earlier, any attempt at inculturating faith which begins by selectively "picking-and-choosing" some aspects of a culture and rejecting others can only be described as "cultural mutilation." Moreover, since there are no two living oak trees alike, we do well to speak of specific cultures—in the plural—rather than of culture in general. No two cultures are identical; each carries within itself its own immanent validity and autonomy, each with its own pattern of development, its own inner dynamic growth and evolution.

One way to view a culture, I am suggesting, is to visualize it as comprising several superimposed but interrelated "layers" or levels of cultural reality, in descending order from the outer to the inner, from the more visible and tangible level to its more mysterious center and "heart," or what I like to call its inner "fiery furnace." One must explore and plumb these deep levels of culture reality *before* the process of inculturating faith can really begin in earnest. Otherwise, one will invariably end up with a superficial "grounding" of the faith and a thinly disguised form of cultural adaptation.

A Visual Inscape of Culture

If we compare culture to a floating iceberg, and if we could view the iceberg in its total configuration and not just the one-tenth portion of it which is visible above the surface of the water, it would probably look something like the following diagram:

Figure 7.1

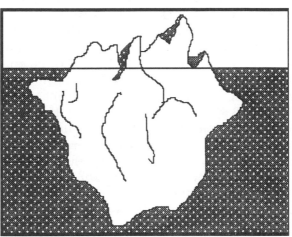

If we now let ourselves imagine, for purposes of analysis, that our cultural iceberg has four distinct layers or strata, our configuration might look something like this:

Figure 7.2

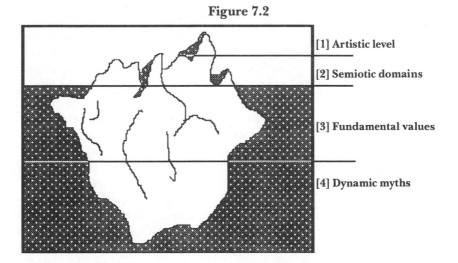

[1] Artistic level

[2] Semiotic domains

[3] Fundamental values

[4] Dynamic myths

According to the above diagram (Fig. 7.2), culture is made up of four distinct "layers" of meaning, two of which can be seen or observed (empirically) with the naked eye; the other two, comprising by far the greater and more impressive portion of culture reality, lie well out of sight in the deeper recesses of a people's collective unconscious and memory. In this and the following chapter, I will examine the distinguishing features of each of the two deeper cultural "layers" [4 and 3], and what each of these entails for inculturating faith. But first, two preliminary observations are in order. *First*, it is important to note that culture is more susceptible to change in its upper levels, and more resistant to change in its deeper levels. While cultures can and obviously do change, such changes take place *most readily* at the uppermost two "visible" levels, *less frequently* at the third level of fundamental values, and *least subject* to change at the deepest, most interior level of a culture, which I have identified as a culture's dynamic myths. Thus changes in a culture are above all *surface* changes in comparison to the more resilient and unchanging deeper levels of that culture. Cultures have been known to disappear from the face of the earth, but what is more remarkable is their ability to endure even under decades of cultural domination or in the face of tremendous social upheaval, transformation, and change. This is important to note because external changes in a culture, however many or spectacular these may be, always belie the more enduring quality and identity of a culture. Thus the changes that one "sees" taking place in a culture can be very misleading since a culture's more profound durability and tenacity often go unnoticed because of being less "observable."

Second, it is also important to note that these four cultural levels or strata do not merely "sit" statically one on the other, as it might be said, for example, of a multilayered wedding cake. Rather they are dynamically interrelated, the deepest fourth level (dynamic myths and symbols) giving rise to the third (fundamental cultural values), which in turn inspires and informs the more "manifest" second and first levels. This "upward" inner dynamic of culture might be compared to the way vital circulating sap *rises* in a tree, from the bottom up. To ignore this *intrinsic upward directional flow* within a culture is to "misread" a culture, and this, perhaps more than anything else, may explain why the church has hitherto been unsuccessful in its attempt to inculturate the faith deeply in most cultures. It has generally approached inculturation as though what "meets the eye" at the surface level of a culture, the visible and more phenomenal, is more important than the undisclosed ground and deeper resources of a culture. In the mistaken belief that minor concessions or surface "adaptations" of Christian faith to culture could bring about an eventual in-depth transformation of that culture, it is no wonder that the church has often had cause to be disappointed.

Thus the real challenge facing the church can be summed up this way: the "heart" of the gospel message must somehow *be exposed* to the "heart" of a culture. That is to say, their respective dynamic "founding" myths must somehow be open and laid bare to one another. This is what inculturation is all about. Anything short of such an immediate in-depth exposure and consummation renders the nuptial union between faith and culture less than mutually engaging and as a rule quite superficial. Christian faith certainly is an export-import item between cultures, as we will see, but in the long run it can only exist authentically when it has put down deep roots. This in fact is what gives faith its indigenous authenticating quality and the church its catholicity. What follows is an attempt to explore the two "hidden" strata of a culture, with particular reference to the American culture, and to indicate what this might mean in terms of inculturating the faith more deeply in this country.

A Culture's "Dynamic Myths"

Contemporary social sciences today explicitly recognize that the "rational analysis" of human behavior, whether in its *individual* tendencies or in its *collective* propensities and systems, must now reckon with the profound and (apparently) "irrational" impulses of the human spirit. In order to properly interpret personal or societal actions, one must not only take into account the environmental factors that contexualize these actions, but also the "social imaginativeness" of human subjects that lies behind them. I mean, the power of those imaginative impulses, mechanisms, and pre-reflexive workings which are usually more subtle, more fluid, and therefore harder to circumscribe than the objects of formal logic or empirical reason. Despite their more elusive contours, which have always bedeviled the positivists, these profound imaginative social "stirrings" are nevertheless now recognized as being pregnant with meaning for the human spirit and do in fact have a decided causal impact on collective human behavior.[5]

Many of these social "imaginings," when strong enough, come to be translated and concretized in a people's habits, customs, or rites, as well as in what jurists of all times have called "customary laws." Cultural myths—like all myths—provide unquestioned assumptions about the forms of behavior appropriate to various broad fields of behavior and activity within a culture. They give rise to the fundamental value orientations and indeed the most important values of the culture [level 3].

While cultural myths are not values and can be distinguished from them, they are intimately associated with them and have to be kept in consideration if the dynamic myths in that culture are to be properly understood. This is why anthropologists and ethnologists are turning their attention and research more resolutely to the role of people's social imaginativeness and how it impacts on who a people take themselves to be and how they actually live together as a *distinct* people or culture. Epistemologically, one of the main instruments of imaginative thinking is the unconscious forms we call "myths." Unfortunately, myth is still an ill-defined category in the mind of many today and its meaning often seems ambiguous.[6] Edmund Leach explains:

> Some people use the word [myth] as if it meant fallacious history—a story about the past which we know to be false; to say that an event is "mythical" is equivalent to saying that it didn't happen. The theological usage is rather different: myth is a formulation of religious mystery—"the expression of unobservable realities in terms of observable phenomena" (Schniewind). This comes close to the anthropologist's usual view that "myth is a sacred tale."
>
> If we accept this latter kind of definition the special quality of myth is not that it is false but that it is divinely true for those who believe, but fairy-tale for those who do not. The distinction that history is true and myth is false is quite arbitrary.[7]

The word "myth" comes from the Greek *mûthos*, which means word, narrative. A myth is basically a story, the story of how a people came to *be* and *think* of themselves as a distinct people: its origins, its "founding" aspirations, the goals it initially set for itself and pursues, and the way all this eventually unfolds as the sacred history of that people. The birth of a people marks the beginning of a new culture, the collective awakening of a people to a new order of reality, a new vision of the world that often comes as a surprise revelation. In the beginning, this new vision is almost palpable in the collective consciousness and behavior of a people; it becomes so real, so captivating, so mobilizing that it fires the social imagination of this people and gives it sufficient courage to embark upon a hitherto unique venture and a new "way" of life. This venture is experienced and perceived as something so utterly original and therefore different that it gives a people its unquestionable sense of being quite *distinct* from all other peoples.

The collective awakening of a people to this new reality, to their distinct self-image and the way a people now begins to view the world around it with new eyes and a new creative mindset, is precisely what myths capture and seek to convey in narrative form. We call these myths "functional" or "dynamic," as we will see shortly, to emphasize their inherent orientating and energizing power, even when revisited and properly attended to by subsequent generations—the power, that is, to stir the most profound impulses and creative energies in the "soul" of a people, the power to again mobilize and unite this people around some new cause, some new threat, some new aspiration or challenge. It is at this lower fourth level of a people's culture and sacred history that the gospel must somehow reach and be exposed to if the process of inculturation is to be anything more than superficial window-dressing. Only at this deeper level does the nuptial union between faith and culture have a reasonable chance of becoming fruitful and mutually enriching.

Another quality of every dynamic myth is that it invariably marks a "break" with what has hitherto preceded in terms of the accepted wisdom or some traditionally accepted norm(s) or law(s), beginning obviously with the way people view and interpret the laws of nature. In short, the birth of primordial cultural myths constitutes something of a liberating "rupture" with the past and a new way of thinking and imagining.[8] The point of a myth is that it ushers in a whole new way of conceiving the traditionally accepted canons of behavior and human relationship. Myth-making is above all that uniquely human capacity to re-evaluate an existing situation and imagine how things could very well be different from what they are or appear to be. "What is is not determinative of what might be."[9] According to Freud and Lévi-Strauss, myths express unconscious wishes which are somehow inconsistent or at odds with conscious experience. They project an imaginative "circumvention" of all that is repressive in society; in so doing, they grant us permission (freedom) to re-evaluate the accepted rules and canons and hence the possibility of envisaging other and perhaps better alternatives. In that sense, a myth parts company with the factual "truth" of history, only to remain open to the conditional "truth" of what should or could conceivably be in the future. James J. Liszka makes the point clearer than most:

> Myth is seen as a *displacement* of the rules and values which impose an order on the culture. Within this framework it *suspends* these rules imaginatively out of their typical employment and reanimates them, simultaneously reevaluating them, within the narrative of the tale.[10]

Myths therefore would not have us take a holiday from the real world of everyday life; instead they set us free and would open us up to the *infinite potential* that being truly human holds for us. Now this intrinsic *openness* of the human spirit lies at the very "heart" of every culture, in its primordial, mobilizing myths, and these are precisely what gives a culture its deep advent-like receptivity to the gospel message. Thus the so-called "objective truth" of history can never be dissociated from the "truth" of a people's myths and social imaginativeness.

This undoubtedly explains, in part at least, why so many people today are fascinated by and attracted to the New Age movement, with all its esoteric "networking" and imaginative "feats of association." It also explains today's renewed attempts to reread the mythical and pre-scientific past with "new eyes," as Thomas Moore has recently done, for example, in his study of the fifteenth century Marsilio Ficino, whose fundamental tool for the spiritual well-being of the human soul was imagination.[11] What much of today's seemingly "irrational pursuit" tells us and points to is the human soul's propensity to "break" with what is in order to "envisage" what might be, to "suspend" what is in order to "renegotiate" what could be. The cultural soul of a people, like the human soul of an individual, is necessarily "restless" and forever dissatisfied with what is, in its quest for what could be. We thus give birth, laboriously or through sheer genius, to whatever is needed to confer on our dreams all the power and precision of reality itself. What all this points to is the incontestable fact that we humans (individually as well as culturally) possess a profound, albeit unconscious, sense of *openness*. This is why cultural receptivity is so high, and why cultural diffusion, absorption, and innovation are so great.[12] What is important to understand, for our purpose, is the crucial role that social imagination plays, through the dynamic cultural myths that it engenders and surrenders to, and the way these in turn give rise, at another level, to the fundamental values of a culture.

The Power and Function of Dynamic Myths

Although a myth is generally articulated and conveyed to us in story form, we do well to pause here for a moment and consider the power and dynamic function of these cultural stories. They function *for us* in at least four remarkable ways. Briefly, I would describe this fourfold dynamic as follows:

   1. *Fear-eliminating:* A living myth serves to remove, first of all, those great fears in us (real or imaginary) that would otherwise prevent us from acting as free and truly human subjects. I mean, the excessive and paralyzing sort of fears that can overtake one in the face

of death, the unknown, risk, insecurity, uncertainty, absurdity, or alienation. A functional myth would remove or lessen these fears and give us the "courage to be" (Tillich) by putting us more "in touch" with our collective unconscious, with our history and tradition, and especially with the primordial experience out of which our culture family or society came into being and survived.

2. *Revelatory:* They also function to have us re-examine and scrutinize anew things which we may have blindly taken for granted, and in so doing they help us to discover new meaning or a new dimension of the "truth" about ourselves, our society, and the universe. A myth is therefore eminently *exploratory*: it invites us to explore those other more elusive, ambiguous, and sometimes "terrifying" borders of human existence that so often elude the faint-hearted or the overly "distracted" (in Pascal's sense). They function, in the words of Joseph Campbell, "to awaken and maintain in the individual a sense of awe and gratitude in relation to the mystery dimension of the universe."[13]

3. *Unifying:* Dynamic myths also serve to unify and bring coherence to those contradictory or mutually exclusive aspects of life which constantly threaten to polarize or divide us. They bring harmony where division might prevail, unity where discord is likely, inclusion where separation is a very real possibility. In this sense, myths function much like symbols; in their unifying role, they have within them—as little else does—the capacity to "build bridges" for us between those yawning dichotomies such as heaven/earth, matter/spirit, female/male, sacred/profane, life/death, conscious/unconscious, obedience/autonomy, etc. To all these bipolar *centrifugal* forces that tend to divide or disperse our cultural soul, dynamic myths and symbols oppose a unifying *centripetal* inducement to remain "centered" in our being and thus integrate these antimonies.

4. *Mobilizing:* Functional myths are above all dynamic accelerators of change. They function to energize and motivate us, to harness and release our human potential and creative discourse as social beings. Far from being an "escape" from reality, they "insert" us even more resolutely in our natural and social environment; they would have us participate and make a difference in it. In short, myths allow us to "live" the tensions and inherent anomalies of human life more creatively, and so enable us to forge, together with others, a renewed human community and a new future.

Again, James Liszka's summary statement illustrates the point well. "Myth," he says, "should be seen as a prelude to discourse; discourse can be viewed as reasoned elaboration of the values and rules found in myth. Where myth no longer generates discourse, it becomes the static repetition of dogma; where discourse fails to avail itself of myth and fable, it loses the chance to regenerate itself, and severs the tie to community. In the end, true art, true myth, is moral, transvaluative, not because it intends to teach its audience a lesson, but because it should engender evaluation."[14]

Before we turn our attention to the dynamic myths that lie deep within our American culture, and as a way of illustrating the more abstract explanation given above concerning the power of dynamic myths, a few concrete examples are in order here. Biblically, one has only to think of the powerful "creation myth" in Genesis and what it seeks to do for us—if we "surrender" to it—in the midst of our experience of human contingency, dependence and limitation. The creation myth in Genesis serves, *first* of all, to eliminate fear. It tells us that however awesome, frightening or threatening the cosmic forces of nature may appear at times, they are fundamentally benevolent and not malicious forces. God himself said they were "good." The myth allays any excessive fears or undue pessimistic views we might otherwise entertain about our created world. It configures our existence in what might seem like a "hostile" world, supplies an interpretation of it, and, in a prodding kind of way, lets us get on with life in the belief that our quest for happiness is not altogether unreasonable.

Second, the creation story is also revelatory. It illumines and discloses to us what "being human" really means: the created handiwork of God and therefore with an innate openness to and capacity for relating to this God (the *capax dei*, as the ancients defined human nature). The biblical creation myth of our primordial origins would reveal to us, lest we be distracted or have cause to believe otherwise, that we come from God and that the incessant restlessness which pulsates in our created human being is in fact God's discreet way of inviting us to seek and find our ultimate "rest" in him, as St. Augustine wondrously suggested.

Third, our creation myth has an uncanny way of keeping alive the notion that despite all our attempts to divide, discriminate and tear asunder, we are in fact a real "family" of human beings, brothers and sisters to one and all, and that whatever happens to any one of these—anywhere in the world—I cannot remain indifferent without betraying my very self and something of the human solidarity inscribed in my deepest being and nature. The creation myth has the power of transforming us into more human, more compassionate men and women. It would bring us closer together, as a human family, and that even with all the strife and tangled density of human existence, it would remind us that God did *not* make a mistake in creating us the way he did. And, *fourth*, the creation myth has the power to mobilize us—indeed this is what it does best—by encouraging us to become, "in the image of God," creators of new life and new worlds. Rather than living our lives as resigned creatures of fate or passive bystanders to the world around us, the creation myth would empower us to imitate our creator and have us become creative agents in helping to bring about "a new heaven and a new earth." In short, the creation myth helps us to rediscover the basic unity of *being* human, underscores our role as responsible stewards of the universe, and provides a holistic vision of our world that includes suffering, chaos and disaster. In that sense, myths are both timely and timeless.

The dynamic myth of the exodus story is another example of how powerfully myths can and do function. Without this myth, it would be virtually impossible to recognize the religious identity of Israel. The exodus story marks the genesis of the Israelite people and has impressed the national Israelite consciousness for all time. One has only to observe the completely unique importance given to the exodus story in the total religious praxis and tradition of the Jewish people, a story that also helped Christians to interpret Christ's paschal mystery. Jesus' own personal story, that of the "coming of God's kingdom," is another good example.[15] Remove this myth from his message and ministry—indeed from his *personal* identity—and the Jesus of the gospels would not be recognizable. Through this kingdom myth the church is mobilized and given to see something of how God "steps" into our world, into relation with us human beings, and how he always *acts* in relation *to us*.

Or again, were we to survey the truly great missionary epochs in the church's history (there have been five or six at most), we would also discover at the heart and center of each such era some particular mobilizing myth that "captured" the missionary heart and imagination of the church. In the sixth and seventh centuries, for example, when the monks left the British Isles for the continent, the mobilizing myth that prevailed was the "pilgrim's journey." It was this myth that fired the imagination of such missionaries as St. Columban and his companions and accounts for their dauntless energy and missionary zeal. With this myth, the church was smitten with what can only be described as a "sacred wanderlust." Its motto became "*Stabilitas in peregrinatione*" and its entire spirituality was encapsulated in the phrase: "We must constantly meditate on the God of our journey which is our life here on earth." In the sixteenth and seventeenth centuries, following the great discoveries, another truly remarkable missionary epoch took place. Typified in the person of St. Francis Xavier, the creation of the Congregation for the Propagation of Faith in 1622, and the founding of numerous new missionary orders, the mobilizing myth that informed and propelled the church in this period was the myth of "saving souls," a myth that fostered an even greater sense of "urgency" since it was closely allied to another powerful myth, namely: "Outside the church no salvation." Later, in the nineteenth century, the dominant functional myth in the church was that of "implanting the church" (*plantatio ecclesiae*) in those countries where its institutional structures did not yet exist.

This would be the obvious place also to consider the "founding myths" of the great religious orders in the church. Renewal in religious life since Vatican II has always consisted in going back to an order's earliest days and, once again, getting "in touch" with its original myths or charism, that is, the sacred stories and events surrounding the order's birth and founder or foundress. Indeed in any serious attempt at renewal, we are invariably brought back to "primordial" times and "founding" myths (what the French call *ressourcement*, renewal by going back to the original source). Ancient stories of birth and rebirth continue to have a powerful place in our psyches and culture. They endure and retain their transforming power despite a tidal wave of change that has taken place not only in our social landscape but also in our fundamental notions of the nature and destiny of humankind.

In all the above examples, the power of dynamic myths is palpable: enabling the church to overcome any paralyzing fears it might otherwise have had, opening its eyes to some new dimension of its own ecclesial identity, giving it greater unity of vision and purpose, and, above all, instilling it with greater missionary incentive to proclaim the gospel to all nations. Something very similar takes place with the dynamic myths in every culture [level 4], and it is to this deep level of American culture that we now turn our attention.

The Dynamic Myths of American Culture

Studies have shown that one of the primordial mobilizing myths in American culture has been the myth of the "wilderness," the "frontier," the "far west." These of course are all spatial images, but as Jurij M. Lotman has pointed out,

One of the universal peculiarities of human culture, possibly connected with the anthropological features of human consciousness,
is the fact that world view invariably acquires features of spatial
characteristics. The very construction of a world order is invariably conceived on the basis of some spatial structure which orga-
nizes all its other levels.[16]

Frederich J. Turner's frontier school of historiography has become
classic—that is, the belief that "the existence of an area of free land, its
continuous recession, and the advance of American settlement westward explain American development."[17] From this process there
emerged a unique people and culture, radically different from any other
and deeply marked by the frontiering experience. This belief derives
from the conviction that the experiences of place and space profoundly
structure our experience of self and others. As Ortega y Gasset declared:
"Tell me the landscape in which you live and I will tell you who you
are."[18] In recent years, the frontier hypothesis which Turner advanced
has been re-examined and many of his basic insights confirmed. In
1962, for example, historian Ray Allen Billington could write:

> Economists, applying the principles of wage theory, have found
> that the frontier did serve as a safety valve for labor, although not
> exactly in the manner that Turner believed. Sociologists have
> begun to retest his statements on frontier-induced mobility, and
> to picture the moving American as a product of his pioneering
> heritage. Historians, using the tools of the statistician, have
> demonstrated through exact case studies that the West did stimu-
> late, if not originate, democratic theory and practice. Today the
> frontier hypothesis is increasingly recognized as a valid interpre-
> tation of American history, and the pioneering experience as one
> of the causal forces responsible for the distinctiveness of the
> nation's social order.[19]

Henry Nash Smith has brilliantly demonstrated how the myth of the
frontier and the west found its most overt and intense expression in
American literature and social thought during the nineteenth century.
In his *Virgin Land: The American West as Symbol and Myth*, Smith traces
the myths and symbols of the westward movement and synthesizes their
imaginative nineteenth century literary expression with their role in
contemporary politics, economics, and society. In his equally insightful
study, *The Rites of Assent*, Sacvan Bercovitch has analyzed the Puritan
myth—migration, venture into the wilderness, a community with an
"errand"—and shows what power this myth had in giving birth to and

shaping America's vision and culture. "The Puritans provided their heirs," he says, "in New England first and then the United States, with a useful, flexible, durable, and compelling fantasy of American identity."[20] In *Landscape and Memory*, Simon Schama has also beautifully illustrated the power of an historical imagination, his main contention being that our perception of the external natural world, even today, is shaped by our inherited myths and traditions.

The intention of this study, however, is not to trace the frontier theme in its overt *material* expressions (whether historical, geographical, political, or literary), but to point out how this cultural myth is appropriated, the way in which its meaning is recovered and gives us a deeper understanding of American culture and who we are as a people. The question then is: What is it that makes an individual or a people *recognize* themselves in a particular myth? And how does this recognition play itself out in the collective "bone-deep" memory of that culture? The two hermeneutic notions of *appropriation* and *belonging to* are especially relevant here since they establish the possibility of such a recognition. In other words, by initially appropriating ("making mine") the meaning of the myth, I am dialectically led to realize that it is not I who chose the myth in question, but rather that the myth has been a part of my being all along, that I have indeed always belonged to this myth, however unconsciously. In short, what may have initially appeared *alien* is not genuinely recognized as one's *own*. This hermeneutic experience is well illustrated in Paul Ricoeur's analysis of the "Adamic" myth in Genesis.[21]

The same holds true for cultural myths. Such myths are generated and come into being when a nation, a people, or a religion is born; they have their origin in the great "founding" events surrounding the birth of a culture or religion. And even when this nation, culture or religion has been in existence for centuries, these primordial myths and symbols remain persistently in the deep collective memory of the people. Moreover, they can be made to surface again at any time, at least closer to the edge of a people's consciousness. When this happens, they have the power to evoke and re-create insights that might otherwise be meaningless or forgotten. They illuminate human experience, Eric Voegelin says, as "a disturbing in-between of ignorance and knowledge, of time and timelessness, of imperfection and perfection, and ultimately of life and death."[22] But the crucial question remains: How do we "tap" into these primordial myths so as to release their power potential? How do we make them "speak" again? The rebirth of their meaning can be achieved, as Voegelin rightly points out, "only by return to the reality experienced which has originally engendered the symbols. The return will engender its own exegesis...and the exegetic language will make the older symbols translucent again."[23]

Thus, for example, when President John F. Kennedy publicly heralded his social program as "The New Frontier," he immediately struck a deep, sensitive cord in the heart of most Americans. An old myth suddenly became alive and "translucent" again. In short order, or so it now seems, the frontier myth was able to galvanize the national will of the American people in a race to the moon against the Russians. A new frontier suddenly came into conscious view, that of outer space. It not only enabled us to overcome great odds, but it mobilized a considerable amount of our tax-paying dollars and best scientific talent, and in the end it succeeded in thrusting the first man, an American, on the moon's surface. The important thing here is not whether one approves or disapproves of such an extravagant venture, but the sheer power potential of any such cultural myth when it is "revisited" and tapped into for its mobilizing energy—in other words, when the myth is invoked and suddenly recognized as being one's own myth.

One should also observe that the frontier myth does not stand alone, in some sort of splendid isolation; like all other primordial myths, it gives rise to a host of other strong emotions, associations and related images which gravitate and cluster around it in "satellite" fashion. It is this bigger constellation which gives the frontier myth its extraordinary richness, suggestive power, and tensive polyvalence. Hence to evoke the pre-eminent central myth of the frontier is to conjure up a number of other closely associated feelings, impulses and ideas. These then "begin to speak to us from the place from which the dominant myth addresses us."[24]

Clustered around our primordial American myth of the frontier, the following can readily be observed in its gravitational orbit:

- A sense of **Adventure**
- A sense of **Freedom**
- A sense of **Ingenuity**
- A sense of **Mission**
- A sense of **Self-reliance**

This by no means exhausts the cogent mythical associations that surround our primordial frontier myth, but it is sufficient, I think, to make our point. One cannot evoke the frontier myth without simultaneously conjuring up some of these other cognate ideas.[25] In terms of inculturating faith in American culture, however, each of these become terribly important since they offer faith a cultural "window" through which the gospel myth and the American myth can indeed become mutually enriched and mutually empowered. In his analysis of American culture and ideas, Russel B. Nye makes the following point:

> One may agree with the thesis that the frontier situation imparted to American life all those qualities of initiative, optimism, and equality of which Turner wrote, but the individualism it engendered had broader implications than simple self-reliance, when placed in the perspective the frontier American had of his world. The decision to follow the frontier, to exchange a settled way of life for an uncertain one, presented the person who made it with the prospect of formidable obstacles as well as great rewards. The challenge of empty land, limitless in expanse and incredibly rich in resources, involved the risk of failure as well as the opportunity for success....The determination to go west—whether it be Bradford's New England, Smith's Virginia, Boone's Kentucky, or Bridger's Rockies—was a personal one....The promise of a new and open society inspired self-confidence in those who decided to go, and expressed itself in the rewards of their individual efforts once they arrived.[26]

The ramifications of all this for inculturating faith in American culture are too numerous to be fully dealt with here, but perhaps we can indicate, by way of illustration, the possible direction and avenues such a project might take. It should be clear to all practitioners of inculturation that the gospel must somehow reach down into this rich "subsoil" of American history and tap into its dynamic primordial myths. Only then can we speak of a real nuptial union between faith and culture, the kind of union, that is, wherein faith and culture truly become "mutually enriched" and "mutually energized." If we take the idea of *adventure*, for example, which is synchronous with the American frontier myth, the following will give some indication of how we might better integrate our faith and our culture.

By any definition, an "adventure" is an exciting or otherwise remarkable undertaking or enterprise, which entails taking risks and requires daring, courage, patience and endurance. The verb "to adventure" means that one is willing to venture forth *for* something that is highly esteemed or valued in the face of risk, uncertainty, and even the possibility of failure or defeat. It is marked by freedom and an openness to possibilities before it, by that spirit of life on the "cutting edge" or "border regions" of things that are anything but routine and settled. Culturally, Americans have always been seen (and see themselves) as being adventuresome, as having a certain passion for original undertakings, for everything that holds out the prospect of some new discovery or breakthrough. As a young, frontier-crossing culture, we are not noted for our prudence and diplomacy (as are, say, the British or French), but more for our innovations and disregard of obstacles. Like the frontier men and women who have gone before us—whether the leatherstocking, the yeoman-farmer, or the western hero or heroine— we still believe we can accomplish what we set out to achieve; although the word "impossible" is in our Webster dictionary, it is not commonly on our lips.

If we accept the above description of an adventure, it is not too difficult to see a correlation with the venture that is the life of Christian faith. Cardinal Newman expressed it well:

> Our duty as Christians lies in making ventures for eternal life without the absolute certainty of success....This, indeed, is the very meaning of the word "venture"; for that is a strange venture which has nothing in it of fear, risk, danger, anxiety, uncertainty....This is the very reason why *faith* is singled out from other graces, and honoured as the especial means of our justification, because its presence implies that we have the heart to make a venture.[27]

If we accept also that the frontier myth (with its satellite connotation of "adventure") still lives on in our cultural psyche and national character, then certain implications would seem to follow for "earthing the gospel" more deeply in American culture. The following suggestions may be helpful:

- The *connaturality* between the American frontier myth and the "boundary-breaking" mission and ministry of Jesus could be emphasized to the mutual benefit of both our faith and our culture.[28] A symbolic reinterpretation of "land" in our frontier myth would also be helpful.[29] Inculturating the faith in the United States will entail reading and interpreting the gospel as consonant with our dynamic myth and not in dissonance with it.

- If a *local American theology* is ever to be constructed, it will most certainly have to begin with a rereading of the gospel message as a frontier, "boundary-crossing" adventure. Such a theology will give pride of place to the "New" Testament, the startlingly new "breakthrough" that Jesus inaugurates, the liberating new "space," new "freedom" and utterly new "possibilities" he opens up before us. It will also emphasize the way Jesus would rather deny the validity of all previous social or religious existence than deny the right of human suffering to be eliminated. It will also take special note of the way Jesus himself disregarded the "barriers" (religious or social) that stood in the way of his Father's kingdom.[30]

- The church might also wish to re-evaluate its own criteria of ecclesial identity. In the American cultural context, one can foresee that the faith of its members will be evaluated or assessed less by the conforming yardstick of *orthodoxy* and more by that of *orthopraxis*, that is, a yardstick that can measure faith as a *verb* ("faith-ing," as in "frontier-ing") rather than as a *noun* or as a possession "to have" and "hold on to."

- In the process of inculturation, faith will be appropriated and heralded as a real gamble, with its intrinsic risk of failure as well as its chance of success. In other words, Christian faith will be viewed as a real adventure and undertaken, as it were, at one's own personal *risk and peril*. This translates into a more "stout-hearted" faith, one that is fully alive to the fact that putting one's faith in the God of Jesus Christ is always a risky affair, that fellowship with Jesus can only mean a real, if costly, grace and venture. Such an inculturated faith will also take St. Paul's statement very seriously: "If Christ has not been raised, your faith is futile" (1 Cor 15:17); it will interpret this as not just a pious rhetorical statement, but a bold challenge to gamble and, if necessary, to even put one's very life on the line. An inculturated American Catholic Church will also come to know that when the Christian community invokes or prays for the Holy Spirit, it is asking for—indeed inviting—the unexpected, the unpredictable, and the divinely incalculable one to "come" into its life and its church. This can be quite unsettling in any adventure, where the "unexpected" can never be prematurely ruled out, but in a church that is sensitive to those unexpected movements of a divine Spirit that "blows where it wills," this can be most daunting. It is here that the "adventuresome" quality of our frontier myth can perhaps best serve us: by putting us more "in tune" and "in touch" with God's own creative Spirit.

8 | A Model for Analysis of Culture (2)

As we move "up" to level 3 in our visual inscape of culture, namely, that of *fundamental cultural values*, we come to a much more problematic and contentious issue. Problematic because it is attended by the difficulty of properly identifying the "core" values of a culture, and contentious because when it comes to distinguishing *these* particular values from the many other non-cultural values one may hold, there is a bewildering array of conflicting views about this. We have already seen the temptation of equating the cultural myths of a culture with certain prevailing "ideologies." Another temptation is to think that some cultural values are "good" while others are "bad." The confusion surrounding the notion of culture generally becomes particularly acute and concentrated at this third stratum of a culture. It would not be an exaggeration to say that the process and the theology of inculturation have most often floundered on this cultural shoal. Clearly, the difficulty involved in accurately discerning the fundamental "core" values of a culture is very real since we are still dealing with that dimension of culture reality that is largely hidden from empirical view. Hence the need to be as clear and precise as possible in defining what we mean by fundamental values. This is all the more important if the nuptial union between faith and culture is to take place and be properly celebrated. Within the context of our proposed model for analyzing a culture, therefore, three major questions will preoccupy us in this chapter. (1) What exactly do we mean by a fundamental cultural value? (2) How must we go about identifying such values? (3) What might be the reciprocal benefits in a nuptial union between these American values and the gospel values?

Since the issue of fundamental values (whether American or gospel) is fraught with so many different interpretations, two preliminary points need to be made. In the first place, while it is true that American culture is pluralistic and made up of conspicuously different traditions and ethnic groups, each claiming its own cultural heritage, cultural pluralism in America still represents a utopian dream more than a cultural *fait accompli*, a surface phenomenon rather than an in-depth reality. Indeed ethnic diversity in the United States still remains more of an outward sign of tension than a real cultural sign of acceptance. While it is true that the rise of ethnicity and the legitimate desire and aspirations of both old and recently arrived immigrants to retain something of their native cultural heritage are more vocal and visible today than in the past, these have not yet met with what one could call genuine cultural receptivity. Moreover, the melting-pot image of U.S. culture, a policy that may have had some political expediency in another age, does not represent the best possible goal for the nation today.[1] It should be obvious by now that when dealing with a culture, "what you see is not necessarily what you get!" Not that what one actually *sees* or can *point to* in a culture is unimportant, especially for its sign value; but it cannot be the ultimate basis for judging and interpreting a culture any more than one can properly size up an iceberg by just looking at the small exposed portion of it above the surface of the water.

A second preliminary point to be made is the following. The dynamic positive interaction between American values and gospel values is not as diffuse, nebulous and elusive as some would have us believe. Admittedly, as in any marriage, one is often struck more by the points of tension and overt disagreements that exist between the partners in the relationship. What makes this couple otherwise deeply united and supportive of one another is not always immediately apparent or obvious. In other words, their basic compatibility, that mutual promotion of the "other," is not always publicly exhibited or readily discernible. Here again, if one were to judge the nuptial union between faith and culture merely on the basis of what transpires in the public political forum or what can be observed, polled, or otherwise empirically verified in any of the surface semiotic domains [level 2], one is not really doing justice to either their radical compatibility or their potential to create together what neither could achieve alone.

In any such vital union, what brings the couple together must be emphasized over what separates them. This more optimistic approach to inculturation, the reader is by now fully aware, is one of the leitmotifs running through this entire study. The reason for this is both theological and cultural. It is theological first of all since the mystery of the redemptive incarnation upon which the process of inculturation is patterned and grounded is also the very foundation of Christian hope, without which there can be no genuine inculturation. This is not to deny that things can and often do go wrong—indeed sometimes terribly wrong—even in a sacred nuptial union. Wherever there is real love, the "cross" is never far off! Nor is this to deny that Christian faith must at times be counter-cultural. However, our theological optimism rests on the faith-conviction that when the Son of God became human, the sovereign initiative of God's love was not a calculated decision based on what might go wrong, but the saving design of his gracious hope in what might succeed and be accomplished through such a partnership and shared destiny.

Even when unassisted by Christian hope, every culture harbors within itself a secret impulse to strive for a brighter future. We see this most notably in those times when a people's culture and identity are being threatened or oppressed. Such a culture, too, will then "hope against hope." It would be a serious misreading of human culture to think that there is no authentic hope in the world save that which Christian believers might bring or provide. Moreover, there is no empirical evidence that human beings, regarded as a cultural family, are any less hope-filled than Christian believers in their church. Cultural hope, like Christian hope, derives from being in solidarity with the past, the present, and the future; and like Christian hope also, it is maintained and kept alive through its own dynamic myths.

Fundamental Cultural Values

The first issue that we must clarify is what we mean exactly by a fundamental cultural value. Perhaps we can begin by saying that cultural values, as I define them, have four main characteristics; they are indeterminate, definitional, non-ethical, and familial. Unlike the values that an individual or group of individuals may otherwise hold, cultural values are not the result of self-conscious acquisition; they are not freely chosen but are transmitted and acquired in an unthinking, unreflective way. They came with the cultural "turf," as it were, with the unsolicited grace or accident of being born into one peculiar culture rather than another. Fundamental cultural values are not necessarily those values that individuals in a country affirm, profess or hold dear. This is true whether the values in question are aesthetic, ethical, political, religious or social. Even when a particular value is claimed by a majority of citizens in a society, this does not mean that it constitutes a fundamental cultural value. It is possible, for example, that a majority of citizens may make wealth, security, or honesty their primary value. This does not *ipso facto* make any of these a real cultural value. Statistical evaluation is perhaps the least reliable means of discerning cultural values.

To say that cultural values are *indeterminate* is to say that they are open and unspecified. Unlike the values that may be held by individuals, cultural values do not have a formal object or specific content; they are indeterminate in that they are not aimed at a *specific* objective or sought-after goal. In that sense, they seek "to inflame, not instruct" (Pascal). They mobilize us and send us on our "way," but without any precise road signs or maps. Because of this indeterminate quality, they are able to "inform" and "inspire" *any* enterprise, *any* undertaking, and *any* human activity within that particular cultural "landscape"—including, we may add, those gospel or kingdom goals that the church sets for itself.

Semiotic analysts describe culture in terms of what they call *semiotic domains*. By this is meant a constellation of meaning in a particular field or area of culture. "A semiotic domain," Robert Schreiter says, "could be considered an assemblage of culture texts relating to one set of activities in culture."[2] The following would each constitute a semiotic domain: economic, political, religious, social, sexual, etc.[3] The point I wish to make here is that when we speak of fundamental cultural values, these do not discriminate between the semiotic domains of culture. On the contrary, they are indeterminate in the sense that they are capable of informing and inspiring any and all activities within a culture, irrespective of its semiotic domains. Different as these may be, and however highly "specialized" the human activities, rules, and inner logic may be within these fields, cultural values, if truly *fundamental* and truly *cultural*, will invariably leave some sign, mark, or telltale "fingerprint" encoded in many of the semiotic domains. However, cultural values are not manifestly or even necessarily disclosed on a culture's visible surface [level 2] at any one time. Hence great care must be taken when reading or interpreting the semiotic texts at this cultural level.

Another characteristic of fundamental cultural values is that they are *definitional*. That is to say, they are deeply inscribed in the national character and spirit of a people as well as in its history. As such, therefore, these basic values define something of the spiritual nature of a people who have traveled long and far with them. When combined and regarded as a "family" of cultural values, they have been called the *Volksgeist* (Hegel), the spirit or spiritual "genius" of a nation, that which gives a people its collective creative impulse and which emerges time and again as its guiding spirit. Closer to home, Walt Whitman's expression "American totality" (or "ensemble") points in the same direction: the people of the United States are not a traditional people in the European sense of the term. For him, the national spirit is an expression of the whole people, not the privileged few. As long as the American people remain unsupplied with autochthonous song, he felt, they would lack first-class nationality. Another American nineteenth century writer, Philip Schaff, likewise believed that all depends ultimately upon the *national character* of a people. In spite of the confusing diversity of peoples in America, Schaff recognized that a basic unity exists between them and that traces of a specifically American national character could be discerned. Among the features of this character he identified the impulse toward freedom and the sense of law and order resting on moral basis.[4] With Whitman, then, we might say that cultural values reveal themselves best in the new songs we create and sing together, in the new art forms we produce and celebrate [level 1].

There is a close affinity between the idea of *national character* and that of *cultural values*. When we speak of "character" in a nation or "values" in a culture, we find that both conjure up similar implied connotations: on the one hand, both suggest the idea of a specific solidity, security, and taken-for-granted naturalness; and, on the other, both evoke something which attracts, stimulates, and fascinates. It is no wonder then that traces of a people's character and fundamental values can be discerned in their historical accomplishments, though the latter may never be completely identified with the former. These are two distinct levels of culture reality: the deep underlying cultural values [level 3] and the more manifest public institutions and life [level 2], and while they may be interrelated, they are not synonymous. Our public institutions and lifestyle are only "inspired" by our cultural values, not predetermined or forcibly shaped by them. This explains why culture signs or "texts" at the surface level can be so misleading and difficult to interpret properly.

A third characteristic trait of fundamental cultural values is that they are *non-ethical* or "metaethical." Unlike the personal values that individuals may hold and affirm, cultural values are not value-judgments about specific things that are deemed abstractly *good* or *bad*, or about acts that are abstractly *right* or *wrong*. Indeed, correctly understood, there is no such thing as a "negative" cultural value; they are all intrinsically positive and potentially constructive. They need not therefore be purified, transformed, or otherwise "redeemed." It is because we have somewhat indiscriminately transferred the moral notion of "values and virtues" to culture that so much confusion has surrounded and bedeviled the process of inculturation.[5]

The fundamental "values" in a culture (if we must continue to use the term) are non-ethical in much the same way that being "right-handed" or "left-handed" is a non-ethical inborn aptitude or inclination. In and of themselves, cultural values are metaethical, that is, beyond the realm of morality, just as are, for example, having a definite musical or artistic talent, a proclivity for contemplation, a genius for exploring and investigating, a special gift for mediating, a natural ability to run fast or be a good teacher or leader. Since our idea of a value is so stubbornly associated with the moral notion of "good-and-bad," "right-and-wrong," and since it is so easy to make value judgements about our own and the culture of other people, perhaps the expression "cultural values" has been poorly designated; maybe we would do better to speak of "cultural gifts" and "charisms." Perhaps then at least we might come to view culture values as cultural enhancements, not as moral impera-tives. We might then better understand how faith and culture were indeed created *for* each other, and why it is that a nuptial union between the two can never be ruled out.

A fourth important characteristic of cultural values is that they cling together as siblings do in a closely knit family; they are *familial* in that they "hold" together and form a family system of values, a family more-over that has a long tradition and history. Cultural values must be acknowledged and accepted as a "family unit," not as isolated or totally unrelated entities. There exists between these "brothers" and "sisters" a real *kinship*, a special bond-in-being or innate connaturality. Even when the church has shown itself to be moderately favorable to the idea of inculturation, it has frequently overlooked this important point. This explains why its encounter with the cultures of the world has often been tentative, haphazard, and somewhat superficial.

Cultural values are distinct but consanguineous. They support one another in good times and bad; they hold hands and lock arms in the face of oppression as well as depression, in time of war and in time of peace. We can press our *familial* image even further and say that among these cultural values, like typical brothers and sisters, some are more dominant, others more modest and self-effacing; some are older, others younger; some are more initiating and outspoken, while others are more introverted; some are family-oriented, others more worldly-oriented; some are peace-makers, others adventure-seekers, and still others merry-makers. Add to this, also, the fact that *living* cultures are never sterile, and that other additional values may yet be born into this cultural "family" and so take its place as the "last-born." In any event and whatever the historical circumstances that brought these sibling values together, they are definitely and incontrovertibly the offspring of the primordial dynamic myths we spoke of earlier.

The foregoing description of cultural values should help us under-stand why any local church that is seriously bent on inculturating the faith cannot discriminate between a culture's values, but must embrace and promote all the fundamental values in a culture. The real challenge does not consist in approving some cultural values and condemning others; it consists rather in knowing how to assist a culture in recogniz-ing its *kairos*, the opportune and divinely-appointed moment of its fullest potential. In order to do this, it must help a culture to *choose*, among its many sibling values, which one(s) must be called upon to "step forward" at a strategic point in time to respond to a new challenge. In other words, the crucial issue here lies, not in showing partiality to this or that cultural value, but in being present to a people in such a way that it can effectively discern, decide, and make the *right choice* as to which of its basic values must be "enlisted" in the service of a gospel or a kingdom challenge. In his book *Pascal for Our Time*, Romano Guardini stated the case perhaps better than anyone:

> Everything is endowed with value, but every value is not urgent. All values as such have validity, but only a certain one is ever appropriate. A wrongly chosen value is good in itself, but has a harmful effect, or at least represses the appropriate value.[6]

Any discussion of inculturation must therefore begin by respecting a culture's own way of deciding how it might best marshal its inner resources to meet a gospel challenge. The issue above all is *accuracy of choice*, that is, knowing which fundamental value in a culture could most appropriately be pressed into service at the right time. This is where the discerning spirit of a competent midwife comes into play. For as scripture has it, there is a time for driving the flock (Gn 29:7), a time of harvest (Mk 4:29), a time for giving birth (Mi 5:2; Lk 1:57; 2:6); there is a proper season for a tree to bear fruit (Ps 104:27; Acts 14:17). Indeed there is a special time, a *kairos*, for every matter under the sun (Eccl 3:1).

We might compare this important discerning exercise with a golfer who finds himself or herself on a difficult par 5 hole and must choose the right golf club for the challenge at hand, especially when in clear view of several yawning bunkers and water hazards. Even a good swing with the wrong club can be self-defeating. So too when dealing with inculturation: it lies above all in knowing when and what cultural value might appropriately be called upon and enlisted at any given time for a particular purpose. At the risk of oversimplification, we might suggest that the process of inculturation begin by asking ourselves the following four sets of questions:

- Among the ten or twelve fundamental values (think: "charisms") that I have come to discern and am able to "name" in my American culture, when was the last time I heard any of these expressly *affirmed, ritualized,* or *celebrated* in the liturgy of my parish or church? And were they ritualized in such a way that the *correlation* between the American value and a corresponding gospel value was made sufficiently manifest so that my parish community was able to

experience something of the "messianic intermezzo" we spoke of
earlier?

- After listening to last Sunday's gospel reading, have I ever asked
  myself what fundamental value in U.S. culture might best be summoned and pressed into service, like Jonathan's armor-bearer,[7] in
  order to meet a gospel challenge? And in trying to discern and
  make this choice, have I reminded myself how often throughout
  salvation history it was the forgotten or neglected family member
  who was "elected" or "chosen" by God for a special mission?

- The next question to ask oneself concerns the *integrity* of one's cultural family. Is it complete? Does my culture have all the core values it will ever have or need, or is it perhaps even now "pregnant"
  and "with child"? And if so, how is my parish or church making all
  possible haste to be in the right place, at the right time, and like a
  good *midwife* assist in this birthing process of a new cultural value?
  Like the women after the resurrection appearances, has my
  Christian community been among the first to announce and celebrate these cultural tidings of great joy? In short, how exactly does
  my church prepare the way for and usher in new life?

- And, lastly, the question must be asked: Are there any intruders or
  imposters in the house? Any ideology, toxin, or false spirit that may
  have surreptitiously crept into my culture, unnoticed, and that now
  masquerades as a legitimate member of the family? How exactly
  does my parish community conduct its rite of exorcism? Is it still
  done in secrecy or in public? by a "phantom" priest or by the whole
  Christian community? And, most importantly, is the exorcism
  effective?

Some Criteria for Discerning "Core" Values

When approaching the issue of criteria, one must be very circum-
spect, and if one is to err, it is better to do so on the side of caution and
restraint. With cultural values, not only are we dealing with something
beyond strict empirical verification but divergent opinions about
American cultural values have multiplied in recent years rather than
diminished. In searching for valid, trustworthy criteria for discerning
these values, one must begin by affirming a culture's particularity. The
distinctiveness of America culture does not make it superior to or paradigmatic for other cultures—only different. Nor does this difference

consist in possessing certain key values that no other culture possesses. The difference consists rather in the peculiar "cluster" of cultural values it enshrines (its "family" profile, if you will) and the way these values play themselves out together in that particular configuration. We need to bring this distinct profile into view and be able to "name" it as our own. Putting one's name to something can mean many things: commitment, ownership, accountability. And cultural values, whether consciously held or not, are all about the commitments we have made in the past, the way we own up to them and stand ready to be identified by them. In order to help uncover our basic values with a certain degree of reliability, then, the following list of recommendations is put forward without any pretension of being either exhaustive or infallible.

First, such an exploratory exercise is best carried out with other people, in small groups or seminars. Just because we were born and grew up in a country does not mean that we "know" our culture well. We come to a better understanding of our uniqueness by exploring it with others, sharing our ideas with them and listening to their observations. Reaching a general consensus with others about our culture is important since along with value sharing there exist great differences in individual personalities, motives, life experiences, habits, and human talents and capacities. We cannot assume that all persons from a particular group or culture have *exactly* the same needs and behaviors, substituting symbiotic stereotypes for the real differences that exist among people of the same culture. "Nor can one be satisfied with having listened once to a culture," as Robert Schreiter makes abundantly clear; "there must be a commitment to continue to listen." Among the tasks of developing a "listening heart," Schreiter invites us to ask: How does one listen to a culture in such a way as to hear Christ already present in it?[8] Another way is simply to ask a group of individuals to list what they consider to be the ten most basic positive traits of their culture, with as many supporting cultural signs and instances as possible, and then from this purview try to discern the salient convergence of values that predominate. The group must try to identify specific situations and concrete examples of actions which reflect or manifest the values in question. Since there is always the danger of cultural encapsulation and therefore bias, it is always wise to include people who are not native to our culture in this exercise, the "outsider," whose *etic* interpretations and insights can corroborate or serve to test our own assumptions.[9] Needless to say, it is particularly important to undertake this exercise with as much disinterestedness as possible.

Second, borrowing a criterion from biblical scholars, we can employ what they call the criterion of "multiple attestation" (N. Perrin) or what is sometimes referred to as the criterion of "cross-section" (Schillebeeckx) in the historical quest for Jesus of Nazareth. We saw earlier how culture exhibits at its surface level several "semiotic domains" and what this means. After having made a thoughtful preliminary list of the ten or twelve "core" values (as suggested above), the exercise would now consist in taking each value individually and, using the criterion of multiple attestation, try to find cultural signs or expressions ("texts") of this value encoded in the divergent and independent semiotic domains of the culture. Assuming, for the sake of illustration, that "*being strong*" and "*being free*" and "*being venturesome*" are three of the fundamental values in American culture, one would then scrutinize the various semiotic domains for traces of each, that is, how the value in question "translates" and perhaps finds expression in different cultural fields: athletic, economic, judicial, religious, social, political, etc.—the assumption being that if sufficient factual traces or signs of a value occur in more than one semiotic domain, the chances of this value being an authentic "core" value, though not established, are nevertheless increased proportionately.

Third, in our quest to "name" our fundamental cultural values, and lest we rely too exclusively and too superficially on the outward semiotic signs for verification of authenticity, we should also employ what I am calling the criterion of historical "displacement" (or "dislocation").[10] If it is true that our fundamental American values stem from the dynamic myth of the "frontier," that is, are generated by the primordial "founding" events of our nation and the powerful symbols associated with these, then the question of *dislocation* or *displacement* lies at the very heart of the American experience. This indeed is where our "core" values derive their cultural affinity and cluster together as a distinct "family" of values.

As a frontiering, adventurous, on-the-move, boundary-crossing society such as ours (and I use these terms in their purest mythical sense), it is inevitable that we should have experienced physical and mental displacement of every description throughout our history. Displacement, in one form or other, seems to be as American as apple pie and certainly as indigenous as anything we might point to in the American experience. It has been our passion as well as our pain, the source of our greatest achievements as well as of our biggest disappointments. It has shadowed us persistently in the past and there is every indication that it will accompany us well into the third millennium. If a society is culturally "cut out" to be a frontiering, ground-breaking, and mobile nation, then it must follow—"as night the day"—that a certain dislocation is part and parcel of our heritage and destiny. If considered closely, it is indeed one of the hallmarks of our past history, our language and artistic creations, our religiosity, the way we do business, and our stature and presence in the world today.

According to the criterion of dislocation, therefore, our authenticating exercise would now consist in looking at the *cluster* of our basic values (as identified thus far) to see how this "family" of values holds up and interrelates in those times of greatest dislocation or displacement in our history. These were undoubtedly moments of great promise and great stress; they must have been of such a nature that they were bound to cause deep consternation if not offense to some (to cultural "insiders" as well as "outsiders"), while at the same time holding out great promise and hope to others. This is certainly an historical criterion, but as such it calls only for concentration on the search to see how our cluster of basic values deploy themselves in such times of restless creative tension, and to what extent they still cohere and interrelate as members of the same cultural family. In other words, can we find historical evidence of the supporting role of each value in these critical moments of displacement?

Were we to put all this in psychological terms, we could say that our attention here should focus on those moments when a society undergoes some significant and protracted periods of change. "Transitional space" is the name given by Donald Winnicott to those times in one's life in which a transition is being negotiated from one "holding environment" to another. The "holding environment" (sometimes called "cultures of embeddedness") refers to those phases in life when a certain integration, balance, and stability are achieved.[11] It is in the "transitional spaces," particularly, that the creative power of culture itself is summoned and that one can "witness" more directly the interplay and creative workings of a culture's fundamental values. This is where the work of creative cultural reconstruction is more evident even though unsettling. It is precisely in "transitional spaces" such as these that the experience of dislocation and disjunction is very real and where we can test the authenticity and "staying power" of our "core" family of cultural values.

Fourth (which is not to say "less importantly"), another valid, positive criterion for authenticating our "core" values is based on the principle of "free artistic imagination," or what we might call the criterion of "cultural fantasy." The reader will have noticed that in my visual inscape of culture, the uppermost stratum or "tip" of our cultural iceberg is designated as the *artistic level*. There is good reason for this. Although the artistic world constitutes a semiotic domain unto itself, much like the others, it stands above them, at a *higher* level of culture reality. The reason for this preeminence is twofold. First, because there is a recognized yet uncanny synchronicity between what takes place in the artist's creative imagination at the border regions of human existence, on the one hand, and what actually takes place in the lower reaches, the "fiery furnace," of a culture on the other. Whether they are conscious of it or not, artists, more than most, are intuitively "in tune" with the deep mythic dominants of a culture. As Joseph Powers correctly states: "In touch with and stirred by the deepest human values, the 'artist' is capable of incorporating and articulating these deep human realities in a way which makes the artist a prototype of the creative will in everyone. He articulates what is deep (and usually suppressed) in every human being, so that others can experience their own latent creativity through him."[12] In her book *The Hero: Myth/Image/Symbol*, Dorothy Norman puts it this way:

> Is it not by way of the swifter eye of the artist that we become most acutely conscious of reality beyond, behind, and beneath appearance? Is it not the artist who—like our dreams—dissolves the pretenses that hide us from ourselves, disclosing both our self-serving fantasies and our unsuspected potentialities?[13]

Rose Marie Scissons, also with good insight, says:

> To paint an image, to make a photograph, to recreate a true vision from within, an artist must be able to articulate, bring to the surface, and to communicate to others this moment of truth....We have always relied on the artist to explain us to ourselves, to articulate for us our deepest longings, our hidden dreams, our fearful secrets and our present joys.[14]

There is yet another reason why artists have an unusual power to tell for us the real stories of our lives, and why we must rely on them as a privileged criterion for evaluating our fundamental cultural values: their *exceptional freedom*. More than the average citizen, they are free from all ideology, anecdote or propaganda, free from immediate material appeal or gain, free also from the need to disguise their own vulnerability. For them, the accepted canons are but norms from which they feel free to depart. It is this remarkable freedom that gives them the power to reawaken in us our dynamic cultural myths, the collective roots of our personal struggles and our ideal of quest, and thus the ability to recall to us the too easily forgotten fact that *what is without is within*.

It is because the Catholic Church has not respected or honored this artistic freedom that our best artists today have become alienated from the church, and why their homeless art has had to look for a new home. Recognizing this alienation, the sensitive Pope Paul VI made what can only be heard as a magisterial "mea culpa" when he told an assembled group of artists in Rome:

> To be courageously honest...we recognize that the church has above all imposed on you the rule of imitation....We told you in effect: "We have this style, you must conform; we have this tradition, you must be faithful to it; we have these masters, you must follow them; we have these rules, you cannot depart from them." It has to be said that at times we imposed a mantle of lead on you; for this, forgive us! And the fact that we, too, have abandoned you.[15]

An excellent way to begin acquiring a "listening heart" is to examine some of the thoughtful analyses that have been made by scholars about our literary American artists. As a "primer" bibliography, I would recommend such readings as Charles Mabee's *Reimagining America*, Belden C. Lane's *Landscapes of the Sacred* (which contains an excellent bibliographical essay of its own), Ihab Hassan's *Selves at Risk: Patterns of Quest in Contemporary American Letters*, and Stanley Romaine Hopper's *The Ways of Transfiguration*, edited by R. Keiser and T. Stoneburner. We would do well also to heed Harold Bloom's advice and put Walt Whitman on our reading list, one of the greatest figures in our literature who sums up and commits to poetry the passionate aspirations of America and does so out of our deepest cultural myths.[16] Apart from the verbal arts, one should also consider the other equally important forms and modes of artistic expression in America.

Some Basic American Values

Having thus far elucidated our model for analyzing culture and some criteria for discerning its "core" values, I would like now to indicate something of what this means when applied to American culture and what it might mean for inculturating the faith more deeply in our culture. Using the above criteria, I think we can agree that Being...FREE, STRONG, ENTERPRISING, and INNOVATIVE, for example, are among some of our basic American cultural values. There are others, to be sure, but these will suffice to illustrate the points we wish to make.

First, the present participle "Being...." refers to the fact that all cultural values are eminently *spiritual values* in that they define the collective identity of a people and should not be confused with a people's possessions or material constructs. Cultural values speak to the qualities of our "being," not our "having." On this point Pope John Paul II is clear and correct: "Herein lies the main distinction," he says, "between what man is and what he has, the distinction between being and having. Culture always relates to man in the essentials, while his relationship to what he owns or 'has' is not only secondary, but completely relative."[17] Hence it is important not to prematurely judge a culture on the basis of its external material affluence (or lack thereof).

Second, no attempt has been made in the above enumeration to give more weight to one value over another; they are indeed all fundamental, even though at certain times and in varying circumstances one or other will predominate over the others. There exists, as we have said, a familial solidarity or kinship between them. The recognition of this cultural consanguinity is most important. Whenever a culture is summoned, threatened, or otherwise challenged, its basic values will tend to coalesce and function together even more. Thus they can be "co-pacifists" when it's time for making peace and "co-belligerents" when it's time for making war; "co-celebrants" when it's time to laugh and dance, and "co-mourners" when it's time to cry; "co-conservatives" when it's time to stay the course and "co-liberals" when it's time to change course. A familial solidarity or kinship exists between them. One can say therefore that they are values "for all seasons."

Third, it is important to note that these cultural values (in the strict sense) are all intrinsically good. As we indicated earlier, there is no such thing as an inherently evil cultural value. Thus we value a *strong* dollar just as we value a *strong* faith, or *free* speech and association (as Jesus certainly did) just as we cherish *freedom* of conscience and religion, etc. The point is: all basic cultural values, if evoked and properly appealed to, can serve any gospel imperative. Indeed one can say that they are the cultural "windows" *par excellence* through which the gospel is given to enter deeply into any culture. Recall, too, as we indicated earlier, that all the above values originate and stem from the primordial dynamic myths in early American history.

While cultural values can be mobilized as a family unity, they also form what might be called a *cultural keyboard*, a set of distinctive "keys" (as on a piano or computer), and because of their number they can be combined in an almost indefinite number of ways. Hence there are an unlimited number of possibilities that a culture has to "compose" itself in history. This is what gives culture its extraordinary "plasticity" in the face of historical events and circumstances. It has the quality of surprise—hiddenness brought to light—the quality of the unexpected and unpredictable. This surprise factor is no doubt what makes every *latest* public opinion poll so tantalizingly attractive. It also helps to explain why the public "mood" of a country can be so fickle, why it can change so swiftly, say from one of confidence to one of general depression (or vice versa). From time to time, a country is overtaken or possessed by a "mood" when it has become disconnected from its basic value structure. This malaise, though often attributed to external factors, in fact stems from having temporarily lost a sense of meaning—where one belongs, where one's allegiance is, where one's roots are—which only a culture's value structure can truly provide.

At this point in our study, the reader may feel that my approach to inculturation has been too idealistic, or that my choice of metaphors (nuptial union), myths (frontier-crossing venture), and cultural values (being free, strong, etc.) are overly optimistic ones and hardly in keeping or "in tune" with the real troubled world and times we live in today. There is indeed much negativity, skepticism, loss of patriotic pride, and a myriad number of other social ills over which as a people we seem to have little or no control. Clearly, there are sufficient "apocalyptic" signs of alienation, sorrow and suffering—at home as well as abroad—to make one think more readily of the prophetic battlefield of Armageddon (Rev 16:16) than envisage the possibility of an immanent "second spring" (Newman). Yet it is precisely in a time like ours, with all its "encircling gloom," that the best impulses of both faith and culture must be summoned forth and their respective strengths and gifts conjoined. If there is ever a time when hope itself becomes prophetic, then it must surely be when we are given so few signs of hope, when we have to "hope against hope."

However, it is necessary, I believe, to call into question some of the current social criticism of American culture. Many such studies do not focus upon a particular flaw in our culture; rather they call into question the whole fabric of contemporary American culture. It is not so much the somewhat extremist character of the cultural critics that is objectionable, but rather the secular despair or fatalism that their readings of culture entail. Charles Mabee sums it up this way: "It sounds creative, even prophetic, to ask for 'searing criticism.' Yet such criticism can degenerate into a moralistic exercise, bereft of vitality and the power of persuasion, unless kept in close affinity with the realities of American identity."[18] Political and social analysts are not the only ones who hold somewhat pessimistic views about contemporary American culture. As Monika Hellwig correctly asserts, the Vatican exhibits the same bias, especially in regard to the way we value freedom and our spirit of enterprise, initiative, and creativity. Hellwig says:

> There has been a subtle, and sometimes not so subtle, tendency on the part of the Vatican to view these aspects of American life and activity as regrettably worldly in their concerns—a tendency some-

times shared in preaching, teaching and writing even by American church leaders, clergy and theologians. I believe that this condemnatory attitude needs to be unmasked as yet another echo of gnosticism in the church....There is evidently a seductive power in the notion that the spiritual in the biblical sense is to be identified with the immaterial, the a-historical, the other-worldly and the unpractical. Yet in the orthodox doctrine the spiritual in the biblical sense is the revitalizing of all creation by the redeeming breath of God drawing all things to their true purpose and focus.[19]

Whether the basic American values listed above are considered as forming a "whole" or envisaged separately, they provide the anchor points on which the inculturation process must be moored if it is to be successful. The real task of inculturation consists in creating the *interface* between these cultural values and the gospel or kingdom values. *Interfacing is another word for inculturation.* The dictionary defines the word "interface" as the means or place of interaction between two systems (for example, the interface between psychology and education). In a more technological sense, it signifies the computing apparatus for connecting two pieces of equipment *so that they can be operated jointly*. To say therefore that inculturation is concerned above all with the interface between faith and culture is in perfect keeping with our original root metaphor of a nuptial union. It also has the advantage of evoking Paul Tillich's method of correlation, which lies at the heart of any attempt to inculturate the faith. Moreover, it is consistent with my theological conviction that like the mystery of the incarnation itself, the mutual embrace of faith and culture is first and foremost a *conjunctive* encounter rather than an *adversarial* one.

How does interfacing faith and culture begin? How does it translate into mission praxis? To date, Charles Mabee has provided one of the most constructive attempts to establish such an interface, to project, as he says, "an encounter between the American self and the biblical tradition that already exists at the deepest layers of the American mythos."[20] I would like to indicate some other steps that can be taken to foster such an interface. Since we have few precedents to go on, such a task will demand considerable creativity, in terms of convergent as well as divergent thinking.[21] What follows is not a detailed blueprint but a few practical suggestions that may help to make a modest beginning.

- We can begin by rereading the gospels and the New Testament writings through the prism or "eye" of each basic value identified above: Being...FREE, STRONG, DEMOCRATIC, SELF-RELIANT, FAIR, and INNOVA-

TIVE (or any other that the reader may identify). Such a first reading has the decided advantage of engaging the American reader at a deep fiducial level and brings the reader into the hermeneutics of the text as an "insider." It also allows us to then consider which of these values (or which combination thereof) might best be summoned and called upon at any given time to further the claims of the gospel.

- From this initial reading there should result the isolation and selection of certain key ("privileged") gospel texts and events that evoke a particularly deep resonance in the reader: (1) a set of texts wherein faith and culture evince a close correspondence or correlation, and (2) a set of texts wherein the disjunction or distance between them appears greatest. Such a dual inventory, when compiled and allowed to "communicate" with one another, can then serve as a basis for a second and third reading of the gospels.

- The kingdom of God is Jesus' preferred root metaphor for God's immediate activity in the world. Reflecting further upon the interface established thus far between faith and culture, it now becomes possible to read the signs and better appreciate the richness of this divine immediacy, a visitation that often lies beneath conscious prehension but is nevertheless real and immediate. This can be understood in terms of the parable of the seed growing secretly in Mark 4:26-29, which C.H. Dodd interprets as follows: "It is not that the Kingdom of God will shortly come, but that it is a present fact; and not a present fact in the sense that it is a tendency towards righteousness always present in the world, but in the sense that something has now happened which never happened before."[22]

- The question then becomes: What new, valuable, perhaps unprecedented, light does this reciprocal correlation between faith and culture shed on both the gospel message and American culture? How does it urge upon the perceiver a reinterpretation of the gospel in our local context, and also a re-creative need to modify one's world view, one's sense of identity and reality? The thoughtful answers to emerge from such an exercise might then well serve as a theological basis "from below" upon which we can begin constructing a local American theology, and perhaps even a supporting local spirituality in the context of the United States.

PART FOUR

New Paths and Spirituality of Mission

9 | New Postmodern Paths in Mission

The immediate task before us now is to contexualize everything we have seen thus far in the broader perspective of our profoundly changing times. There can be no doubt that as we approach the third millennium, the world and our times are experiencing a profound ground swell of historic proportions, one that is leaving very little untouched, unquestioned or securely anchored, either within the church or in society at large. I am referring of course to the present transition from modernity to postmodernity, a liminal "betwixt-and-between" period in history that is very disconcerting and the cause of much confusion and soul-searching. It is in this epochal transition period that the church is being challenged to re-vision its mission priorities and spirituality. We will begin by "tracking" this postmodern ground swell, and then move on, in the second half of this chapter, to consider some new paths and priorities that are being suggested by our changing times for the church in the United States.

The Postmodern Divide

The term *postmodernity* renders accurately the defining traits of the social condition that now prevails in the affluent countries of Europe and North America. The term is accurate since it draws attention to the continuity as well as the discontinuity between the present social condition and the *modern* era that preceded and gestated it. The discontinuity arises from the fact that many of the major presuppositions of modernity can no longer be upheld in the light of the new postmodern experience: the myth of unending progress, the clear and distinct ideas of universal reason, the power of the self-contained and self-directed individual, and the over-confident ascendancy of human control over nature. By contrast, we are conscious today of the end of progress, the limits of reason, the sorry state of isolated and unconnected individuals, and the ecological catastrophes that can and do result when nature is disrespected. Zygmunt Bauman is quite right when he says:

> Postmodernity is not a transitory departure from the "normal state" of modernity; neither is it a diseased state of modernity, an ailment likely to be rectified, a case of "modernity in crisis." It is, instead, a self-reproducing pragmatically self-contained social condition defined by *distinctive features of its own*.[1]

One of the major preoccupations of postmodern discourse in the late twentieth century has been the quest for wholeness. A quest for the overcoming of fragmentation, a search for connectedness and integration, a "recognition of the existing interactions between the natural systems and the cultural systems, between biology and ethics, between attitudes and historic events,"[2] characterize a new way of thinking which has been called constructive or revisionary postmodernity. This new mindset stems from a need to "heal thought" by overcoming the rigid dualisms of modern scientific rationalism, by countering the individualism so cherished by the enlightenment, combined with a desire to achieve a new unity of scientific, ethical and religious intuitions.

This can be seen in the concerted attempt to find an "intellectually defensible way of allowing for the possibility of a reenchanted science."[3] It is the view of constructive postmodern theorists that natural science itself can be utilized as a "witness against the adequacy of the modern world view."[4] We are living at a time when the most fruitful scientific models are examples of what could be called physiological world mending models: models which seek to reunify what has been segmented. Unlike enlightenment models, according to which science alone seeks truth and delivers realistic insight, and unlike the perspectives of deconstructive postmodern theorists which ascribe only a functional value to a word like "truth"—a perspective being true only in the sense that it is capable of illuminating a partial aspect of reality—constructive postmodernist models regard the reality of truth (and the truth of reality) in much more holistic terms, that is, in terms of the interconnectedness and interplay of all beings, human and non-human.[5]

David Griffin supports his claim that contemporary science itself is exposing the limitations of the world view of classical modernity by referring to a range of twentieth century developments. He cites the mysterious theoretical developments in quantum physics, for example, with its emphasis on internal context-dependent relationships between parts and wholes that has fired the imagination of religious thinkers, east and west. Similarly, organismic rather than mechanistic models are "re-enchanting" molecular biology. As Sheldrake notes: "While a mechanistic start-ing point cannot account for genuine organism, an organistic starting point can account for all the mechanistic phenomena evident in the world."[6] And for those involved in ministries of physiological healing, the exploration of what is called the mind/body debate is of considerable significance. The contours of the problem are unpacked in what Griffin sets forth as the logical interplay between a fact, an apparent fact and an inference. The fact is that we have or are a mind, in the sense of a stream of experiences. Apparently, minds and bodies interact, yet the inference has been that the human body is composed of things devoid of experi-ence. The problem then and what necessitates a new explanatory model lies in the question: "How is it understandable that these two totally unlike things appear to interact?" In his article, "Of Minds and Molecules: Postmodern Medicine in a Psychosomatic Universe," Griffin argues that contemporary medicine has no plausible theory which can incorporate evidences of psychosomatic interaction in matters of health as genuine data. The usual way of dealing with phenomena that cannot now be seen to fit into a formal framework is to set them aside. According to Griffin,

> The idea that people's bodily health is intrinsically and importantly tied up with the state of their souls will not become part of the general lore of our culture unless a generally acceptable frame-work makes an idea seem natural. Only a new paradigm, a gener-ally accepted model of the human person—and in fact of reality as a whole, because the human person incorporates all levels from subatomic particle to self-conscious mind—will allow psychoso-matic medicine to become the new orthodoxy and orthopraxis instead of a fading fad.[7]

If the re-enchantment of science is one of the major preoccupations of postmodern discourse, a renewed emphasis on communal vision is another. In Barbara Ehrenreich's insightful analysis of western middle-class ideology in the final decades of the twentieth century, *Fear of Falling*, she characterizes the modern mindset as follows:

> Left and right, we are still locked in by a middle-class culture that is almost wholly insular, self-referential and in its own way parochial. We seldom see "the others" except as projections of our own anxieties or instruments of our own ambitions, and even when "seeing them"—as victims, cases or exemplars of archaic virtue—seldom hear.[8]

The need to "see others" for accurate assessment of a population's health and well-being is increasingly recognized in official public health statements. What is stressed is a need for a holistic model, this time of humans in society. There is growing recognition that social, economic and environmental factors outside the health care system are the most important influences on individual and collective well-being. There is also a new openness to religious systems and intuitions. A response with integrity to our changing times demands a more fully articulated declaration of the manner in which God, not only the church, stands in relation to the world.

The holistic quest of postmodernity, combined with its reassertion that mission is primarily, whatever more it might entail, attention to the *whole* person, needs an appropriate "word" as well as deed for what Sallie McFague describes as "the totality of reality; hunger, fear and suffering unite beings, both human and nonhuman in a wordless community where a cry of pain is the universal word."[9] McFague's metaphorical theology, especially her development around the metaphor "God-as-Lover-of-the-World," is entirely congruent with our own nuptial root metaphor and the underlying theology developed in this study. The metaphor speaks both to the inherent value of the beloved, namely creation, and to the persistent hesitancy of our human response to that love. McFague's model would have us re-vision salvation as "the making whole or uniting of that which is attractive and valuable rather than the rescuing of what is sinful and worthless."[10] In this model, healing is the manner in which making whole is brought about. It is a model that emphasizes reconciliation and seeks above all the reunification of our disordered world.[11]

Such a perspective is also entirely congruent with the biblical story of salvation history. In this "peculiar" story, salvation is depicted as the absence of every form of alienation—whether it be alienation within one's self, from one's neighbor, from nature or from God. Alienation is basically the degree to which a person feels or believes that he or she cannot fulfill in society that which is his or her perceived rightful role and place in community. As Eric Fromm says: "By alienation is meant a mode of experience in which the person experiences himself as an alien."[12] Those who feel that their actions are meaningless would make them meaningful *if they could*; those who feel that they do not belong would cause themselves to belong *if they could*; those who feel manipulated would cease to be so *if they could*; and those who are or feel isolated in society would be recognized and accepted *if they could*. This is what salvation is all about: the deliverance from alienation in all its variables, whether it be a sense of powerlessness, meaninglessness, self-estrangement or isolation, and whether it be alienation in the personal sphere or alienation in the social, political or ecclesial spheres. Throughout the biblical narrative, reconciliation is another name for salvation and alienation is but another name for sin. In the Christian perspective, this is why mission has always consisted primarily in some form of "boundary-crossing," some ecstatic form of going beyond and outside the boundaries of one's own comfortable *chez soi* in order to meet and "see others" as they themselves see and feel.

It should be clear from the start, though, that the church cannot halt, reverse or otherwise substantially alter the postmodern ground swell we are now experiencing as it once perhaps could in another age and another era. An "epochal rupture" (Rahner) of this magnitude, combined with the growing overpopulation of the world, the ubiquitous presence of technology in our daily lives, the emergence of what Peter Drucker calls the "knowledge society,"[13] the radical transformation of our thought processes as a result of electronics and the global information society, means that the church must learn to live *with* and *through* these tempestuous times. "These phenomena," as Walter Ong quite rightly pointed out, "are not additions to God's creation, but are simply the normal developments of what he created."[14] Nor can the church hope to stand "unaffected" or "outside" these global trends; it does not enjoy the kind of immunity or a-temporal exemption that is said to have been granted to Noah's ark in the book of Genesis. On the contrary, the church, to its incarnational credit, is very much *in* the real world and it must accept all the limitations (and opportunities) that being an historical and temporal community of believers implies. If the Catholic Church experienced something of a paradigm shift in its life as a result of Vatican II in the 1960s,[15] postmodernity will affect church life in ways no less profound. What may prove even moｒe unsettling for it in this transition from modernity to postmodernity is that the present ground swell is not of its own making, as Vatican II was, and it does not enjoy even the relative control over these forces that it has had over those forces unleashed in the post-Vatican church.

That the gospel has to be articulated and proclaimed in tune with this new postmodern sensitivity and quest for wholeness is certainly one of the major challenges facing the Catholic Church in the United States today. What follows, in this and the next chapter of our study, is an attempt to suggest some new mission priorities whereby the church can meet this daunting challenge.

New Mission Paths and Priorities

Until we actually cross the threshold of the third millennium, we can expect a host of projections about what this epochal turning point has in store for us and what new direction the future of mission will take in the coming decades. John Paul II has already trained the eyes of the faithful and the church on this great turning point of Christian history and will no doubt continue to do so with increasing urgency. Robert Schreiter and Walbert Bühlmann, among others, have also invited us to seriously consider what shape the mission of the church can be expected to take as we move into the new millennium.[16] I would like in turn to suggest some mission priorities for the Catholic Church in America. While the projections about the future of mission by both Schreiter and Bühlmann are framed in a global or world perspective, mine, intentionally, will focus on the local Catholic Church in North America.

On the basis of everything we have said about inculturating faith more deeply in U.S. culture, three new mission priorities have already surfaced: a significant change of emphasis (1) from an anxious, problem-oriented church to one that clearly radiates *hope* and, as St. Peter himself stipulated, is ready to give a credible account for its hope "with gentleness and reverence," (2) from a church that would unilaterally try to transform U.S. culture to one that seeks rather to evangelize the existing *marriage union* between faith and culture, and (3) from a church that is prone to be exclusive to one that is more *inclusive*. Clearly, any "new evangelization" in the United States will only succeed if it is appropriate to the faith-culture matrix it addresses; this means seriously taking into account the dynamic currents of interrelatedness that lie deep within this matrix instead of focusing primarily on the often tormented surface of it.

It is fair to say that the above three shifts in mission priorities stem from the church's own internal debate and reflection about what inculturation means and the new challenges it presents. Again recently, as he so often has in the past, John Paul II underscored the importance of this challenge: "Inculturation," he says, "thus appears as *one of the most necessary and vital tasks* of evangelization and catechesis, but also as one of the most difficult and delicate....*The paradigm for this task is the Incarnation of the Word of God itself*, a historical and saving event on which Christian faith is based."[17] There are other equally important mission priorities, however, that are not the result of the church's self-reflection but are dictated by the postmodern transformation that is presently taking place in our society, changes that will certainly continue well beyond the year 2000. In his article, "The Age of Social Transformation," already referred to, Peter Drucker sums it up this way:

> No century in recorded history has experienced so many social transformations and such radical ones as the twentieth century.

They, I submit, may turn out to be the most significant events of this, our century, and its lasting legacy. In the developed free-market countries...work and work force, society and polity, are all, in the last decade of this century, *qualitatively* and *quantitatively* different not only from what they were in the first years of this century but also from what has existed at any other time in history: in their configurations, in their processes, in their problems, and in their structures.[18]

Below the surface of all the material factors and objective processes that account for the social transformations that Drucker describes, however, there is an even more vital area of concern for mission, namely, that of the "subjective reality" or social consciousness of a people. Changes in work and work force, the market situation, the global economy, and the intensifying of technology do not explain per se how Americans think of themselves or their world, nor do these material factors explain their social behavior or motivations, which at times can appear quite contrary to what is generally accepted as contemporary "common sense." The central concern of mission, therefore, must focus on the way Americans think and feel about life, their beliefs, ways of thinking, social and aesthetic values, attitude toward nature, experience of time and space, ideas about death and the other world, their interpretation of ages in human life, etc., which are all interconnected and form a kind of whole, a *mentalité* that is being increasingly described by observers of contemporary history as *postmodern*.

It is in this postmodern frame of reference and consciousness that the unresolved issues and uneasy dialogue outlined at the beginning of this study must be seen and new mission priorities formulated. What we are in fact experiencing today is nothing short of a major historical transition period, a radical paradigm shift from a *modernist* to a *postmodern* social consciousness. Evidence and signs of this epoch-making change in consciousness are too numerous to be ignored and are being increasingly documented and studied.[19] Hence any thought of a "new evangelization" or new mission priorities must be grounded and centered in the reality of this ongoing paradigm shift. The central issue then becomes: How do we tell the Christian story meaningfully and with credibility to a people who are in the very process of crossing this great historical divide between modernity and postmodernity? Is the church ready or able to undertake this exodus journey with its people or will they increasingly have to fend for themselves and go it alone?

Transition periods of this magnitude are no time for the church to "drop anchor," as it were, in the hope of weathering the storm changes by conservatively holding fast or still. Nor is it possible during this axial period to elaborate a definitive, long-term mission policy or plan for a future that cannot yet be fully determined or foreseen. What can be done, however, is to foster a mission spirituality that equips the church for this *interim* transition period, one that is fitted and better suited for a new exodus/desert experience. When Moses undertook to lead his people out of Egypt to a new land, when Abraham left Ur of the Chaldees for an unknown country, and when Pope John XXIII convened Vatican Council II and summoned the church into a new era, there were no blueprints to show the way, no crystal balls to foretell the future, no way of being absolutely certain what the eventual outcome would be. Any discussion of mission priorities at this point in time therefore must be geared to a world in transition, a people on the move, a liminal time in history. The movement of the Christian community, the people of God, into the desert means that mission and ministry in the church will have to be conducted differently. In order to be truly present to this historical transition so that it may be a time of grace instead of a time of utter confusion and dismay, I set out below schematically and somewhat baldly some mission priorities that the present "signs of the times" would seem to suggest. The postmodern paradigm shift that is marking the close of our century is certainly one of those signs, and it is in the light of this emerging new social consciousness that the following should be read.

1. The Courage to Re-Vision Our Conventional Image of God

Crossing the postmodern divide for the Christian community today will not be unlike the desert experience that the people of God underwent in the wilderness, and many of their temptations will no doubt be similar to the ones we may experience. One is the nostalgic temptation to return to the old sacred securities of the past, the "fleshpots" of a pre-Vatican church, so to speak, when obedience and conformity were regarded as more pleasing to God than the creative capacity and self-expression of faith itself. Another temptation will be to cling to a fixed and static image of God (the one we grew up with and perhaps never changed), thus resisting the idea that God can manifest his presence differently today than in the past, or thinking that he can only be encountered in the exact same sacred "times" and "sites" where we have always sought his presence. Perhaps the greatest temptation in our new desert experience, however, will be to think that the God of our faith, the God of Jesus Christ, is truly present to us as long as we somehow manage to make ourselves *feel a need* for him amidst our daily concerns and preoccupations. As most Catholics know from personal experience, it is not necessarily when we need him most that God shows his face or makes his presence felt. On this point the utter silence of God on Calvary, when Jesus needed his "Abba" most, should leave little room for any illusions. Yet religious illusions are often the hardest to part with.

Moreover a mission spirituality based solely on the utter reliance on God for help does not correspond to our postmodern experience, as it perhaps once did in the past. As E. Jüngel put it, today we must be ready to explore and exploit the modern discovery of the "worldly non-necessity" of God (which is not to be confused with the "death" or "absence" of God).[20] French theologian Claude Geffré and others have taken up this challenge and suggest that the non-necessity of God in our secular world today means "that utilitarian versions of God are no longer relevant."[21] What we need, instead, is to "take a fresh look at the gratuitousness of the biblical God of the *Alliance*, which is exchange, gift and love, excess and generosity."[22] Perhaps the critical test for faith today, then, is whether or not we can re-vision our traditional image of God, whether or not we can learn to understand the generous, gracious, gratuitous character of God's love, a love that is so free, so wild, so extravagant and yet so unobtrusive, that it does not threaten or demand anything in return. Is it not possible to think that the God of Jesus Christ does not impose himself, does not menace, does not demand or claim something in return for his divine favors and grace— only that we ourselves might be made *free* to love as he loves? Could it be that God is now calling us to love him, no longer out of self-interest or because of his blessings in the past or those promised in the future, but loved in and for himself alone? Loved only for himself, that is, as though he were of no "earthly" use to us? Is this not what John means when he says that "God *is* love" and ultimately what makes the Christian God uniquely *triune*, and the commandment to love God and neighbor uniquely *one*? Is this not, in the end as in the beginning, what Jesus came to reveal and make manifest?

Clearly, this is what Charles Péguy had in mind when he penned the following words:

> *Ask any father whether the best of all moments is not that one*
> *When his sons begin to love him as full-grown men,*
> *To love him as himself a man, freely and for nought.*
> *When subservience is done with, and the sons, grown into men,*
> *Now deal with him and love him man to man, like those who*
> *have a right to judge.*[23]

An anonymous sixteenth century Spanish sonnet, *Al Cristo crucifica-do*, sometimes attributed to St. Francis Xavier or St. Teresa of Avila, also beautifully captures this idea:

> *I am not moved, my God, to love you*
> *by the heaven you have promised;*
> *nor am I moved by the dread of hell*
> *to stay away from sins that might offend you.*

············

> *Beyond all else, it is your love that moves me,*
> *and if there were no heaven I would love you,*
> *and if there were no hell, I still would have my fear of you.*

············

> *For me to love you, there is no need for you to give:*
> *though I should have no hope of what I hope for,*
> *as I love you now, I would love you still.*[24]

2. The Wisdom to Give Mission Priority to Mystagogy over Pedagogy

Lest one think that such religious sensitivity is rare today or sought after by only a few privileged "souls," a second mission priority imposes itself. In his own eminently wise projections of tomorrow's church, Karl Rahner stated that "the Christian of the future will be a mystic or he will not exist at all."[25] If this is true or even falls somewhere within the "ballpark" of God's truth, then a most appropriate priority and focus for church leaders and those who take mission seriously would be a renewed emphasis on the character of faith as *mystery*. This means a shift of emphasis from magisterium to mystagogy, from pedagogy to midwifery, from problem solvers to mystery dwellers. A problem, as the etymology of the Greek word *pro-ballein* suggests, is something that is thrown out in front of us to be solved, an obstacle that can be aggressively cracked open like a nut and "solved." For every problem, theoretically speaking, there is a solution or answer. Mystery on the other hand calls for no such imperious resolution. What is called for, instead, is much more akin to the "active surrender" of a mystic or holy person in the presence of an unfolding mystery. In Gabriel Marcel's phrase, mystery is something "that encroaches on the intrinsic conditions of its own possibility." If properly initiated into, mystery opens us up to unexpected and inexhaustible depths in ourselves, our faith and our world.

The recovery of the notion and significance of mystery and mysticism constitutes one of the major challenges in terms of re-visioning mission in today's postmodern world.[26]

We began this study with a catalogue of some unresolved issues facing the Catholic Church in the United States today. The manner in which one approaches these issues is crucial. If they are viewed as so many *problems* to be solved (as they appear to have been approached in the church thus far), then we can expect a church even more divided by the end of the century. On the other hand, if these same pressing issues are viewed as perhaps the "encroaching" *mystery* of living faith itself, the result of the Holy Spirit's "groaning" within the community of faith and the world, then the church might be perceived as a more discerning and mystagogic church, and not only or primarily as a "teaching" authority.

If Karl Rahner is correct—and the growing *sensus fidelium* among Catholics today in the God of mysticism would seem to support his contention—then mission as mystagogy, the art of initiating into mystery, can no longer be isolated as a "special" ministry in the church and thus entrusted to only a special group of ministers: spiritual directors, "soul friends," spiritual guides and companions. Today's spiritual hunger is of such size and scope, of such manifest density and social relevance, that "feeding the hungry" transcends the traditional "diaconal" function in the church of distributing food to the hungry. It has now become a question of "feeding the multitude" *spiritually*, and today this can only mean fostering the ability of *all* the faithful to see "beyond what meets the eye." Leonardo Boff puts it well:

> Mysticism is not the privilege of the fortunate few. It is rather a dimension of human life to which all of us have access when we become conscious of a deeper level of the self, when we try to study the other side of things, when we become aware of the inward richness of the other, and when we confront the grandeur, complexity, and harmony of the universe. All of us, at a certain level, are mystics.[27]

Many feel that the institutional church has now become a mother who is ill-equipped or knows not how to feed her big family—at least in terms of the spiritual nourishment a growing number of her children long for and feel they now need. The church will have to face this growing challenge with more than a new catechism or a new encyclical; it will have to rethink the way its spiritual "catering" facilities function in today's changing times and become, recognizably and pervasively, a mystagogic church. This means that the church will have to find new ways to meet the deepest "longing" of people today, namely, their radical desire to see beyond what superficially meets the eye and to personally experience the hidden mystery that embraces the totality of all things and all beings, human as well as non-human. Such a deep, widespread longing is clearly one of the more conspicuous postmodern "signs of the times." The church must not simply try to "satisfy" this longing (in the sense that it would eventually disappear and go away), but it itself must become and be seen as the passionate embodiment and bearer of this mystical longing. Otherwise, those who so long will look elsewhere for an appropriate spirituality, as many already have.

In August 1994, *Concilium* published a special issue under the title "Mysticism and the Institutional Crisis." This is how the editorial committee of this review introduced the issue:

> At present there is great curiosity about mysticism; it is inversely proportional to the allergy provoked by the ecclesiastical institutions. Many people feel that these institutions have fallen into disuse because of their failure to respond to the spiritual hunger which marks the end of our century. This desire seeks immediacy with God. In this perspective, many people think that as a result of their dogmatic or practical intransigence the churches are a source of violence and do not encourage spiritual experience....God can only be encountered where one lives in freedom.[28]

3. The Imagination Required to Create More "Go Structures" in the Parish

A third mission priority for the Catholic Church in the United States has to do with its traditional parish structures. The local parish church around which Catholic life gravitates and is nourished is predominantly made up of what might be called "come structures." Catholics "come" to church for mass; they "come" for marriage preparation and the sacraments; they "come" to the rectory to see a priest; they "come" to the parish hall for church functions, etc. With its centralized constellation of "come" structures, the parish complex (parking lot often included) is basically where the church welcomes and receives its members, where they come to pray, to hear the word of God and ritualize their communion. This is what I earlier referred to as the church's mission *ad intra.* As such, the parish is conceived and set up as a *sacred hospitality center:* it receives and provides for those of its own who come to church. In this sense it quietly reminds the faithful that their adherence to religion is an eminently free, voluntary association. What is needed, I am suggesting, is not the dismantlement of the existing parish complex but the creation of more "go structures" within the parish.

Clearly, mission includes hospitality but it is by no means exhausted by it; the *ad intra* life and mission of the church is seriously weakened if it does not have a concomitant *ad extra* dimension, that is, sufficient parish "go" structures. In fact, mission is more properly defined in terms of "go" structures, in terms of an exodus or "going out" experience, as when Jesus said: "Let us go on to the neighboring towns so that I may proclaim the message there also; for that is what I have *come out* to do" (Mk 1:38). It is not enough to dismiss the faithful at the end of a eucharistic service with the words: "The mass is ended; go in peace to love and serve the Lord." They must be given new additional *outgoing* structures that will enable them to effectively reach out to the poor, the forgotten in their deep needs, the marginalized and the "distant," those who for whatever reason no longer "come" to church, those who suffer in distress and have legitimate reason for disbelieving in a compassionate God or church. New parochial structures will have to be created and invested in, much like the Vatican had to finance and create (virtually *ex nihilo*) when our contemporary popes decided they were no longer "prisoners" of the Vatican, but could begin *visiting* the local churches around the world. Indeed salvation history reads like an ongoing succession of divine visits or visitations, as does the ministry of Jesus who had "nowhere to lay his head" except as someone's visitor or guest, not to mention the "boundary crossing" visits and journeys of the apostle Paul. Even Mary, who was herself unexpectedly "visited" from on high, immediately set out and became, in turn, a "visitor" to Elizabeth. Visiting, it must be conceded, is but another name for mission.

What makes this so important for mission *ad extra* is that in taking the gratuitous initiative of visiting someone, I am obliged to tear myself away from the familiarity of my own sacred space and private securities, and venture out to someone else's doorstep and sacred "interior." To cross another's threshold is to enter into that person's or that family's private and highly personalized world. For most people, divine grace and human nature commingle best in their own home, in their *chez soi*, and this is where any church with a mission would want to make haste to be present, knowing of course that God always gets there first.

Every visit, including the missionary visit or visitation, supposes some intervening distance which I must cross. In the past, this generally meant leaving hearth and kin, crossing the ocean, and venturing to some distant land or people. Hence the classic expression: "foreign missions." Today, however, there are some even more formidable "distances" to be crossed right here at home if the Catholic Church in America is to become truly missionary. I am referring to those wrenching, boundary-stressing divides of a social, economic, racial, sexual or religious nature, those distances that separate people who otherwise *now* live in close physical proximity within our own city or diocesan jurisdiction—the distance, I mean, that separates the rich from the poor (and vice versa), the young from the elderly, the whites from the blacks, the Catholics from the Protestants, the churched from the unchurched, the gays from the straights, the secure from the abandoned or abused, the sought after from the marginalized, etc., etc. All these unresolved "crossings" must now be deemed the new "foreign missions" in postmodern America—"foreign," I say, because the experience of crossing *these* boundaries on a regular, systematic basis may still be strange and unfamiliar to most of us. Mission always has been (and always will be) about boundary-crossing, whether it be the boundary between class and race, race and gender, gender and status, status and marginality, marginality and religion. The reason for this is because such boundary-crossing invariably brings about healing and reconciliation, and thus foreshadows the coming of God's reign and kingdom *in our very midst!*

In order to meet this challenge, much more will be required of the church than vocal appeals for charity and justice, much more than timely symbolic gestures of goodwill—indeed even more will be required than the fervent "prayers of the faithful" at mass. What the parish community needs are systematic, well-organized "go" structures, structures that are permanent and well-funded and that enable the faithful to become not only a singing community on Sunday, but a boundary-crossing people on weekdays—a need, I suggest, that is aptly symbolized in the notion of "visit" or "visitation."

This changes the whole mission equation: by becoming a "guest," as Jesus so often was, the church thereby promotes the other as "host." The tables are turned, so to speak, and a whole new mission dynamic is in place. When the church assumes the vulnerability and trepidation of systematically crossing the above-mentioned boundaries and thus becoming a "guest" and not merely a "host," it then begins to listen differently, dialogue and tell its stories differently, absorb more sensitively—which is after all the first sign of compassion. As a visitor, my manners alter, my ear becomes more attentive, my language more attuned and precise. I become present to the other in a new way, a way that makes shared existence, dialogue and mutual enrichment and revelation possible.[29] The tact and mission skills required of a visitor are very different from those of a parish custodian or host, especially when the visitor comes "empty-handed" like Christ, the vulnerable visitor of God.

4. A Willingness to Espouse the Quest for Integrated Wholeness

If there is one category that is emerging as a central feature in the new postmodern sensitivity, as we have already indicated, it is that of wholeness—or more precisely, the quest for wholeness. "The cardinal doctrine of postmodernity," Ted Peters says, "is that the whole is greater than the sum of the parts, and the problem with us moderns is that we look only to the parts while ignoring the whole. An important corollary to the cardinal principle is this: everything is related to everything else."[30] The constructive implications of this growing postmodern sensitivity to interrelatedness are explored and developed at great length in such works as *Spirituality and Society* and its sequel *Sacred Interconnections*, both edited by David Ray Griffin in a series published by the State University of New York. As Peters makes abundantly clear, this quest for wholeness comes from many quarters, too numerous in fact to elaborate or go into here. It should be obvious, however, that the present study has consciously attempted to re-vision mission in the light of this postmodern quest for wholeness and the "relational web" or interconnectedness of all things and all life. Hence the insistence throughout this study on (1) the inseparability of the Christian mysteries as we have come to know and fragment them: creation-incarnation-resurrection-redemption, (2) the new vision of faith and culture as interlacing one another in a sacred connection, a nuptial union, and (3) why mission *ad intra* and mission *ad extra* must be seen as interpenetrating one another and thus forming an organic whole.

In *An American Strategic Theology*, John Coleman has correctly underscored the inseparability of another sacred couple, namely, justice *and* charity:

> Contemporary society needs once again to take a long look at charity as a social ideal and its role in American society....If charity without justice is impotent, a mockery of love, justice without charity is harsh, sometimes narrowly calculating and inhumane. Without a vision of an earthly city informed by charity, justice all too easily disintegrates into the solitary question of who gets what from whom under what form of coercive organization.[31]

Such an essential connection between the virtues is not new, of course; it harks back to scholastic theology, as when Saint Thomas says: "Justice without mercy is cruelty; mercy without justice is the mother of laxity." "Mercy does not cancel out justice; it is rather, in a manner of speaking, the plenitude of justice."[32] What is new, however, is a growing hunger and quest for a recovery of the sacred connection between justice and charity.

Clearly associated with wholeness is the ability to ask for forgiveness. One of the first things our Christian parents urged us to do early in life was: "Tell your brother [or sister] that you're sorry!" Who does not remember being so enjoined? In this respect, one of the more promising postmodern invitations of John Paul II, in his apostolic letter *The Jubilee of the Year 2000*, is his call for admissive social forgiveness on the part of the church. In both our Catholic Church and society, forgiveness has been first and foremost an event or act between individual persons. Even sacramental reconciliation is still largely a *privatized* ritual between priest and penitent. What is emerging is a public awareness that asking for social forgiveness between larger groups (for example, nations, churches, ethnic groups, etc.) is also a missionary task.[33] Like charity, the witness value and importance of asking for social forgiveness begins at home, with the institutional church itself, and must not be confused with what German theologian Dietrich Bonhoeffer called "cheap grace" or what Robert Schreiter calls a "hasty peace." The price or cost involved is nothing short of a "change of heart," or what we have traditionally called a *conversion*.

5. A Welcoming-Acceptance of Ambiguity as a Blessing Instead of a Curse

During any epoch-making transition period, such as the conjunctural paradigm shift we are now experiencing, the analogy of the "desert experience" seems most appropriate. If there is one thing that can be predicted about a desert experience, especially for a people or a church not accustomed to such an experience, it is the inevitability of having to face and live with confusion and uncertainty for a protracted period of time. The shifting, whistling sands of the desert make for poor visibility and considerable ambiguity. Many will experience a sense of strangeness and disorientation, as if the ground had been pulled out from under them. In Christian terms, the desert experience has traditionally been described as a "dark night"—indeed a dark night of the senses as well as the soul. This is a time when the faith of the Christian community is tested and purified. It can be a time of grace provided we have an appropriate spirituality to sustain us on this new journey, a spirituality, I will argue in the next chapter, that must make generous allowance for ambiguity.

10 | A Spirituality for Crossing the Postmodern Divide [1]

Langdon Gilkey has described our contemporary situation as a "time of troubles," a stormy sea or tempest, through which Christian theology must pass like a ship on the high seas.[2] The metaphor is certainly fitting and correlates with the epoch-making paradigm shift we have been discussing. There are significant points of similarity between being caught in a "tempest" on the open sea and finding oneself thrust suddenly in the swirling sands of a "desert." In either case, we feel out of sorts and out of place, vulnerable and precarious. The institutions, customs, and beliefs that gave us security and well-being in the past now appear more and more problematic and ineffective, and the same question invariably arises: How is it possible credibly to speak of hope in a situation such as this?[3] For many Catholics in America, this question is bound to sit persistently on the edge of their consciousness well into the third millennium. In fact, as we continue to make our way across the postmodern divide, we can expect that this soul-searching question will loom ever larger in the spiritual life of Christians. Increasingly, it will come to dominate any meaningful discussion of the church's mission *ad intra* as well as *ad extra*.

The first thing that must be said about any new spirituality for our times is that it must be provisional and transitional, one that is intentionally geared to our postmodern rite of passage. Such a spirituality must foster what the French call *le dynamique du provisoire*, the ability to seize and make good use of fleeting opportunities. It will also make generous allowance for raising fundamental doubts and questions instead of raising false expectations and bogus spiritual security. Letting God be God for us in times such as these means traveling with him as a pilgrim people with questions. The poet Rainer Maria Rilke suggests the right inner attitude when he invites us

> to be patient toward all that is unsolved in your heart and try to love the *questions themselves*....Do not now seek the answers, which

159

cannot be given you because you would not be able to live them. And the point is, to live everything. *Live* the questions now. Perhaps you will then gradually, without noticing it, live along some distant day into the answer.[4]

Living the questions, wrestling in the darkness of faith and ambiguity, must come to be seen as a blessing in disguise and not necessarily a curse. What is needed, therefore, is a spirituality of openness and honesty, one where those who question or doubt have no need to fear being condemned or marginalized in the church. In any crucial rite of passage, learning to ask the right question is always more important than knowing the answer—as Perceval's quest for the holy grail makes abundantly clear:

> It is a very remarkable fact that just at the time of the high flowering of chivalry (Perceval), whose most essential characteristics were a spiritual search and an undoubted lack of certainty, amounting even to a burden of guilt, should take the stage alongside the perfect Christian knights (Gauvain, Galahad) as the most important figure in the Grail legend. A higher value is placed on the more human hero than on the conventional noble knight, for to be able to doubt oneself, to grope one's lonely way, step by uncertain step, appears to represent a higher achievement of consciousness than naively to follow collective ideals.[5]

It is also a remarkable fact that Pope Paul VI, very much in tune with the religious sensitivity of our time, should express the same idea and sentiments we find in the above quotation. This he does, for example, on the occasion of the beatification of a certain Leonard Murialdo:

> We want to discover in the saints whatever brings them close to us rather than whatever sets them apart; we want to put them on our level as human beings, plunged into the sometimes unedifying experiences of this world, and to find in them sharers of our labor and, perhaps also, of our misery so that we might have confidence in them and share with them the common and burdensome state of our earthly existence.[6]

How one "befriends" and "lives with" a deep question, how one learns to "carry" and "hold" it—*preciously* (as one might when finding a pearl of great value), and *tenderly* (as one would an infant close to our heart)—is of the essence of a mission spirituality. The principal reason why this is important is because the Spirit of God uses our deep questionings to lead us through the desert. Alan Ecclestone, in *The Night Sky of the Lord*, is right in saying:

> It is a function of the Spirit, as Jews and Christians have known it, to enter searchingly into man's house, and there to put questions, now like a breath, and now like a wind, to try all things that it finds there, to question their fitness to endure. The process in our own night-sky is one of near gale-force winds. It is a delusion to suppose that the disturbing questions will, if ignored, go away, if suppressed, be forgotten, or that by hiding ourselves like naked Adam we can escape them. It is no less delusive to expect that we shall get comforting answers to our questionings. To live with our uncertainties is not simply a necessary part of our education at all levels: it is the very truth of faith. To endure the sifting process of interrogation is the hall-mark of discipleship.[7]

To ask the question "Is hope possible in today's changing world?" raises the concomitant question: Can I live with ambiguity? Is my tolerance of ambiguity such that I am able to grow spiritually in and through the present historical paradigm shift? Far from being the enemy of the spiritual life, a tolerance of ambiguity, I will argue, is vital to our life of faith, especially during a rite of passage such as the one we are experiencing today. We forget too often that tolerance also is a grace of God—indeed a divine attribute of the God of Jesus Christ—and that ambiguity is a summons to believe, not a cause to despair.

Ambiguity is a phenomenon with which we are all familiar. If we think about it at all, it probably appears to us as something rather unsettling, unpleasant, perhaps even threatening. The experience of ambiguity, especially as it impinges upon those vital areas of our Christian life and identity, is not something we welcome, nor are we inclined to see it as a positive element in our life of faith. Although there is much ambiguity in our world today, at home as well as abroad, here I want to focus on that peculiar ambiguity which attaches itself to Christian faith, and hence also to the unresolved issues we surfaced in Part One of this study. I will argue that ambiguity is not hostile or inimical to faith, but on the contrary is an integral dimension of faith itself, an abiding and necessary summons to believe, and that to have lost this important ability to hear God sing in the night is to have lost a singular opportunity to possess our faith in a deeper and more vital way.

To say that ambiguity is an integral part of Christian existence is a theological and pastoral understatement. Not only do we experience ambiguity at certain awkward moments, as when we have to make difficult moral decisions or on those special occasions when we deliberately place ourselves in a posture of Christian discernment. Ambiguity exists at the very heart of our life of faith. Faith never yields that kind of certainty which would eliminate all ambiguity and doubt in the believer's consciousness and lived experience. On this score, the Council of Trent was very explicit: "No one can know with the certainty of faith that he has obtained the grace of God" (Denz. 802). Nor do we know for sure that our sins have indeed been forgiven by God, or that we will in fact persevere to the end and be saved (Denz. 823, 806). In more recent times, Karl Rahner has shown in what sense the reformation formula *Simul justus et peccator* (justified and sinner at the same time), when properly understood, is in accordance with Catholic teaching and theology.[8]

In a seminal and truly remarkable study some years ago, Johannes Metz showed how it is no longer possible to make a clear-cut distinction between belief and unbelief in the actual life of a Christian, that belief and unbelief are real, conflicting elements within the activity of believing itself.[9] The failure to recognize or appreciate this theological truth, I am convinced, has contributed to a certain misguided fundamentalism within the church and to the unwarranted alienation of many believers who now find themselves on the so-called periphery or margin of the church. It is my contention that the church's intolerance of ambiguity and its overconcern with certitude are part of the problem, not the answer, and that ambiguity cannot be eliminated from the mysterious ways God "seduces" and lovingly draws us to himself. This is why we must pay much closer attention to the manifestations of the Spirit "in the lives of those who have been pushed or shoved to the margins of church and society."[10] Their personal experience of ambiguity can teach us many things about the life of faith. Through them, the church has the good fortune of discovering anew that true mission goes hand in hand with evangelical poverty. To accept, as they do, our own ambiguous insecurities is already to live poverty.

Belated Acceptance of Ambiguity in Western Culture

In our western culture, "ambiguity" has long been a pejorative term, something to be eliminated if at all possible. This reflects the general bias in our civilization which, from classical Greek times, put so much confidence in reason and gave such pride of place to the unbroken quest for clarity, precision, exactness, and certainty. In such a cultural context, ambiguity could only be regarded as an *enfant terrible*, a temporary annoyance or threat that was to be eliminated as quickly as possible. It represented a failure in the reasoning process and was generally attributed to either excessive brevity, to a deliberate attempt to distort the truth, or just simply to faulty logic. In philosophy, the acceptance of ambiguity came only in the twentieth century. Earlier thinkers, like Russell, Wittgenstein in his *Tractatus*, and Husserl, tried to overcome ambiguity and leave it behind. The later Wittgenstein, Merleau-Ponty, and the existentialists like Sartre and Simone de Beauvoir accept ambiguity and make it the basis of their philosophies.

It was only some forty years ago that psychologists began studying the question of ambiguity explicitly and why it is that certain individuals have more difficulty than others coping with ambiguous situations. They discovered, for example, that authoritarian personalities had a lower tolerance for ambiguity than did people in general.[11] In psychological terms, intolerance of ambiguity is the tendency to perceive (or interpret) an ambiguous situation as a source of threat. Many studies of intolerance of ambiguity have since been conducted by means of questionnaires, interviews, projective tests, systematic observation, and experimental research. The focus of most of this research has been to determine how intolerance of ambiguity relates to other personality traits.[12] Their research findings have shown—indeed have shown quite convincingly—that people who are intolerant of ambiguity are more than likely to evince one or more of the following traits: low self-esteem, rigidity in thinking, close-mindedness, dogmatism, anxiety, strong ethno-centrism, religious fundamentalism, conformity, prejudice, and low creativity. Carl Jung had of course perceived ambiguity as an inescapable dimension of being human, indeed at the heart of the human psyche—what he called the *animus* and the *anima*. More significantly, he saw it as a necessary precondition for any real growth and development, a point well made in the following passage:

> Life itself flows from springs both clear and muddy. Hence all excessive "purity" lacks vitality. A constant striving for clarity and differentiation means a proportionate loss of vital intensity precisely because the muddy elements are excluded. Every renewal of all life needs the muddy as well as the clear.[13]

Of course there has always been a significant minority of individuals in our cultural history who looked more kindly on ambiguity—indeed who seem to have actually thrived on it. I am referring of course to the artists, the poets, and the mystics. For them, ambiguity was often the very focus of their creative talents and insights. One need only think of the multiplicity of meanings and hence the ambiguity in a work like

Dante's *Divina comedia*, or Shakespeare's *Hamlet*, a play and a character which have both become synonymous with ambiguity. The same is true of visual or aesthetic ambiguity, as in Da Vinci's "Mona Lisa" or Vermeer's "An Artist in His Studio." And the great mystics in our western culture, too, those who experienced a "close encounter" with God, with the Holy One, invariably speak of this experience as most ambiguous—something bewildering yet fascinating beyond compare. Were we to excise all the ambiguities in the works of John of the Cross, Teresa of Avila, Meister Eckhart, or Ruysbroec, for example, there would be little or nothing left of their mystical experiences and stories. In a moment of great candor, Saint Bernard will tell his fellow monks for example:

> Now bear with my foolishness for a little. I want to tell you of my own experience....I admit that the Word has also come to me—I speak as a fool—and has come many times. But although he has come to me, I have never been conscious of the moment of his coming. I perceived his presence, I remembered afterwards that he had been with me; sometimes I had the presentiment that he would come, but I was never conscious of his coming or going. And where he comes from when he visits my soul, and where he goes, and by what means he enters and goes out, I admit that I do not know even now....He never made known his coming by any signs, not by sight, not by sound, not by touch....Only by the movement of my heart did I perceive his presence.[14]

What is noteworthy in this passage is the way Bernard describes the mysterious elusive presence of the Word and his own ambiguous yet no less real experience of it. I am convinced that every Catholic in America, if invited or given a chance, if given some little spiritual self-confidence, would be able to voice their own similar mystical experiences, and do so, moreover, with as much faith conviction and Pauline "foolishness" as Bernard has succeeded in doing. I am also suggesting that their personal stories of such "close encounters" with God will be, like Bernard's, of a divinely elusive and ambiguous nature. This also means that intolerance of ambiguity has enormous implications for mission *ad intra* and *ad extra*, as well as for the way one's "Catholic identity" or affiliation to the church is perceived and reckoned. Throughout history the ongoing debate about who belongs to the church and the criteria against which Christian identification is measured have always been conditioned by the degree of intolerance of ambiguity that prevails in the church at any given time. Thus it comes as no surprise that Saint Augustine acknowledged the ambiguity of church membership when he wrote: "Some seem to be inside [the church] who are in fact outside, while others seem to be outside who are in fact inside."[15]

Clearly, there are many ambiguities in Catholic Church life today, many different ways of interpreting scriptural texts, many differing theological viewpoints, a plurality of convictions about what *really* constitutes a Christian lifestyle in today's world. Indeed many of the faithful are presently living in what can only be described as a "limbo" of ecclesiastical ambiguity: the divorced and remarried, the gay and lesbian members of the Christian community, those whose conscience compels them to use artificial means of birth control, those who are in favor of a married clergy and the ordination of women, the feminists in a church that is still male-dominated, or the many who are spiritually hungry and who are looking elsewhere for spiritual enrichment. What we need, therefore, is a theology and spirituality of ambiguity, one that can capitalize on the ambiguous times in which we live and that will secure or at least steady our passage across the postmodern divide. What follows is an attempt to articulate the theological basis of just such a spirituality.

The God of Biblical Revelation

The God of Abraham, Isaac, and Jacob reveals himself but always with an essential and ambiguous reserve: as the one who is far and yet near, who is unapproachable and yet who beckons us to come closer, who is intangible and yet can be violated. He reveals himself in history and yet always seems to be receding from it. In the biblical account of salvation history, the free, unsolicited advances that God is forever making on our behalf are always steeped in profound ambiguity. At times he appears as wonderful (in the sense of performing wonders that cause amazement), aweful (in the sense of inspiring awe), terrible (in the sense of awakening terror), and overwhelming (in the sense of being beyond our control or manipulation). At other times he appears gracious, inviting, comforting, enabling and fulfilling. In short, he is the Holy One, the *mysterium tremendum et fascinans*: absolutely terrifying and utterly fascinating.

It comes as little surprise, then, that those who put their trust in such a God will themselves be ambiguous in their stance before him. On the one hand, we want to distance ourselves from him, like Simon Peter who said: "Depart from me, O Lord, for I am a sinful man" (Lk 5:8). But even as we say this, we also experience that secret longing which the disciples of Emmaus knew so well: "Stay with us, for it is nearly evening and the day is almost over" (Lk 24:29). Thus our identity as believers is always ambiguous: we are secure and yet homeless, "in the world yet not of the world," restless seekers and yet the prodigal who has already made it home. One would have thought that with the incarnation, things would have become much clearer, less ambiguous. What we often forget is that incarnation always means more ambiguity—not less! Of all the *magnalia dei*, the great acts of God, surely the incarnation is by far the one that generates the most ambiguity. Human nature is ambiguous in itself. Even St. Thomas recognized this when he said: "In us there is not only the pleasure that we share with the beasts, but also the pleasure we share with the angels."[16] But when human nature and divine nature are conjoined in a hypostatic union, one has the makings of untold ambiguity.

Let us examine some of the basic ambiguity that surrounded the historical figure of Jesus: how he deliberately created ambiguity and how he himself experienced it. This will help us to see that ambiguity need not be something which has to be avoided or eliminated at all cost, but can indeed be a divinely-appointed grace, a "blessing in disguise," a positive invitation to trust in the Lord.

Jesus Creates and Endures Ambiguity

When we focus on the life of Jesus, ambiguity seems to surround him at every turn. Moreover, he was very conscious of this: "Who do people say that I am?" he asked, and the answers he received varied considerably (Mt 16:13-16). Those who encountered him felt a basic strangeness in his nature. They did not know quite how they stood with him. Again and again they tried to fit him into their ordinary scheme of things, but they never succeeded. He struck them as being too ambiguous—open, that is, to too many possible and even contradictory interpretations. We see this inherent ambiguity of Jesus, for example, in the way he presented himself to his followers as both master and servant. Jesus is Lord and master—he knows it and says so (Mt 10:25). Yet he is also one who came "not to be served by others but to serve" (Mt 20:28). And even when he tries to remove the distance between himself and his disciples, he nevertheless underlines it, as when he says: "A servant is no greater than his master. If they persecuted me, they will persecute you too" (Jn 15:10). The ambiguity here stems from the fact that he presents himself as absolute master and as absolute servant. He is a servant who remains a master and a master who never ceases to be a servant. We know that Simon Peter, in particular, had difficulty coping with this ambiguity when Jesus tried to wash his feet (Jn 13:4-11).

Jesus was being deliberately ambiguous when he told the high priests and elders that even the village prostitutes were further on the road to the kingdom of God than they were (Mt 21:31-32). The Old Testament prophets had often used this image of the prostitute to symbolize Israel's infidelity and estrangement from God. How could prostitutes now be signaled out for commendation? If there was any truth in Jesus' words—even a grain of truth—why wrap it in such ambiguity? Why run counter to the well-established norms and criteria of favor in God's sight? Not only does Jesus reverse the existing identities through the prostitute symbol (the righteous becoming the sinners and sinners becoming somehow justified), but he actually calls into question the way in which one's neighbor was hitherto perceived and judged.

Nor can we overlook the ambiguity created by the sort of company Jesus kept and the way he freely associated with women of ill-repute: the notorious sinful woman of the city (Lk 7:36-50), the adulteress (Jn 8:2-11), the Samaritan woman known to have had six husbands (Jn 4:5-27), or the one with a long-standing "flow of blood" (Mk 5:25-34). Public comportment of this kind was bound to send out "mixed" signals and give rise to some contentious ambiguity. Jesus' own tolerance of ambiguity can be seen in the remarkable patience he had with those of his followers who were hesitant and still very tentative in their response to his message. When the twelve were tempted one day to eliminate some of the existing ambiguity in Jesus' following, he told them the parable of the weeds (Mt 13:24-30): how the good and the bad must be allowed to live together until the final judgment. By his own reckoning, Jesus' followers would always be ˜n improbable, unseemly, ambiguous lot! It was not so much *despite* this ambiguity but rather *because* of it that Jesus was able to reveal God's loving patience. What was yesterday's useless weed may become, through grace, tomorrow's fruitful plant. The misfits of society may turn out to be its prophets; today's sinner, tomorrow's saint. Jesus was not one to crush the bruised weed or quench the smoldering wick (Mt 16:20). He would be patient, but patience, as we know, creates its own ambiguity.

So does deliberate discretion and silence (and our four gospels attribute a lot of both to Jesus). It is curious and doubtless revealing that Jesus never once on his own took the floor to say who he was. Formal statements concerning his person in the synoptics always come from someone other than he. Moreover, Jesus left many questions unanswered, and it certainly wasn't for lack of opportunity that he didn't make his positions clearer and less ambiguous. This silence and reserve on the part of Jesus was without doubt a major cause of ambiguity for his contemporaries.

The gospels not only give evidence that Jesus created ambiguity for others, but that he himself experienced it also. It is one of the truly great divine ironies that the very ambiguity which Jesus created through his silence would be visited upon him when the drama of his own life was about to reach its climax. At Gethsemane and on the cross, Jesus experiences the real agony of ambiguity since it stemmed from the utter silence of precisely the One he had grown accustomed to call "Abba"—Daddy, dear Father! The God that he had known up to this hour was almighty and all-good, a God who could have chosen for him an entirely different mission path to arrive at the same goal. Now he appears as the inexorable God of justice. Hence the ambiguity: "My God, my God, why have you forsaken me?" (Mt 27:46)

What this great mystery illustrates is that ambiguity, however threatening, harbors a singular grace: it can unleash the most ferocious instincts of fear and abandonment, while at the same time it can expand the souls of those who put their complete and ultimate trust in God. As with Jesus, or Mary, who on more than one occasion exclaimed "How is this possible?" or Abraham, our father in faith, ambiguity invites us to reach down deeper within ourselves and there, in the "dark night of the soul," to surrender more completely to the God of mystery. In short, ambiguity provides the invitation, while the Spirit within gives us the grace to respond.

Thus we come to discern the divine mystagogy of ambiguity, its dynamic pattern and "inner logic." The ambiguity that Jesus created stems basically from the dialectic of veiling and unveiling which characterized his humanity. In Jesus, the incarnate Word, God is both unveiled and veiled, manifested but still hidden, self-declared yet not forced upon us with the kind of clarity and overwhelming evidence that would remove all ambiguity—and thus our very freedom. The mystery and deeper reality of Jesus' person is never given as a clear and indisputable fact. Then as now, he reveals himself only in the shadowy light of the human condition and through the "clair-obscur" of human mediations, symbols that are by nature polysemic and therefore ambiguous.

In order for Jesus to truly reveal himself, it was not enough to speak clearly or even act decisively: what he said had to be understood and believed. He could not simply say who he was and expect people to really understand him; he could not express the full mystery of his person in any known word or human form of expression. Otherwise we would have been left with just that—*human* concepts and nothing more! Of course he had to use human words and vocabulary to reveal himself, words whose meaning would make some sense to us. But he also had to draw us beyond these human parables and symbols, beyond these finite, human forms of expression. He had to do this so that we might surrender to a higher wisdom, a *divine* revelation, and hence something beyond our natural capacity to comprehend.

The only way Jesus could do this was through a mystagogy of ambiguity, that is, by telling us only as much as we needed to know, yet not enough to make us think that he was only communicating human wisdom and not a divine revelation. Thus much of the ambiguity that Jesus created was intended as an *invitation* to explore and probe deeper, to come closer, and be asked that only meaningful and deeply personal question: "And you, who do *you* say that I am?" Jesus' ambiguity—whether in his words, silence, or actions—always placed the witness in a position in which this question could not be avoided. Only then might the mystery of a divine revelation become effectively received as invitation, as a personal R.S.V.P., with the real possibility of either surrendering to it or forever being culpable for rejecting it. In short, *ambiguity creates the kind of space necessary for the possibility of faith.*

The Ambiguous Truth About Faith

From everything we have seen thus far, ambiguity can be described as the *climate* of faith, the *condition of its possibility*: neither its ground, nor its goal or perfection, but rather a penultimate means of grace in a world whose final salvation remains an object of hope. For as St. Paul says, "In hope we were saved. But hope is not hope if its object is seen; how is it possible to hope for what one can actually see? But hoping for what we cannot see means awaiting it with patient endurance" (Rom 8:24-25). The New Testament writers affirm in various ways that "we walk by faith, not by sight" (2 Cor 5:7), and that faith only allows us to see "dimly" or "indistinctly," as in a mirror (1 Cor 13:12). Thomas Merton the monk would put it this way:

> The very obscurity of faith is an argument of its perfection. It is darkness to our minds because it so far transcends their weakness. The more perfect faith is, the darker it becomes. The closer we get to God, the less is our faith diluted with the half-light of created images and concepts.[17]

Church authorities and church leaders would do well to concede that this describes fairly accurately the actual experience of many believers today—including the many who have taken some distance from external religion and the church as institution. This is another way of saying that if in the past the church has been a good teacher, a good *pedagogue*, it must now become an even better *mystagogue*. And the difference, as we said earlier, is crucial. It was Jean Guitton, I believe, who said: "Dans le domaine des problèmes, il faut être enseigné; mais dans le domaine du mystère, il faut être initié." The language and discourse of a teacher, for the most part, will be conceptual, rational, and logical. It will focus mainly on what can be known, validated, and reasonably expressed. The language of a mystagogue, on the other hand, is essentially a language of mystery, a language of the religious imagination, one that invites us to cross over and beyond what meets the eye, beyond what can be known or seen directly—in short, one that initiates us into the mystery by which "we live and move and have our being."

The ultimate conviction and decision to believe does not depend on the degree of manifest certitude that the church possesses or displays, but on the inner promptings welling up and bursting forth within us of God's playful and absolutely free Spirit. Meister Eckhart, another great mystic, captured something of this playful divine ambiguity when he says: "God is like a person who clears his throat while hiding and so gives himself away."[18] Saint Augustine is no less mystical or profound when he says of the ascension: "Admirable is the mystery of Christ sitting at the right hand of God: he hid himself from us that we might believe in him; he was taken from us that we might hope in him."[19] In his great text *On Christian Doctrine*, Saint Augustine even maintains that God provides some ambiguities and obscurities in the bible *for our benefit*! In his close examination of this classic work, David Tracy concludes: "In sum, for Augustine, the principle of the theological value of obscurity and ambiguity allows him to argue for the scriptures as the new classic signs—wiser and even more eloquent than his own beloved pagan classics."[20] It was Pascal, however, who made the ambiguity of God's manifestations central to his whole theology. The following passage is worth quoting since its relevance for our own time in the postmodern desert of ambiguity is too great to ignore. In a letter to Madame de Roannez, he says:

> This great secrecy into which God has withdrawn, impenetrable to the gaze of men, is a great lesson for us....He remained hidden, under the veil of nature which hides him from us, until the incarnation; and when it was necessary for him to appear, he hid himself even more by covering himself with humanity. He was much more recognizable when he was invisible than after he made himself visible. And finally...he chose to remain in the strangest and most obscure secrecy of all, the species of the Eucharist. It is this sacrament which Saint John calls, in the Apocalypse, a hidden

manna; and I believe that Isaiah saw him in this state when he said in the spirit of prophecy: Truly you are a hidden God.[21]

Troublesome, disconcerting, and at times pervasive, ambiguity has always been experienced by "those who have gone before us, marked with the sign of faith." Ambiguity is nothing new in the history of the church and our experience of it today is neither unique nor unprecedented. We need only recall (to take but one example) the extent to which the early church was plunged into ambiguity as a result of the ongoing delay of the *parousia*, the "second coming." What is significant here is that despite their fervent expectation of the imminent return of Jesus in power and glory, the early Christians never allowed the delay of the parousia to develop into an acute crisis of faith. Their ambiguity was real, however, and it ran deep! While they became increasingly involved in the day-to-day running and organization of the visible church, they were never quite sure this was the Christian thing to do. Was it not a betrayal of Jesus' promise to return soon? Was it not tantamount to planting shade trees under which the church felt it would never sit?

Throughout this time of uncertainty and ambiguity, the early church forced no pseudo-clarity into the picture. The Christians not only learned to live with this ambiguity but, even more significant, it was this very ambiguity that quickened their faith and taught them to renew—on a daily, ongoing basis—their abiding trust and unqualified hope in the risen Lord. Even the apostle Paul himself gradually came to realize that he had misread Jesus' ambiguous statements about an imminent end of the world. The delay of the parousia certainly raised many questions. But it is precisely because these questions were never stifled, never prematurely foreclosed, never given a final or overly authoritative answer, that sufficient space was created in the church for Christian hope to become contagious. Like the mysterious *manna* that nourished the Israelites in the desert, the early church came to rely on God, *one day at a time*! In this, especially, it proved to be inspired and boldly creative.

At any time, then, but especially in a time of pervasive ambiguity such as the turn of our century is proving to be, we see faith operating at its best when it trusts in God amid an encircling lack of security, that "dark night of the senses" which the great saints and mystics describe so well.[22] Such faith may seem like a "leap in the dark"—for indeed that is what it is—but it is in taking such a risk that faith is purified, our chances of a closer encounter with God are enhanced, and our beliefs become more fully aligned and integrated with our real life experiences. Moreover, it is fitting to recall that God sings some of his best songs in the night, or as Léon Bloy put it: "DEUS DEDIT CARMINA IN

NOCTE." From a very tender age, every Catholic seems to have known the wonder and truth of this mystery. This is no doubt why the church has always liked to keep night vigils, and why we continue to chant the venerable words at the Easter vigil: "*O vere beata nox*"—O truly blessed night! Whether in a stable in Bethlehem or at an empty tomb in Jerusalem, Jesus seems always to have awaited the world at night to hear his Father sing. To follow Jesus in this "way" seems most appropriate as a spirituality for our time and our mission today.

Notes

1. Why a New Utterance About Mission?

[1] Amos N. Wilder, *Early Christian Rhetoric* (Cambridge: Harvard University Press, 1978), pp. 1-17. See also Christine Mohrmann, *Etudes sur le latin des chretiens*, Tome I (Roma: Editioni di Storia e Letteratura, 1961), especially Chap. 5, "Linguistic Problems in the Early Church," pp. 103-111.

[2] Thomas Moore (ed.), *A Blue Fire: Selected Writing of James Hillman* (New York: Harper & Row, 1989), pp. 28-29.

[3] Karl Rahner, "Priest and Poet," in *The Word: Readings in Theology* (New York: P.J. Kenedy & Sons, 1964), p. 4.

[4] Norman Perrin, *The New Testament: An Introduction* (New York: Harcourt Brace Jovanovich, 1974), p. 295.

[5] David Bosch, *Transforming Mission: Paradigm Shifts in Theology of Mission* (Maryknoll, NY: Orbis Books, 1991), p. 511.

[6] Edouard Loffeld, *Le problème cardinal de la missiologie et des missions catholiques* (Rhenen: Editions "Spiritus," 1956), p. 17.

[7] Bosch, *op. cit.*, p. 1.

[8] Vatican II, *Ad Gentes* 2.

[9] Eugene Lapointe, "Le paradigme contemporain de la mission," in *Kerygma*, 25 (1991), p. 237.

[10] See A.-M. Henry, "Missions d'hier, mission de demain," coll. "Unam Sanctam," 67 (Paris: Editions du Cerf, 1967), pp. 411-440.

[11] See Henri Holstein, "Quel est le sens du mot 'mission'?" in *Spiritus*, 25 (December 1965), pp. 371-380.

[12] A.-V. Seumois, *Introduction à la missiologie* (Schoneck-Beckenried, 1952), p. 62.

[13] John Paul II, *Redemptoris Missio*, 31-34.

[14] Carlos Mesters, "Listening to What the Spirit Is Saying to the Churches: Popular Interpretation of the Bible in Brazil," in *Concilium* 1 (1991), pp. 100-111.

[15] For a comprehensive overview and rigorous evaluation of these major changes in the discipline of hermeneutics, see Anthony

173

Thiselton, *New Horizons in Hermeneutics* (Grand Rapids: Zondervan Publishing House, 1992).

[16] Charles Mabee, *Reimagining America. A Theological Critique of the American Mythos and Biblical Hermeneutics* (Macon, GA: Mercer University Press, 1985), p. ix.

[17] See also the excellent issue of *Concilium* 1 (1991), which carries the title "The Bible and Its Readers."

[18] Pontifical Biblical Commission, "The Interpretation of the Bible in the Church," in *Origins*, Vol. 23, No. 29 (January 6, 1994), esp. pp. 500-510.

[19] Claude Geffré, *The Risk of Interpretation: On Being Faithful to the Christian Tradition in a Non-Christian Age* (New York: Paulist Press, 1987), p. 167. On this point see also the summary E. Schillebeeckx makes of his theological methodology in *Expérience humaine et foi en Jésus-Christ* (Paris: Ed. du Cerf, 1981), esp. pp. 29-64.

[20] Sandra M. Schneiders, *The Revelatory Text: Interpreting the New Testament as Sacred Scripture* (New York: HarperCollins Publishers, 1991) and *Beyond Patching: Faith and Feminism in the Catholic Church* (New York: Paulist Press, 1991).

[21] While pluralism has always existed in one form or another in theology, Karl Rahner describes today's pluralistic situation as a "qualitatively new" state of affairs. For a theological analysis of pluralism, see his "Pluralism in Theology and the Unity of the Creed in the Church," in *Theological Investigations,* Vol. 11 (New York: Seabury Press, 1974), pp. 3-23.

[22] C.G. Jung, *Collected Works*, Volume II, "A Psychological to the Dogma of the Trinity," pp. 109-111, 117, 153, 188; "The Psychology of Christian Alchemical Symbolism," pp. 174-176, 181.

[23] See Karl Rahner's caution about putting unrealistic expectations on faith, *Grace and Freedom* (New York: Herder and Herder, 1969), p. 69.

[24] John Riches, "Present-day Eucharistic Spirituality," *Theology* (April 1974), p. 177. For an excellent in-depth study of the erosion of Christian symbolism, see Jean Borella, *La crise du symbolisme religieux* (Lausanne: Age d'Homme, 1990).

[25] Paul Tillich, "The Lost Dimension in Religion," in *The Religious Experience*, George Brantl (ed.), Vol. 2 (New York: George Braziller, 1964), pp. 590-591.

[26] See Monica Wilson, *Religion and the Transformation of Society: A Study in Social Change in Africa* (London: Cambridge University Press, 1971).

[27] See Wayne Meeks, *The First Urban Christians: The Social World of the Apostle Paul* (New Haven: Yale University Press, 1982).

[28] James W. Heisig, "Symbolism," in *The Encyclopedia of Religion* (New York: Macmillan Publishing Co., 1987), Mircea Eliade (ed.), Vol. 14, p. 207.

[29] Langdon Gilkey, "The Crisis of Christianity in North America," in *Morphologies of Faith: Essays in Religion and Culture in Honor of Nathan A. Scott, Jr.,* ed. Mary Gerhart, Anthony C. Yu (Atlanta: Scholars Press, 1990), p. 41.

[30] See John Kirby, "Symbolism and Dogmatism: Voegelin's Distinction," in *The Ecumenist* (Jan.-Feb. 1975), pp. 26-31.

[31] See Karl Rahner, "What the Church Officially Teaches and What the People Actually Believe," in *Theological Investigations* (New York: Crossroad, 1991), Vol. XXII, pp. 165-175.

[32] Ernest Skublics, "Psychologically Living Symbolism and Liturgy," in *Carl Jung and Christian Spirituality*, ed. Robert L. Moore (New York: Paulist Press, 1988), p. 216.

[33] See Bernard J. Cooke, *The Distancing of God: The Ambiguity of Symbol in History and Theology* (Minneapolis: Fortress Press, 1990).

[34] Walbert Bühlmann, *With Eyes to See: Church and World in the Third Millennium* (Maryknoll: Orbis Books, 1990).

[35] David Bosch, *Dynamique de la mission chrétienne* (Paris: Karthala, 1995).

2. An Uneasy Dialogue in the American Catholic Church

[1] Robert Schreiter, *Constructing Local Theologies* (Maryknoll: Orbis Books, 1985), pp. 25-36.

[2] Hans Urs von Balthasar, *Science, Religion and Christianity* (London: Burns & Oates, 1958), pp. 142-155.

[3] David O'Brien, "The Church and American Culture During Our Nation's Lifetime, 1787-1987," in *The Catholic Church and American Culture,* ed. Cassian Yuhaus (New York: Paulist Press, 1990), pp. 1-23. For a lively history of the American Catholic Church from colonial days to the present, see William Faherty, *American Catholic Heritage* (Kansas City, MO: Sheed & Ward, 1991).

[4] Richard McBrien, "Conflict in the Church: Redefining the Center," *America* (August 1992), pp. 78-81.

[5] José Casanova, *Public Religions in the Modern World* (Chicago: University of Chicago Press, 1994), p. 223.

[6] Quoted in *National Catholic Reporter* (May 29, 1992), p. 20.

[7] The expression is from Sister Maureen Fiedler, a director of Catholics Speak Out.

[8] For a comprehensive coverage and the findings of this poll, see *National Catholic Reporter* (October 8, 1993), pp. 21-31. The same religious phenomenon has been well documented in the Canadian church as well: see Reginald Bibby, *Fragmented Gods: The Poverty and Potential of Religion in Canada* (Toronto: Irwin Publishing, 1987).

[9] Ibid., p. 23.

[10] For more national data collected and analyzed, see "The End of American Catholicism?—Another Look," in *America* (May 1, 1993), pp. 4-9; George Gallup, Jr., and Jim Castelli, *The American Catholic People: Their Beliefs, Practices, and Values* (Garden City: Doubleday & Co., 1987); Eugene Kennedy, *Tomorrow's Catholics Yesterday's Church: The Two Cultures of American Catholicism* (New York: Harper & Row, 1990); Andrew Greeley, *The Catholic Myth: The Behavior and Beliefs of American Catholics* (New York: Collier Books, 1991). See also the more extensive National Survey of Religious Identification (NSRI) in Barry A. Kosmin and Seymour P. Lachman, *One Nation Under God: Religion in Contemporary America* (New York: Harmony Press, 1993).

[11] See Ralph Della Cava, "Vatican Policy, 1978-90: An Updated Overview," in *Social Research* 59:1 (Spring 1992).

[12] Quoted in *National Catholic Reporter* (May 18, 1990), p. 3.

[13] Quoted by Dolores Leckey, in *The Future of the Catholic Church in America* (Collegeville: The Liturgical Press, 1991), p. 82.

[14] See Katarina Schuth, *Reasons for Hope: The Future of Roman Catholic Theologates* (Wilmington: Michael Glazier, 1989).

[15] For a timely discussion of "Catholic Identity" today, see *Concilium* 5 (1994).

[16] Andrew Greeley, *Crisis in the Church: A Study of Religion in America* (Chicago: Thomas More Press, 1979), especially Chap. 6, "Who Are the Communal Catholics?" See also his article, "Why Catholics Stay in the Church," in *America* (August 8, 1987), pp. 54-57, 70.

[17] Karl Rahner, *Theological Investigations*, Vol. 12 (London: Darton, Longman & Todd, 1974), pp. 112-113.

[18] José Casanova, *Public Religions in the Modern World*, p. 206.

[19] Augustine, *De bapt.*, V: 27, 28. See also *De civ. Dei*, I:35 and *In Joan. Ev.*, tr. XXVII: 11 and tr. XLV: 12.

[20] Robert Kress, "Religious Indifference—Definition and Criteria," in *Concilium* (5/1983), pp. 11-19. See also his article, "Religiously Indifferent or Religiously Different?" in *Kerygma* (24/1990), pp. 143-159.

[21] Kress, ibid., p. 13.

²² John Coleman, "American Culture as a Challenge to Catholic Intellectuals," in *The Catholic Church and American Culture* (New York: Paulist Press, 1990), Cassian Yuhaus, ed., p. 44.

²³ Paul VI, *Evangelii Nuntiandi* (December 8, 1975), 20.

²⁴ William Faherty, *American Catholic Heritage* (Kansas City, MO: Sheed & Ward, 1991), pp. 42-43.

²⁵ See Eugene Bianchi & Rosemary Ruether, eds. *A Democratic Catholic Church: The Reconstruction of Roman Catholicism* (New York: Crossroad, 1993).

²⁶ Kosman and Lachman, *One Nation Under God,* p. 256. For statistical data, see pp. 256-269.

²⁷ Richard John Neuhaus, *The Catholic Moment: The Paradox of the Church in the Postmodern World* (San Francisco: Harper & Row, 1987), p. 283.

²⁸ For more on this, see Gustave Weigel, *The Modern God: Faith in a Secular Culture* (New York: The Macmillan Co., 1963), especially Chapter 5, "The Church and the Public Conscience," pp. 153-168.

²⁹ José Casanova, *Public Religions in the Modern World,* p. 204.

³⁰ *National Catholic Reporter* (October 27, 1989), p. 11.

³¹ Allan Deck, *The Second Wave: Hispanic Ministry and the Evangelization of Cultures* (New York: Paulist Press, 1989), p. 2.

³² Ibid., p. 12.

³³ Joseph P. Fitzpatrick, *One Church Many Cultures. Challenge of Diversity* (Kansas City, MO: Sheed & Ward, 1987), pp. 125-161.

³⁴ Kosman and Lachman, *One Nation Under God,* pp. 127-128.

3. Re-Visioning Inculturation

¹ See the conference given by Fr. Segura entitled, "L'initiation, valeur permanente en vue de l'inculturation," in *Mission et cultures non-chrétiennes. Rapports et compte rendu de la XXIXe Semaine de Missiologie. Louvain 1959* (Bruges: Desclée de Brouwer, 1959), pp. 219-235.

² Cited by Msgr. Coffy, in *Documentation Catholique,* no. 1731 (December 4, 1977), p. 1036. My translation.

³ For the genesis and early interpretation of this term, see P. Arrupe, "Lettre et document de travail sur l'inculturation," in *Acta Romana Societatis Jesu,* XVII, 1-2 (1978), pp. 282-309; A.A. Roest Crollius, "What Is So New About Inculturation? A Concept and Its Implications," in *Gregorianum* 59 (1978), pp. 721-738.

⁴ Stephen B. Bevans, *Models of Contextual Theology* (New York: Orbis Books, 1992).

[5] Robert Schreiter, "Faith and Cultures: Challenges to a World Church," in *Theological Studies* 50 (1989), pp. 744-760. For an informative survey of the debate on inculturation, see L.J. Custodio, "Understanding Culture," in *Philippiniana Sacra* 25, 1992, no. 80, pp. 279-292.

[6] It should be noted here that the Catholic Theological Society of America has taken up the theme of inculturation several times at its meetings and that the Institute for World Concerns at Duquesne University held a major seminar in 1985 on "The Integration of Faith and Culture: The Mission of the Church."

[7] For an extensive review of Pope John Paul II's teaching on faith and culture, see Francis George, OMI, *Inculturation and Ecclesial Communion* (Rome: Urbaniana University Press, 1990); Joseph Gremillion (ed.), *The Church and Culture Since Vatican II* (Notre Dame: University of Notre Dame Press, 1985), especially Part II: "Documents of the Church on Culture."

[8] Gregory Baum, "Faith and Culture," in *The Ecumenist* 24 (November-December, 1985), p. 12.

[9] Schreiter, "Faith and Cultures," p. 752.

[10] Typewritten document, signed January 25, 1994, p. 2.

[11] Paul VI, *On Evangelization in the Modern World,* December 8, 1975, no. 20.

[12] Robert Schreiter, *Constructing Local Theologies* (Maryknoll: Orbis Books, 1985), p. 61.

[13] H. Richard Niebuhr, *Christ and Culture* (New York: Harper & Row, 1951), chap. 5, pp. 190-229.

[14] Robert Schreiter, "Inculturation of Faith or Identification with Culture?" in *Concilium* 2 (1994), p. 16.

[15] Ibid., p. 17.

[16] Niebuhr, *Christ and Culture*, p. 103.

[17] Paul Ricoeur, *The Rule of Metaphor: Multidisciplinary Studies of the Creation of Meaning in Language,* trans. Robert Czerny et al. (Toronto: University of Toronto Press, 1981), pp. 4, 99, 180; see also Ricoeur, *Interpretation Theory: Discourse and the Surplus of Meaning* (Fort Worth: Texas Christian University Press, 1976), pp. 46-53.

[18] For an excellent analysis of the marriage metaphor in the Old Testament, see Nelly Stienstra, *YHWH Is the Husband of His People* (Kampen, The Netherlands: Kok Pharos Publishing House, 1993).

[19] Jean Leclercq, *Monks on Marriage: A Twelfth-Century View* (New York: The Seabury Press, 1982).

[20] Jean Gaudemet, *Droit de l'Eglise et vie sociale au Moyen Age* (Northampton, Eng.: Variorum Reprints, 1989), pp. 110-123.

[21] *Sermons from the Latins*, trans. James J. Baxter (New York: Benzinger Brothers, 1902), pp. 554-555. Translation slightly modified, with emphasis added.

[22] Abraham Heschel, *Who Is Man?* (Stanford, CA: Stanford University Press, 1965), pp. 88-89.

[23] Mark Johnson, *Moral Imagination: Implications of Cognitive Science for Ethics* (Chicago: The University of Chicago Press, 1993), pp. 53-54. [The italics and capitalization in the above quotation are those of Mark Johnson.]

[24] One is also reminded of the successive stages in the canonical form of penance, the "ordo poenitentium," that existed in the church from the fourth to the sixth century. See Cyrille Vogel, *Le pécheur et la pénitence dans l'Eglise ancienne* (Paris: Editions du Cerf, 1966), pp. 34-41.

[25] John Dominic Crossan, *The Dark Interval. Towards a Theology of Story* (Niles, IL: Argus Communications, 1975), p. 57.

[26] Like the Hebrew verb "to know" (*yadah*) or the Latin word "*commixtio,*" we use the term "co-penetration" with its connotation as typified in the act of sexual union, i.e., one that implies an intimate, experiential encounter between the two partners in question, a communion such that both partners gain a better understanding of their own individuality as well as the way they complement each other. It is a term that even Vatican II did not deem inappropriate or too strong in describing the intimate relationship between the church and the world: *Gaudium et Spes*, nn. 40 and 3.

[27] *L'Osservatore Romano* (English ed.), May 7, 1979, p. 8. Emphasis added.

[28] Address to the Congress of the Ecclesial Movement of Cultural Commitment, January 16, 1982, *The Pope Speaks*, 27 (1982), p. 157.

[29] *Puebla and Beyond: Documentation and Commentary*, edited by John Eagleson and Philip Scharper (Maryknoll: Orbis Books, 1979), p. 177.

[30] Richard G. Cote, *Universal Grace: Myth or Reality?* (Maryknoll: Orbis Books, 1977), pp. 110-123.

4. Mapping the Process of Inculturation

[1] Andrew Ortony, "Why Metaphors Are Necessary and Not Just Nice," in *Educational Theory* 25 (1975), pp. 45-53.

[2] "Unde oportet modum istius scientiae esse metaphoricum, sive symbolicum, vel parabolicum." *In I Sent. Prol., q. I, a.v.*

[3] Paul Ricoeur, *Time and Narrative* (Chicago: The University of Chicago Press, 1984), Vol. 1, pp. 66-67.

[4] Arthur Schlesinger Jr., "An Informal History of Love U.S.A.," in *The Saturday Evening Post* (Dec. 31, 1966), p. 30.

[5] On this whole issue of the teaching authority of the believers, see *Concilium* 180 (4/1985).

[6] David M. Thomas, *Christian Marriage: A Life Together* (Wilmington: Michael Glazier, 1983), p. 79 [emphasis added] and p. 80. See also Richard G. Cote, *Universal Grace: Myth or Reality?* (Maryknoll: Orbis Books, 1977), whose central thesis is that the incarnation of God in Jesus is not simply a prelude to or a "launching pad" for redemption, but is redemptive in and of itself.

[7] See Roger Finke and Rodney Stark, *The Churching of America, 1776–1990: Winners and Losers in Our Religious Economy* (New Brunswick, NJ: Rutgers University Press, 1992), pp. 112-113.

[8] See Jean-Marie Mayeur, "Catholic Parties, Christian Democratic Parties and the Catholic Church," in *Concilium* 157 (7/1982), pp. 21-26.

[9] Karl Rahner, *Concern for the Church: Theological Investigations XX* (New York: Crossroad, 1981), p. 149.

[10] St. John Chrysostom, quoted in Josef Pieper, *In Tune with the World. A Theory of Festivity* (Chicago: Franciscan Herald Press, 1973), p. 18.

[11] Jürgen Moltmann, *The Church in the Power of the Spirit* (New York: Harper & Row, 1977), pp. 272-275. See also Josef Pieper, *Leisure: The Basis of Culture* (New York: New American Library, 1963), pp. 56-64.

[12] Moltmann, *The Church in the Power of the Spirit,* p. 271.

[13] T.S. Eliot, *Four Quartets* (New York: Harcourt, Brace, 1943), p. 38.

[14] Harvey Cox, *The Feast of Fools. A Theological Essay on Festivity and Fantasy* (Cambridge, MA: Harvard University Press, 1969), p. 22.

[15] Diane Vaughan, *Uncoupling: How and Why Relationships Come Apart* (New York: Random House, 1990).

[16] Edward Schillebeeckx, *The Mission of the Church*, tr. by N.D. Smith (New York: Herder and Herder, 1973), pp. 43-50.

[17] Yves Congar, *Sainte Eglise: Etudes et approaches ecclésiologiques* (Paris: Editions du Cerf, 1964), pp. 155-161, and *L'Eglise: une, sainte, catholique et apostolique* (Paris: Editions du Cerf, 1970), Mysterium salutis 15, pp. 160-175.

5. Theological Foundations

[1] Aylward Shorter, *Toward a Theology of Inculturation* (Maryknoll: Orbis Books, 1988), pp. 81-83.

[2] On the limitations of classical Christology, see Karl Rahner,

Foundations of Christian Faith (New York: The Seabury Press, 1978), pp. 289-293.

[3] Ibid., p. 87.

[4] Ibid.

[5] See Karl Rahner's "The Concept of Mystery in Catholic Theology," in *Theological Investigations*, Vol. IV (Baltimore: Helicon Press, 1966), pp. 36-73.

[6] T.W. Manson, *Ethics and the Gospel* (London: SCM Press, 1960), p. 68.

[7] *De Trinitate*, IV, 3, 6; PL 42, 891.

[8] On the way St. Leo uses the formula "sacramentum et exemplum," see Dom Marie-Bernard de Soos, *Le Mystère Liturgique d'après Saint Léon Le Grand* (Münster Westfalen: Aschendorff, 1958), pp. 78-98. See also Germain Hudon, *La Perfection Chrétienne d'après les Sermons de Saint Léon* (Paris: Editions du Cerf, 1959), pp. 157-164.

[9] Sermon 67, 15-18; CCL 138, 411. Elsewhere St. Leo will say: "If Christ were not true God, he would not be for us a remedy; if he were not true man, he would not be an example for us," Sermon 21, 2; PL 54, 192.

[10] *Epistle* 190, ch. 9; PL 182, 1072.

[11] *S. Bernardi Opera*, III, ed. J. Leclercq (Romae: Ed. Cistercienses, 1963), p. 190.

[12] *Song of Songs* I, Sermon 15, 4 (Kalamazoo: Cistercian Publications, 1979), p. 111.

[13] For one such attempt, see E.-J. Penoukou, *Elgises d'Afrique: Propositions pour l'Avenir* (Paris: Editions Karthala, 1984).

[14] Dom Marie-Bernard de Soos, *Le Mystère Liturgique d'après Saint Léon le Grand* (Münster Westfalen: Aschendorff, 1958), p. 78.

[15] Sermon 23, 3: "peccatum mundi in Jesu Christi nativitate ac passione deleri."

[16] Cf. Sermons 22, 2; 25, 1.

[17] Cf. Sermons 25, 4; 26, 2; 25, 5.

[18] Sermon 67, 5: "et sua nobis insereret et in se nostra curaret."

[19] For an anthology of patristic and liturgical texts on this "wonderful exchange," see Joseph Lemarie, *La Manifestation du Seigneur* (Paris: Editions du Cerf, 1957), pp. 145-160.

[20] Cf. Edmond Barbotin, *The Humanity of Man* (Maryknoll: Orbis Books, 1975), pp. 289-298.

[21] "Quod non est assumptum, non est sanatum." See St. Gregory, *Epist.* 102; PG 37, 181; and Cyril of Alexandria, *In Joh.* 12; PG 74, 700.

[22] Sermon 54.

[23] Sermon 72, 2.

[24] Sermon 39, 3(265 A): "non quasi a Deo jam, sed ab homine vinceretur." Cf. also Sermon 63, 1(353).

[25] *In Joh.* 8; PG 74, 92. The same idea is expressed by John Damascene, *De fide orth.*, 3, 6; PG 94, 1005.

[26] St. Irenaeus, *Adversus Haereses*, III, 18, 7.

[27] Ibid., II, 22, 4. PG 7, 783-784. Hans Urs von Balthasar has significantly developed this notion of Jesus' "passage through time" and proposed a theological anthropology of the "Word as child," the "Word as youth," and the "Word as man" in *A Theological Anthropology* (New York: Sheed and Ward, 1967), pp. 234-274.

[28] *Adversus Haereses*, III, 22, 1-2.

[29] M.-D. Chenu, "Dimension nouvelle de la Chrétienté," in *La Vie Intellectuelle*, Vol. 53 (Dec. 25, 1937), pp. 327 and 331.

[30] Edward Schillebeeckx, *Christ the Sacrament of the Encounter with God* (New York: Sheed and Ward, 1963), p. 42.

[31] For a more extensive treatment of biblical anthropomorphism, see Richard G. Cote, *Holy Mirth: A Theology of Laughter* (Mystic, CT: Twenty-Third Publications, 1986), pp. 39-46.

[32] On this crucial issue, see Robert Schreiter, *Constructing Local Theologies*, pp. 63-70: "Identity in semiotic description."

[33] For a thoughtful clarification of the church as the "body of Christ," see Hans Küng, *The Church* (London: Burns & Oates, 1967), pp. 230-241.

[34] Cf. Schillebeeckx, *Christ the Sacrament*, pp. 47-89.

[35] Paul Poupard, *L'Eglise au défi des cultures. Inculturation et Evangélisation* (Paris: Desclée, 1989), p. 44. The cardinal's emphasis; my translation.

[36] Edward Schillebeeckx, *Christ: The Experience of Jesus as Lord* (New York: The Seabury Press, 1980), pp. 731-743, wherein he explores these six anthropological constants in terms of what it really means to be human.

[37] Edward Schillebeeckx, *Church: The Human Story of God* (New York: Crossroad, 1993), p. 36.

[38] Ibid., p. 33.

[39] Alfred T. Hennelly, ed., *Santo Domingo and Beyond: Documents and Commentaries* (Maryknoll: Orbis Books, 1993), p. 140, no. 248. Emphasis added.

6. Culture Revisited: Some Misconceptions

[1] For general discussions of the concept of culture, see A.L. Kroeber and Clyde Kluckhohn, *Culture: A Critical Review of Concepts and*

Definitions (Cambridge, MA: Harvard University, 1952); Raymond Williams, *Keywords: A Vocabulary of Culture and Society* (London: Fontana, 1976) and *Culture* (London: Fontana, 1981); Milton Singer, "The Concept of Culture," in *International Encyclopedia of the Social Sciences,* ed. David L. Sills, Vol. 3 (New York: The Macmillan Co., 1968), pp. 527-543.

[2] Edward B. Tylor, *Primitive Culture: Researches into the Development of Mythology, Philosophy, Religion, Language, Art, and Custom,* Vol. 1 (London: John Murray, 1903), p. 1.

[3] *Gaudium et Spes,* no. 53.

[4] *Evangelii Nuntiandi,* no. 20.

[5] From the pope's address reprinted in *Origins,* Vol. 10, no. 4 (June 12, 1980), p. 60.

[6] *Gaudium et Spes,* no. 41.

[7] Leslie A. White, *The Science of Culture: A Study of Man and Civilization* (New York: Farrar, Strauss and Cudahy, 1949).

[8] Clifford Geertz, *The Interpretation of Cultures* (New York: Basic Books, 1973), p. 5.

[9] Ibid., p. 89.

[10] Leopold Pospisil has shown, for example, that there is a relationship between pig-breeding, polygyny, and political power in the culture of the Kapauku Papuans of New Guinea, in *The Kapauku Papuans of West New Guinea* (New York: Holt, Rinehart and Winston, 1963).

[11] See Anthony Giddens, *Central Problems and Social Theory* (London: Macmillan, 1979).

[12] See Margaret Archer, *Culture and Agency: The Place of Culture in Social Theory* (Cambridge: Cambridge University Press, 1988).

[13] Quoted in John Staudenmaier, *Technology's Storytellers: Reweaving the Human Fabric* (Cambridge, MA: The MIT Press, 1985), p. 241, note 45.

[14] Langdon Winner, *Autonomous Technology: Technics-out-of-Control as a Theme in Political Thought* (Cambridge, MA: The MIT Press, 1977), p. 25.

[15] Ibid., p. 327. John Staudenmaier has attempted to show how and in what ways we could have a limited influence over modern technological systems with his model of the three constituencies in technological change, in *Technology's Storytellers,* pp. 192-201.

[16] Ibid., p. 326.

[17] See Allan Deck, *The Second Wave: Hispanic Ministry and the Evangelization of Cultures,* Foreword by Virgil Elizondo (New York: Paulist Press, 1989), xv. Emphasis added.

[18] Stephen L. Carter, *The Culture of Disbelief: How American Law and Politics Trivializes Religious Devotion* (New York: Basic Books, 1993).

[19] See Barry Kosman and Seymour Lachman (eds.), *One Nation Under*

God: Religion in Contemporary American Society (New York: Harmony Books, 1993).

[20] John B. Thompson, *Ideology and Modern Culture: Critical Social Theory in the Era of Mass Communication* (Stanford, CA: Stanford University Press, 1990), in which the author shows how the modern electronic media, especially television, have fueled the circulation of ideologies as a *mass* phenomenon.

[21] Ibid., p. 63. For a further discussion of some of the links between ideology and rhetorical figures of speech, see Olivier Reboul, *Langage et idéologie* (Paris: Presses Universitaires de France, 1980), ch. 4.

[22] Karl Rahner, "Christianity and Ideology," in *Concilium* 6 (May 1965), p. 43. Emphasis added.

[23] See Magnus Lohrer, "Theologische Wurzeln des Konfessionalismus," *Reformatio* 24:3 (March 1975), pp. 154-164.

[24] Joseph Cardinal Ratzinger, "Der Christliche Glaube vor der Herausforderung der Kulturen," in *Evangelium und Inkulturation (1492-1992)*, ed. Paulus Gordan (Graz: Verlag Styria, 1992), p. 12. [Trans. Norma Lelless].

[25] Joseph Cardinal Ratzinger, "Christ, Faith and the Challenge of Cultures," in *L'Osservatore Romano*, n. 17 (26 April 1995), p. 6.

[26] "The Interpretation of the Bible in the Church," in *Origins*, Vol. 23 (January 6, 1994), p. 521.

[27] For an extensive overview of the theological publications on the "hierarchy" of truths since Vatican II, see William Henn, "The Hierarchy of Truths Twenty Years Later," in *Theological Studies* 48:3 (September 1987), pp. 439-471.

[28] Karl Rahner, *Expériences d'un Théologien Catholique*, trans. Raymond Mengus (Paris: Cariscript, 1985), p. 22. Emphasis added. See also Karl Rahner, "Hierarchy of Truths," in *Theology Digest* 30:3 (Fall 1982), pp. 227- 229.

7. A Model for Analysis of Culture (1)

[1] David J. Bryant, *Faith and the Play of Imagination: On the Role of Imagination in Religion* (Macon, GA: Mercer University Press, 1989), p. 5.

[2] Robert Schreiter, "Faith and Cultures: Challenges to a World Church," in *Theological Studies* 50 (1989), p. 757.

[3] For an excellent introduction to the systems theory in science, psychology and religion, see Linda E. Olds, *Metaphors of Interrelatedness: Toward a Systems Theory of Psychology* (Albany: State University of New York Press, 1992). See also Margaret J. Wheatley, *Leadership and the New*

Science: Learning about Organization from an Orderly Universe (San Francisco: Berrett-Koehler, 1992).

[4] This image was in fact used by Giambattista Vico in his *New Science*, tr. from the 1744 third edition by Thomas Bergin and Max Fisch (Garden City, NY: Doubleday & Co., 1961), p. 72.

[5] These dynamic cultural myths are what Joseph Campbell has called "society's dreams," as distinct from an individual's private dream.

[6] In Chapter 10, I will deal expressly with the positive role that "ambiguity" plays in the life of faith.

[7] Edmund Leach, *Lévi-Strauss* (London: Collins/Fontana, 1970), p. 54.

[8] For more on this, see Michel de Certeau, *La faiblesse de croire* (Paris: Editions du Seuil, 1987), pp. 40-46. See also his article, "La rupture instauratrice ou le christianisme dans la culture contemporaines," in *Esprit* 39 (1971), pp. 1180-1183.

[9] Lynn Ross-Bryant, *Imagination and the Life of the Spirit* (Chico, CA: Scholars Press, 1981), p. 94.

[10] James Jakob Liszka, *The Semiotic of Myth: A Critical Study of the Symbol* (Bloomington: Indiana University Press, 1989), p. 215. Emphasis added.

[11] Thomas Moore, *The Planets Within. The Astrological Psychology of Marsilio Ficino* (Hudson, NY: Lindisfarne Press, 1990).

[12] For a comprehensive study of how something new arises in the midst of all that is accepted and traditional in a society, see H.G. Barnett, *Innovation: The Basis of Cultural Change* (New York: McGraw-Hill Book Co., 1953). See also A.L. Kroeber, *Anthropology: Culture Patterns and Processes* (New York: Harcourt, Brace & World, 1963), pp. 66-67, 194-252, 219-223.

[13] Joseph Campbell, *Myths To Live By* (Toronto: Bantam Books, 1972), p. 221.

[14] James Liszka, *The Semiotic of Myth*, p. 219.

[15] For the "kingdom of God" viewed as a symbol, see especially Norman Perrin, *Jesus and the Language of the Kingdom: Symbol and Metaphor in New Testament Interpretation* (Philadelphia: Fortress Press, 1976).

[16] Jurij M. Lotman, "On the Metalanguage of a Typological Description of Culture," in *Semiotica* 14:2 (1975), p. 101.

[17] Frederich J. Turner, *The Frontier in American History* (New York: Holt, Rinehart and Winston, 1947), p. 1.

[18] Quoted in Martin Marty, *The Public Church: Mainline-Evangelical-Catholic* (New York: Harper & Row, 1981), p. 95.

[19] Ray Allen Billington, in his 1962 Foreword to *The Frontier in American History*, p. xviii.

[20] Sacvan Bercovitch, *The Rites of Assent: Transformation in the Symbolic Construction of America* (New York: Routledge, 1993), p. 7. See also Rollo May, *The Cry for Myth* (New York: Dell Publishing, 1992), in which the author, a psychiatrist, elaborates on the American myth of the frontier in Chapter 6, "The Great Myth of the New Land," pp. 91-107.

[21] See Paul Ricoeur, *The Symbolism of Evil* (New York: Harper & Row, 1967), pp. 232-260.

[22] Eric Voegelin, "The Gospel and Culture," *Jesus and Man's Hope*, Vol. 2, eds. D. Miller and D. Hadidian (Pittsburgh: Pittsburgh Theological Seminary Press, 1971), p. 63.

[23] Eric Voegelin, "Immortality: Experience and Symbol," in *Harvard Theological Review* 60 (1967), p. 257.

[24] Paul Ricoeur, *The Symbolism of Evil*, p. 309.

[25] For more on this, see Victor Turner, *Dramas, Fields, and Metaphors: Symbolic Action in Human Society* (Ithaca, NY: Cornell University Press, 1974).

[26] Russel B. Nye, *The Almost Chosen People: Essays in the History of American Ideas* (East Lansing, MI: Michigan State University Press, 1966), p. 211.

[27] Quoted in A.N. Wilson (ed.), *John Henry Newman. Prayers, Poems, Meditations* (New York: Crossroad, 1990), p. 125.

[28] On this notion of "boundary-breaking" in the gospel, see the interesting study of G. Theissen, *The Miracle Stories of the Early Christian Tradition* (Philadelphia: Fortress, 1983).

[29] See, for example, the study of W.D. Davies, *The Gospel and the Land: Early Christianity and Jewish Territorial Doctrine* (Berkeley: University of California, 1974); also B. Malina, *The New Testament World: Insights from Cultural Anthropology* (Atlanta: John Knox, 1981), pp. 122-152.

[30] For a suggestive and thoughtful reading of the New Testament along these lines, see Donald Senior, "Healing as Boundary-Breaking: The Cross-Cultural Impulse of Early Christianity," a conference he gave in May 1985 at a seminar on the Integration of Faith and Culture, which was held at Duquesne University (Pittsburgh, PA).

8. A Model for Analysis of Culture (2)

[1] The statement by the U.S. bishops' Committee for Social Development and World Peace, entitled *Beyond the Melting Pot: Ethnic Diversity*

in the United States, makes the point most convincingly. See *Origins* 10 (January 15, 1981), pp. 481-489.

² Robert Schreiter, *Constructing Local Theologies* (Maryknoll: Orbis Books, 1985), p. 69.

³ In my proposed model of culture, these semiotic domains and the human activities that constitute them correspond to **level 2.**

⁴ Philip Schaff, *America, a Sketch of Its Political, Social, and Religious Character,* ed. Perry Miller (Cambridge, MA: Belknap Press of Harvard University Press, 1961).

⁵ An entire issue of *Concilium* (1987/3) dealt with "Changing Values and Virtues," wherein not only are the terms "virtue" and "value" used interchangeably, but the notion of value itself is cast almost exclusively in ethical terms.

⁶ Romano Guardini, *Pascal for Our Time* (New York: Herder and Herder, 1966), p. 133.

⁷ 1 Sam 14:7.

⁸ Robert Schreiter, *Constructing Local Theologies*, p. 40.

⁹ For a practical guide on how to improve the communication and cultural awareness among culturally different people, see Paul Pedersen, *A Handbook for Developing Multicultural Awareness* (Alexandria, VA: American Association for Counseling and Development, 1988); also Paul Pedersen, ed., *Handbook of Cross-Cultural Counseling and Therapy* (New York: Praeger, 1987).

¹⁰ This criterion was suggested to me by Charles Mabee's insightful analysis of Melville's *Moby-Dick* and the book of Job. In particular see his chapter on "The Hermeneutics of Displacement," in *Reimagining America*, pp. 69-110.

¹¹ See Donald Winnicott, "Transitional Objects and Transitional Phenomena," in *Through Pediatrics to Psychoanalysis* (London: Hogarth Press, 1958), p. 237; also Robert Kegan, *The Evolving Self. Problem and Process in Human Development* (Cambridge, MA: Harvard University Press, 1982), pp. 115-132.

¹² Joseph Powers, "Faith, Morality, Creativity: Toward the Art of Believing," in *Theological Studies* 4 (December 1978), pp. 670-671.

¹³ Dorothy Norman, *The Hero: Myth/Image/Symbol* (New York: Doubleday Anchor Books, 1990), p. 161.

¹⁴ Rose Marie Scissons, "The Artist's Prophetic Voice," in *Celebrate!* (May-June 1990), p. 7.

¹⁵ Paul VI, in *Documentation Catholique* 61 (1964), c. 686-687. [My translation from the French.] For more on the alienation of artists from the church, see Albert Lalonde, O.M.I., "Artists and the Church," in *Kerygma* 27 (1993), pp. 3-37.

[16] See Harold Bloom, *The Western Canon: The Books and Schools of the Ages* (New York: Harcourt Brace, 1994).

[17] In *Origins* 4 (June 12, 1980), p. 60.

[18] Charles Mabee, *Reimagining America*, p. 11.

[19] Monika Hellwig, "American Culture: Reciprocity with Catholic Vision, Values and Community," in *The Catholic Church and American Culture,* ed. Cassian Yuhaus (New York: Paulist Press, 1990), p. 64.

[20] Charles Mabee, *Reimagining America*, p. 11.

[21] For "convergent" thinking, see R.L. Firestein and D.J. Treffinger, "Ownership and Converging: Essential Ingredients of Creative Problem Solving," in *Journal of Creative Behavior* 17 (1983), pp. 32-38. For "lateral" and "divergent" thinking, see Edward de Bono, *Lateral Thinking. A Textbook of Creativity* (New York: Penguin Books, 1970); and J.P. Guilford, "Creativity: Retrospect and Issues," in *Journal of Creative Behavior* 4 (1970), pp. 149-168.

[22] C.H. Dodd, *The Parables of the Kingdom* (New York: Charles Scribner's Sons, 1961), p. 143.

9. New Postmodern Paths in Mission

[1] Zygmunt Bauman, *Intimations of Postmodernity* (London: Routledge, 1993), p. 188. [Italics in original].

[2] Klaus Klostermaier, "From Phenomenology to Metascience: Reflection on the Study of Religions," in *Studies in Religion* 6 (Summer 1976), p. 562.

[3] David Ray Griffin, ed., *The Reenchantment of Science* (Albany, NY: State University of New York Press, 1988), p. 6. For an expansion of this perspective, what Charlene Spretnak calls "ecological postmodernism," see her *States of Grace: The Recovery of Meaning in the Postmodern Age* (San Francisco: Harper, 1992), pp. xi-xv.

[4] Ibid., p. xi.

[5] For a cogent comparison of old versus new paradigm thinking in science and theology, see Fritjjof Capra and David Steindl-Rast, *Belonging to the Universe: Explorations on the Frontiers of Science and Spirituality* (San Francisco: Harper, 1992).

[6] David Griffin, *The Reenchantment of Science*, p. 16.

[7] Ibid., p. 143.

[8] Barbara Ehrenreich, *Fear of Falling* (New York: HarperCollins Publishing, 1990), p. 257.

[9] Sallie McFague, *Models of God: Theology for an Ecological Nuclear Age* (Philadelphia: Fortress Press, 1987), p. 28.

[10] Ibid., p. 130.

[11] Ibid., p. 147.

[12] Eric Fromm, *The Sane Society* (New York: Rinehart, 1969), p. 120.

[13] Peter F. Drucker, "The Age of Social Transformation," in *The Atlantic Monthly* (November 1994), pp. 53-80.

[14] Walter Ong, *Faith and Contexts*, Vol. 1, Selected Essays and Studies: 1952-1991, ed. Thomas Farrell and Paul Soukup (Atlanta, GA: Scholars Press, 1992), p. 222.

[15] See Edward Schillebeeckx, "The Role of History in What Is Called the New Paradigm," in Hans Küng and David Tracy (eds.), *Paradigm Change in Theology* (New York: Crossroad, 1989), pp. 307-319.

[16] See Robert Schreiter, "Mission into the Third Millennium," in *Missiology* 18 (January 1990), pp. 3-12; Walbert Bühlmann, *With Eyes to See. Church and World in the Third Millennium* (Maryknoll: Orbis Books, 1990).

[17] *L'Osservatore Romano*, edition in English, 40 (9 October 1994), p. 4. [Italics in original].

[18] Drucker, "The Age of Social Transformation," p. 53. [Italics in original]

[19] See the SUNY series in constructive postmodern thought, edited by David Ray Griffin and published by the State University of New York Press, Albany. See also Charlene Spretnak, *States of Grace: The Recovery of Meaning in the Postmodern Age* (New York: HarperCollins Publishers, 1991); Hans Küng, *Theology for the Third Millennium* (New York: Doubleday, 1988) and *Global Responsibility. In Search of a New World Ethic* (New York: Doubleday, 1991).

[20] Eberhard Jüngel, *God as the Mystery of the World* (Grand Rapids: William B. Eerdmans, 1983), pp. 14ff.

[21] Claude Geffré, "The Outlook for the Christian Faith in a World of Religious Indifference," in *Concilium* 5 (1983), p. 63.

[22] Ibid., p. 64.

[23] Quoted in Hans Urs von Balthasar, *The Glory of the Lord. A Theology of Aesthetics*, III (San Francisco: Ignatius Press, 1986), pp. 500-501.

[24] Quoted from memory and therefore perhaps not complete or literally exact.

[25] Karl Rahner, *Concern for the Church* (New York: Crossroad, 1981), p. 149.

[26] See Leonardo Boff, *Ecology and Liberation: A New Paradigm* (Maryknoll: Orbis Books, 1995), especially Chapter 8: "Nurturing Our Mysticism," pp. 139-162.

[27] Ibid., pp. 147-148.

[28] *Concilium* 4 (1994), p. viii.

[29] For a more comprehensive and in-depth analysis of the "visitor" and the "visit received," see Edmond Barbotin, *The Humanity of Man* (Maryknoll: Orbis Books, 1975), pp. 289-318.

[30] Ted Peters, *God–The World's Future: Systematic Theology for a Postmodern Era* (Minneapolis: Fortress Press, 1992), p. 15.

[31] John Coleman, *An American Strategic Theology* (New York: Paulist Press, 1982), p. 202.

[32] Thomas Aquinas, *In Matth.* 5, 1; and *Summa Theologica* I, 21, 3 ad 2.

[33] For more on this important topic, see Carl Brakenhielm, *Forgiveness* (Minneapolis: Fortress Press, 1993); also Robert Schreiter, *Reconciliation: Mission and Ministry in a Changing Social Order* (Maryknoll: Orbis Books, 1992).

10. A Spirituality for Crossing the Postmodern Divide

[1] The publishers of *Concilium* have graciously given permission to adapt and publish my copyrighted article, "God Sings in the Night: An Invitation to Believe," which first appeared in *Concilium* 4 (1992), pp. 95-105.

[2] Langdon Gilkey, *Through the Tempest. Theological Voyages in a Pluralistic Culture*, ed. Jeff B. Pool (Minneapolis: Fortress Press, 1991).

[3] Ibid., p. 153.

[4] *Rilke on Love and Other Difficulties*, tr. John J.L. Mood (New York: W.W. Norton & Co., 1975), p. 25. Emphasis in original.

[5] Emma Jung and Marie-Louise von Franz, *The Grail Legend* (Boston: Sigo Press, 1986), p. 215.

[6] Allocution of Pope Paul VI in *L'Osservatore Romano* (French edition), November 15, 1963, p. 4.

[7] Quoted in Kenneth Leech, *Experiencing God. Theology as Spirituality* (San Francisco: Harper & Row, 1985), p. 160.

[8] Karl Rahner, *Theological Investigations* VI (Baltimore: Helicon Press, 1967), pp. 218-230.

[9] Johannes Metz, "Unbelief as a Theological Problem," in *Concilium* 6 (June 1969), pp. 59-77.

[10] Michael Downey, "Christian Spirituality: Changing Currents, Perspectives, Challenges," in *America* (April 2, 1994), p. 12.

[11] T.W. Adorno, E. Frenkel-Brunswick, D. Levinson, and R.N. Sanford, *The Authoritarian Personality* (New York: Harper & Row, 1950).

[12] See S. Budner, "Intolerance of Ambiguity as a Personality Variable," in *Journal of Personality* 1 (1962), pp. 29-50.

[13] C.J. Jung, *Collected Works*, Vol. 6 (London: Routledge & Kegan Paul, 1971), pp. 244-245.

[14] Bernard of Clairvaux, *On the Song of Songs,* Sermon 72, IV (Kalamazoo, MI: Cistercian Publications, 1980), pp. 89-91.

[15] St. Augustine, *De bapt.,* V:27, 28. See also *De civ. Dei.* I:35 and *In Joan. Ev.,* tr. XXVII:11 and tr. XLV:12.

[16] Thomas Aquinas, *Summa theologica*, I-II, 31, 4 ad 3.

[17] Thomas Merton, *New Seeds of Contemplation* (New York: New Directions, 1961), p. 134.

[18] Quoted freely in Matthew Fox, *Meditations with Meister Eckhart* (Sante Fe, NM: Bear & Co., 1983), p. 60.

[19] Saint Augustine, *En. in Ps.* 109, 8; PL 37, 1451.

[20] David Tracy, "Charity, Obscurity, Clarity: Augustine's Search for a True Rhetoric," in *Morphologies of Faith. Essays in Religion and Culture in Honor of Nathan A. Scott, Jr.,* ed. Mary Gerhart and Anthony C. Yu (Atlanta: Scholars Press, 1990), p. 139.

[21] Quoted in Romano Guardini, *Pascal for Our Time* (New York: Herder and Herder, 1966), p. 122.

[22] See the excellent and timely study by Richard W. Kropf, *Faith: Security and Risk. The Dynamics of Spiritual Growth* (New York: Paulist Press, 1990). Also George Aschenbrenner, *A God for a Dark Journey* (Denville, NJ: Dimension Books, 1984), pp. 110-139.

ISAAC HECKER STUDIES
IN RELIGION AND AMERICAN CULTURE
Other Books in the Series